S0-AIK-461

The Art of the Homily

William Spaid
October 1992

The Art of the Homily

Christopher L. Webber

MOREHOUSE PUBLISHING
Harrisburg, PA

© 1992 Christopher L. Webber

All rights reserved. No part of this book may be reproduced or transmitted in any form or by any means, electronic or mechanical, including photocopying, recording, or by any information storage and retrieval system, without written permission from the publisher.

Morehouse Publishing

Editorial Office:
871 Ethan Allen Highway
Ridgefield, CT 06877

Corporate Office:
P.O. Box 1321
Harrisburg, PA 17105

Acknowledgment
Unless otherwise noted, Scripture quotations are from the New Revised Standard Version of the Bible, copyright © 1989 by the Division of Christian Education of the National Council of Churches of Christ in the U.S.A. Used by permission.

Library of Congress Cataloging-in-Publication Data
Webber, Christopher.
  The art of the homily / Christopher L. Webber.
     p.   cm.
  ISBN 0-8192-1567-8
     1. Baptismal sermons.   2. Baptismal sermons—History and criticism.   3. Wedding sermons.   4. Wedding sermons—History and criticism.   5. Funeral sermons.   6. Funeral sermons—History and criticism.   7. Sermons, American.   8. Episcopal Church—Sermons. 9. Anglican Communion—Sermons.   I. Title.
BV4255.2.W43   1991   91-17395
251—dc20   CIP

Printed in the United States of America
by
BSC Litho
Harrisburg, PA 17105

10 9 8 7 6 5 4 3 2 1

Contents

Preface

From my mother I learned to love language and from my father I learned to love liturgy. This book originates in those two loves (which are one) and the writing of it is a consequence of the way life is shared in the body of Christ. I have been invited into the most joyous and painful moments in the lives of others, and I have therefore learned much I would never otherwise have known of the love of God. If, now, I can share with others what has been shared with me, that enlarges the privilege.

I owe a particular debt to those who took the time to read this book before it was finished and gave me the benefit of their own wisdom and caring. My wife is the best proofreader I know and after many years is still willing to point out patiently (in this as in other matters) the things I have overlooked. Clair McPherson and Bonnie Shullenberger noted many small errors and made many helpful suggestions. Richard Corney gave generously of his time and scholarship to save me from misstatements and make this a much better book than it would have been otherwise. I am grateful to them all.

Introduction

The Art of the Homily

The word "homily" has been used in very different ways over the centuries and is used in very different ways in different churches today.

In Greek, the word "homileo/homilia" means to be crowded together and to commune closely with another. The disciples on the road to Emmaus "homilized" with each other as they walked. The implication is of close and personal discourse. Such might be the spirit of the words spoken to a family at the baptism of a newborn child, to a couple being married, or to the bereaved at the time of death. This is not a time to preach a sermon in the usual sense but to speak personally and closely to immediate need.

Nevertheless, the word "homily" has not always conveyed this sense and therefore can be easily misunderstood. In the Middle Ages, the word had acquired a moralistic tone and that sense is still conveyed in the dictionaries which define "homily" as "a serious admonition; a lecture; a tedious moralizing discourse." (OED) Shakespeare asks, "What tedious homilie of Loue haue you wearied your parishioners withal?" (AYL 3:2,164)

Today, in some churches, the word "homily" is used generally to apply to all sermons and, of course, the art of preaching is generally described as "homiletics." The *Book of Common Prayer,* on the other hand, calls for a "homily" at weddings and funerals while speaking of a "sermon" in the eucharist and on other occasions. This terminology is hardly universal but it seems to have value as making a distinction between two very different tasks. Almost instinctively, we feel that preaching at baptisms, weddings, and funerals is not the same task as preaching to a full congregation on Sunday morning. But what are the differences and how should we deal with them?

It is important also to distinguish the homily from the eulogy which is a widely practiced but secular art form. The line between eulogy and homily, like that between homily and sermon, may not be easily drawn and each may, at times, intrude on the other, but each has its appropriate place and distinctive purpose. "The right tool for the right purpose" is a precept as applicable in preaching as in carpentry.

This book, then, is intended to focus attention on one special kind of preaching, to discuss those aspects of setting and style and content which make it different, to look closely at the biblical passages which may be most relevant, and to provide actual examples of the art: real homilies, preached to real people, on real occasions. Phillips Brooks' famous dictum that "preaching is the communication of truth through personality" applies here as well. No two people will communicate the same truth in quite the same way. But perhaps in the case of the homily it should be said that truth is communicated "through personality, by personality." Here, more than in the Sunday or feast day sermon, the personality of those at the center of the action, the one who has died and his or her immediate family, the couple to be married, the family of the child or adult being baptized, becomes also a means of revealing grace. Where personalities are involved, there can be no single formula or universally valid method, but one rule can be stated—at the heart of this ministry there must be a personal relationship with a personal God through which the preacher has learned to value each individual as evidence of the Creator's manifold gifts. From that relationship, the preacher can speak the personal word to personal need which gives immediate life and meaning to the universal word which speaks to the needs of all humanity.

This book has three sections, each with three subsections. Baptism, marriage, and burial are the three central moments of life and, in the Christian understanding, each involves a dying to self. The first subsection, then, is an essay on one of these three moments and the way in which the word and the liturgy can be brought together in each circumstance.

The second subsection is a selection of Bible passages appropriate to the occasion and a commentary on each passage. The commentary is not intended to provide scholarly analysis but rather some indication of the way in which the particular passage might be related to the particular liturgical moment. The biblical selections come from some of the standard prayer books and hymnals in current use in liturgical churches as well as from experience. I Corinthians 13, for example, is a standard suggestion for marriage services and frequently chosen. I have not seen it suggested for funerals, but I have been asked to use it more than once. In the same way, Ecclesiastes 3 is suggested for funerals but not weddings, but I have been asked to use it at weddings also. There are, when you consider it, very definite connections to be made, and rather different connections from those that would be made at marriage for I Corinthians and at death for Ecclesiastes. The unifying theme of death to self, however, is only reinforced by the evidence that some of the same readings can, in fact, be used on all three occasions.

The third subsection is a collection of homilies I have actually preached on these occasions. Some are addressed very directly to the individuals involved while others are much more general. All, however, center on God and the gospel of God's love and attempt to bring that gospel to bear on individual lives rather than the other way round (as a eulogy, for example, might do).

The Occasion of the Homily

St. Paul speaks more than once of baptism as a death to self and burial with Christ. He also makes an analogy between the self-sacrificing love of marriage and the death of Christ. And Jesus spoke of his own death as a baptism through which he must pass. These "three kinds of dying" along the

Christian way—baptism, marriage, and death—are all potential openings to reveal the life God promises his people through the death and resurrection of Jesus Christ. The personalities involved in each occasion often determine the keynote of the homily.

John Schelpert is an obstetrician and a gynecologist. He and his wife, Joanne, raised four daughters; two of whom are married. When his first grandchild arrived, the baptism had to be scheduled for a Sunday afternoon to allow members of the family to come to the New York area from Philadelphia and Boston. It seemed appropriate, in view of his profession, to choose as the Bible reading the story of Nicodemus' visit to Jesus and to use as a text for a homily the words "You must be born again."

Paul Warchol is a professional architectural photographer whose work consists of making studies of buildings from every angle. When he and his fiancee decided to have the thirteenth chapter of First Corinthians read at their wedding, it seemed natural to discuss the way in which St. Paul also explores the building of love from every angle.

John Paul Castagna lived in a church-sponsored residence for the retarded. His winning smile and seemingly endless optimism endeared him to many in the community. When he killed himself in a sudden depression, the reading which seemed most appropriate was the lesson from John's First Epistle which says, "Beloved, now are we the children of God and it does not yet appear what we shall be; but we know that when he appears we shall be like him..." John Paul had been limited in this life (as we all are in many ways) but we have hope of a life in which those limits will be done away, when we will be more fully what we have the potential to be but have not been in this life.

The Audience of the Homily

Baptisms, weddings, and funerals provide a unique challenge to the preacher. On no other occasion is attention focused in so sharply on one or two individual lives. Indeed, it might seem at first glance that the homily on these occasions is entirely directed to only one person or two. The wedding homily, for example, is, in fact, often addressed in very intimate terms to the man and woman standing immediately in front of the preacher.

But the center of attention on these occasions may make the least responsive audience. The baby to be baptized will most likely have its first experience of a sermon going right over its head. The newly deceased will have heard his or her last sermon on an earlier occasion. And even the young couple, so responsive in many ways to the love God is revealing to them, may not have their whole attention centered on the Word of God being proclaimed a few feet from where they stand. Gathered around the ostensible center of attention, however, will be friends and family very interested to hear what words may be spoken on an occasion so important in the lives of those they care for and value.

The preacher's Sunday task is sometimes compared to the effort to fill an array of narrow-necked bottles by sloshing buckets of water over them. Sitting in the congregation may be an elderly woman, lonely and worried about her failing strength, a college student just beginning to read Nietzsche and wondering how true his childhood religion is, the newly appointed vice president of a bank, wondering whether she can maintain her integrity and still keep up with the competition, and a couple whose marriage is being tested to the limit by the demands of careers and children. What word can the preacher say that will fill the needs of each when those needs are so different? These same people may be at the baptism, wedding, or funeral, but they, like everyone else present, will have come there for one reason, out of love for one person. For the moment, at least, their attention will be centered in a way that it seldom is on Sunday.

Indeed, some of those present will seldom if ever be in attendance at all on a Sunday morning. Some will have drifted away from church in their teenage years. Some will have married someone of a different faith and been unable to work out a pattern of life that enables them to continue as active church members. Some will have grown up in a family where faith was not a serious option. Some will know of the Christian faith only secondhand or will have known it only in a form which they could not accept.

Clergy sometimes respond to this opportunity by being merely jovial or trivial. At a marriage, particularly, the words spoken may be more amusing than substantive. The idea seems to be to persuade those present that the clergy of the church are, contrary to the stereotype, actually delightful people to meet and not significantly different from anyone else. This may be a first small step forward with some individuals, but it also sends many people away with the feeling that the clergy are more concerned to be likable than responsible and that they have no word to say that is different from what might be said by anyone of good will.

When human beings come into a totally strange and forbidding environment it may well be helpful to encounter there a charming and humorous host who will assure them of their welcome. A church may be such an environment for many. But birth, marriage, and death are part of the experience of every human being. All of us are born; most of us grow up in the context of a family formed by marriage; all will in due time die. Only the most unreflective can attend the ceremonies that surround such occasions without pondering their own mortality and the significance and value of the life they are living. To that extent, the environment is not strange. On the contrary, it is one we have all known at first hand, or will, and one that "connects" to some of our most fundamental and life-shaping experience. Here, where questions of meaning and value press in most inescapably, is it better to find a host who can charm us, or one who can give us words that throw light not only on the lives of those we care for but also on our own?

Besides all this, it is worth noticing that even a preacher who presides at only ten to fifteen weddings a year and twenty or thirty funerals may, when you subtract vacations and guest preachers from the year's total, speak as often on these occasions as on a Sunday. Moreover, since the Sunday congregation includes few newcomers while weddings and funerals usually bring together a different congregation each time, the ordinary preacher may speak to a far larger total number of individuals on these special occasions than on all the Sundays of the year. It can hardly be assumed that all these are strangers to the Christian faith since many or most may be active members of another congregation. But if they are, then the homily is a prime means of strengthening the ecumenical movement by manifesting the faith we have in common, and if they are not, it is a prime means of evangelism if it manifests the faith on which the church is built.

It seems clear then that one of the greatest opportunities for proclaiming God's word comes precisely at these transition points, indeed that these occasions provide for many clergy a rare and precious opportunity to speak God's word to those who have never heard it clearly. These are moments to be taken with the utmost seriousness in preparation and delivery.

The homilist approaches this moment with one enormous advantage for the moment is, in itself, revelatory. If human beings are ever to be aware of God's claim on their lives, it is likely to be at these three moments. And these three moments are central also to the understanding of the Christian faith. The gospel proclaims a God who was born for us, who died for us, and who calls us into a relationship more intimate and all-embracing than marriage. What better opportunity could we find to relate this gospel to our lives? Perhaps only at Christmas, Holy Week and Easter are we so inescapably confronted with the way God acts in human history. But Christmas and Easter have been so overlaid with centuries of tradition and with distracting secular customs that we can celebrate them without confronting their meaning. And, in any event, these festivals celebrate God's actions at other times and places.

Birth, marriage, and death also have social patterns intended to insulate us from the full impact of the event, but the immediacy of that which changes a life can still cut through the ceremonies and force questions that could otherwise be avoided. The homilist begins with the likelihood that the hearers are ready to hear and to hear that which matters most.

This preparedness and centeredness make possible the one overriding requirement of a homily which is brevity. Baptisms and weddings, in particular, are dominated by a certain urgency: an infant may not be quiet for long; the wedding feast will grow cold. But one fundamental assertion supported by one arresting illustration, analogy, or turn of phrase may serve to link memories of the occasion forever with the truth of the gospel so that the one cannot be thought of without the other. And that, surely, is what preaching is all about—the imbedding of gospel truth in the deepest levels of memory, joined forever with those moments by which our lives are defined.

PART ONE

Baptism

I. The Baptismal Homily

There is a book that has been in my library for years (I have forgotten entirely how I acquired it) called *Manners and Rules of Good Society* by "A Member of the Aristocracy." It was published in London in 1926 but reads like an account of life in a different world and time. Chapter 47 is entitled "Christening Parties" and instructs us as follows:

> **The Christening Ceremony** takes place in the afternoon, usually at 2.30[sic]. The relatives on arrival at the church seat themselves in pews or on chairs near to the font. The godmother holds the infant during the first part of the service, and then places it on the left arm of the officiating clergyman.... (The) godparents are usually the intimate friends of the child's mother. In certain instances the relatives are chosen for the office of godfather and godmother, but oftener not for family reasons.... The officiating priest receives some little gift in old silver or china, but not of money; if, however, the parents of the child are wealthy a cheque is sometimes given with a request that he will devote it to the needs of his parish.[1]

That world, in which baptism was a formal custom but perhaps little more, is now gone. Our world is more like the world of the Reformation and, also, of the early church: a world of rapid change in which the Christian faith is being challenged in many ways. Now, as in those days, those called to the Christian life may find that the decision they have made is constantly tested and needs, therefore, to be frequently renewed. It is not surprising, therefore, to find Thomas Cranmer and Martin Luther calling attention in words that have a very contemporary ring to the primacy of the sacrament of baptism and the need all Christians have to be reminded of that commitment and renew it.

Cranmer, in the preface to the baptismal service in the 1549 *Book of Common Prayer,* directed:

> baptisme shoulde not be ministred but upon Sondayes and other holy dayes, when the most numbre of people maye come together. As well for that the congregacion there presente may testifie the receyuyng of them, that be newly baptysed, into the noumbre of Christes Churche, as also because in the Baptisme of Infantes, euery manne presente maye be put in remembraunce of his owne profession made to God in his Baptisme. For whiche cause also it is expediente that Baptisme be ministred in the Englishe tounge.

---

[1] "A Member of the Aristocracy," *Manners and Rules of Good Society,* London, 1926, pp. 262-3.

Luther, in the same vein, wrote:

You must understand baptism to mean something by which evermore you must die and live: and therefore...you must still return to the very power that baptism exercises, and begin again to do what you were baptized for, and what your baptism signifies... Although you only receive the sacrament of baptism once, you are continually baptized anew by faith, always dying and yet ever living... indeed, we are continually being re-baptized, until we attain to the completion of the sign at the last day.

It is that sense of baptism as both the source and continuing center of the Christian life that is being rediscovered now in all the churches.

The renewed emphasis on baptism in recent years has paralleled a growing realization that the Christian Church in the western world is once again a minority faith in a largely pagan society. In such a society, baptism is beginning to be seen once more as the consequence of a radical, life-changing decision and itself a powerful, transforming action of the God who works in this sacrament to create a new community. The construction of immersion fonts in liturgical churches, the restoration of a catechumenate, the emphasis on baptism at the Easter Vigil, and the reincorporation of baptism into the Sunday eucharist are all evidence of this growing awareness of baptism as the action by which the church bears witness to the new life which the world needs and which Christians have begun to know.

Baptism, so understood, cannot ever be a "private" act. "Private baptism" is a contradiction in terms. Baptism is incorporation into the church, entrance into life in a body, and the life begun at baptism cannot be lived alone. Just as recovering alcoholics need the support of others to keep them in a life of sobriety, so Christians need the witness, guidance, and prayers of other Christians to enable them to continue and grow in the life to which they have committed themselves. They need to be strengthened by regular participation in the corporate worship of the gathered community.

For all these reasons, baptism is ministered more and more often in the midst of the eucharistic assembly on Sunday morning. Often it takes place at the Easter Vigil or on a Sunday with special significance for baptism such as the Feast of Pentecost or the Sunday after the Epiphany when the gospel tells the story of the baptism of Jesus.

If this procedure is right, it might seem anomalous to propose a discussion of baptismal homilies. We have defined homilies as sermons having an especially intimate or personal character, and if baptisms are to be performed only on corporate occasions which have their own importance, a baptismal homily of an intimate character would presumably be inappropriate. While the themes of baptism may indeed be developed in the sermon when the baptism takes place on Sunday morning, the sermon would presumably be of normal length and addressed to the whole congregation. Since baptism is so central to the Christian faith, the assigned readings will almost always be easily connected with the baptismal occasion. Particular reference might, of course, be made to the particular child or children to be baptized on that day. But the community will have gathered primarily for the eucharist of that Sunday or festival and those being baptized should not be completely the center of attention.

Nevertheless, there may still be occasions for a special baptismal homily. There are, to begin with, many churches where private baptism is still common and where the baptismal homily can help place the sacrament in the broader context of the church's corporate life. Such homilies may even help pave the way for a change in parish practice from private to public baptism. Many clergy, too, will find themselves making occasional exceptions to a general policy of Sunday morning baptism. Friends and family, for example, may need to come from a distance that makes the Sunday morning time difficult. They may live too far away to be able to arrive at the church by 10 o'clock in the morning but not so far away that they are willing to go to the expense of arriving the day before and spending the night in a motel. Or it may be that the parents are new to the community and, being young and a little insecure about their faith, are unwilling to appear as the center of attention on Sunday morning in the midst of strangers. Such families, once incorporated into the community, will often regret their initial choice and be happy to schedule the baptism of a second child on Sunday morning when they have seen what a marvelous occasion it can be. And there are also, no doubt, congregations so large, and with so many closely scheduled Sunday services, that it would be difficult if not impossible to hold all baptisms in the midst of the Sunday eucharist.

We live, in short, in a world in which the abnormal may not be unusual and "private baptism," although a contradiction in terms, may still be a pastoral necessity from time to time. Such occasions need not be totally devoid of redeeming grace. After all, as the citation from **Manners and Rules of Good Society** demonstrates, the church has survived long periods of time in the past in which baptisms were celebrated in a way not calculated to reinforce teaching on the corporate nature of the church. But the grace of baptism is not dependent on the number in attendance or the time of the service. Ten o'clock on Sunday morning may be, from God's perspective, not radically different from 2:30 in the afternoon. Baptism, whatever the outward circumstances, is still a rebirth in Christ, an incorporation into the life of the church, and a sharing of Christ's death and resurrection. One value of the sacraments is that they do continue to speak God's love, however poorly it may be understood by the human actors in the drama. It may, therefore, not only be possible but of the greatest importance to use such occasions to speak very directly to semi-converted Christians about the nature of grace, of the church, of redemption, and, because the preacher is clearly speaking to them and not someone else, to be heard in a way that she or he would not be heard on a Sunday morning in the midst of the assembled church.

What then will be the nature of a homily on such an occasion? Like the homilies at a wedding or funeral, the baptismal homily will have three reference points: the Word of God, the individuals involved, and the sacrament itself. The remainder of this section will deal with two of these three reference points: first the liturgy itself, and then the individuals. The Word of God, as it applies to this sacrament, will be discussed in the commentaries in the following section.

A. The Liturgy

The liturgy of baptism should be the clearest expression of God's purpose in human lives. As we have said, the time and place of the service should witness to the corporate nature of Christian life. If, in fact, that witness is not being made in the normal way by the congregation, still the service expects the presence of others. Baptism may be administered in an emergency in a lonely place with only the baptizer and a dying person but, if the newly baptized individual survives, the service should be completed later in the presence of the congregation. The ancient custom of sponsors or "godparents" is, in part, a means of ensuring that witnesses are present and that the membership of the church is represented at the font. This corporate nature of baptism would be an important theme to explore in a homily at a "private" baptism, and there are aspects of the liturgy which can be used to illustrate the point.

Even more importantly, baptism has to do with death and resurrection. Over the centuries, fonts have diminished in size and the custom of pouring (even "sprinkling" in some churches) has replaced immersion as the normal symbol. But sacraments do somehow reassert themselves and fonts large enough for immersion are once again being built and used. When a candidate is buried in the water of baptism and brought up again after having disappeared in the depths, it is clearly demonstrated that baptism has to do with something more radical than a washing and cleansing: it has to do with dying and being returned to life. Just as the corporate nature of baptism needs to be stressed especially when a congregation is not present, so the radical symbolism of water needs to be stressed especially if only a little is used in the service.

Rebirth and a new beginning is, of course, witnessed in other ways in the liturgy. Many churches have fonts placed at the back of the church or near an entrance door to make this point. Where baptisms are held at the main service, such locations are often seen as awkward and sometimes a bowl on a table at the crossing is used instead. Thus the emphasis on "corporateness" diminishes the emphasis on "entrance." "Private baptisms" can more easily be held wherever the font is located and that location will often be dramatically emphasized if a few people gather at the back of an empty church. Such a service is clearly the first step into a new life and leaves many more steps to be taken to arrive at God's throne.

Wherever the font is located and whenever the service is held, the liturgy can bear witness to the sacrament as an entrance both into life and into death. Just as Cranmer's *Book of Common Prayer* directed the priest at a burial service to meet the "corpse" at the door of the church and to lead the body to the grave, so it also instructed the priest to meet the baptismal party at the church door and to lead them to the font. Quite deliberately the two liturgies were set in parallel and the point was made that we are always being led through death to life. All too often the baptismal party arrives at the church to find the priest busy elsewhere or the ushers preoccupied. Whether the baptism is private or at the normal time, it might be better if the priest were at the door and a procession, however informal, were made into the church. In some churches the parents, sponsors, and friends, are seated at the back of the church through the first part of the service and then led on into the church and to the font by acolytes and clergy. But even at a less public service, the priest could arrange to be at the door and lead the baptismal party into the church and to the font, so making the point that they are welcome in God's house and that God is always leading us (more often by means of lay people and the events of our lives than by those who have been ordained) through death into life.

B. The Individual

Infant baptism is the strongest possible witness to the doctrine of prevenient grace. Although we have stressed the "personal" nature of a homily and the value of drawing a direct relationship between the gospel and the individual, there is, in a sense, no individual yet present at baptism. Incipient personality is, undoubtedly, present and beginning to manifest itself even in the smallest infant, but no one expects the child to be able to make a mature commitment to the Christian faith. That is why godparents and parents make the promises they do. And since it is the parents and godparents who make a commitment for the child, so it is probably the parents and godparents who provide whatever particularity can be used in the baptismal homily. It is they who are committing themselves to transmit the Christian faith, they who are being addressed, and therefore they whose circumstances and interests can most readily provide material for the homily. But the very lack of personal development in the child being baptized does provide grist for the homiletical mill. We are all too likely to think that our own commitment is a matter of our own choice. It "feels" as if we had chosen to be Christians, to go to church, to respond to the gospel, and so we act as if it were the case. In fact, as the old hymn says, "thou wert long beforehand with my soul."[2] Parents and godparents are agents of prevenient grace. They choose and act on behalf of the child and deliberately attempt to mold the child in the image of Christ. Most of us are well aware of, and thankful for, the loving care parents have given us from the moment of birth. We are aware of gifts of love and material gifts that came to us undeserved. And it would seldom occur to us to protest that parents have, by so doing, had an improper influence on us or even destroyed our freedom.

---

[2] *The Hymnal* 1940, No. 405.

Baptism, and God's prevenient grace, are like that. Not even the most perceptive parents know what the child will become and the wisest parents know they cannot, and should not, control that outcome. But still they will do whatever they can to offer the child what they believe to be good. And God will work in the child far more wisely, not preempting its freedom, but providing love. There cannot be a response to love if love is not offered. Baptism situates the child in the place where love is offered and where the response can begin to be made even before a conscious, deliberate choice can be articulated. A loving God could hardly act otherwise. Love never holds back, waiting to be sought; love seeks first, and our love of God, like our love of parents, is always a response to another's initiative.

It has been said that we are not human "beings" but human "becomings." Thus the baptismal homily addresses a child who is in the early stages of becoming. The homily, therefore, will speak particularly to parents and godparents since it is in large part through their "becoming" that God will begin to become in the newly baptized child.

Having said all that, it is also true that what is most particular about a child at the time of baptism is the given name. The name may be inherited and indicate the parents' hope that the child will carry on the family tradition as it was embodied in a grandparent, aunt, or uncle. Or the name may be chosen to honor a famous individual or to emphasize ethnic heritage. Few given names are totally unique. Yet the given name remains the symbol of individuality and of God's care for each of us as individuals. The child being baptized is named so that he or she will not be "the Smith girl" or "the Adams boy" to God but Elisabeth or John.

Therefore the chosen name may provide the means of linking the universal gospel with the individual soul. Perhaps the name is a biblical name or saint's name which indicates parental hopes and ideals. But the simple fact of naming is itself significant of the process of individuation: though baptized into the body of Christ and grafted into a common life, the child is, and will become, individual. Neither corporate identity in Christ nor genetic inheritance nor the sometimes almost overwhelming forces of socialization can finally override the singular worth and responsibility symbolized by the given name.

This difficult balance between the corporate and the individual life is at the heart of the baptismal liturgy and will find its place in the homily as the biblical readings provide their own guidance and revealing light.

II. The Readings at a Baptism

Since baptism should normally take place on Sunday morning at the principal service, the lessons read will normally be those appointed for the day. This will not prevent sermons on baptism from being preached since few if any Bible readings will be irrelevant to the subject of baptism. The theme of the Bible is the renewal of the life for which we were made. The fact of a baptism at a public service will frequently throw new light on familiar lessons and be a valuable reminder of our own baptism and the grace at work in our lives.

As we have stated, however, there may be times when exceptions seem justified and these will have the advantage of providing opportunity to look specifically at the subject of baptism and to address the members and friends of one family directly on the meaning of the action in which they are involved. The commentary on suggested lessons in the next section is intended simply to point to some of the relationships between the lesson and the sacrament and to provide starting points for an appropriate homily. Note that almost all of these lessons are also appointed for a Sunday or major festival in the Ecumenical Lectionary and the commentary on them may be useful for preparing sermons for public services as well as homilies for smaller occasions. In most cases the commentary's focus is on one or two texts within the passage. There are, obviously, many other texts that might be used and other points that might be made. The purpose here is simply to suggest some ways of dealing with the text that may be helpful and appropriate.

The texts selected for a baptism will have something to say in the first place about the sacrament itself. That may seem too obvious to need stating but the question does, in fact, arise in two ways. First of all, there are, naturally, no Old Testament texts which deal with baptism as such and, in the second place, it is questionable whether any texts from the gospels deal directly with Christian baptism. The baptismal stories in the New Testament are stories about Jesus' baptism at the hands of John. The implications of that event are hardly the same as when an infant is baptized today.

Some of the Old Testament passages suggested will seem to be "typological." That is, they draw a deeper meaning from the text on the basis of the New Testament. Typology reads the Old Testament in the light of the New and sees Old Testament events as foreshadowings of the Christian dispensation. Thus, when we come to the subject of baptism, the use of water for cleansing and for bringing life out of chaos and death are seen as "types" of the baptismal washing and renewal of life. In the Middle Ages this kind of analysis of the Bible was very popular, but it runs the danger of trivializing the Old Testament and reducing it to a mere series of warm-ups for "the real thing."

In fact, there are many appropriate Old Testament passages which have nothing to do with water. Those that do refer to water have value in showing God's consistent purpose to bring life out of death and to cleanse and purify a creation stained with sin. But other passages will demonstrate that God's purpose has always been to call people into a saving relationship with the love of God, to create a people for God's own possession, and to enable people everywhere to respond to God's love. Use of such passages will serve to emphasize the universality of God's purpose and place the particular baptism in the largest possible context.

In the same way, New Testament passages need not be confined to those which deal explicitly with baptism. There are many stories of calling and healing which will throw light on God's purpose and way of working in human lives. Water, after all, is the means of baptism but not the meaning. The meaning is choice and response and faith and empowerment and cleansing and new life and incorporation into the realm of love.

Although the Bible speaks to us and we must always be careful not to impose our meanings on it, it is also true that God calls us into dialogue. God speaks, but we also respond. So we will inevitably choose certain passages as more appropriate than others in view of the individuals involved. This does not mean that we are shaping or accommodating the Scripture to our understanding, but simply that we are encouraging dialogue: seeking passages that individuals may be better able to hear, or to remember, or with which they may need to continue to carry on a dialogue, rebelling and responding and rebelling and responding again until their lives and God's purpose come into the harmony God intends.

A. Old Testament Texts and Commentary

1. Genesis 7:17-23 (or 7:17-8:5) ♦ "Only Noah was left, and those that were with him in the ark"

a. *Sin, water, and death* are the essential elements in this story. The ancient stories of Genesis portray a creation which was "very good" and yet, upon the creation of the human race, was almost immediately stained with sin. These stories seek to explain where sin came from and how God deals with it. The story of Noah tells us that only death can finally remove sin and that water brings death. At baptism, water is a symbol of death, the death that wipes away the stain of sin. But the story also tells us that God made a way for life to survive and be renewed. The First Epistle of Peter says that the water of the flood corresponds to baptism and that, as Noah's family was "saved through water," (3:20) so baptism now saves us. Life can be destroyed by water or saved by water. The water of baptism is a symbol of death and life: death to the sin that weighs us down and eternal life through Christ.

b. A rather different point can be made by focusing attention on the ark itself. From ancient times, the ark has been seen as a "type" of the church, and the church has been seen as an ark into which we are gathered for protection against the waves and storms of the world and a safe passage into God's kingdom. Even small infants seem to have a natural ability to swim and there are programs to teach swimming to infants who have not yet learned to walk. Depending on our ability as swimmers we may survive for some time even in the ocean. But although many people have swum the English channel and other such bodies of water, no one yet has swum the ocean. For a long crossing, we need a ship. And the church is the ship we are given to ensure our safe crossing into God's kingdom. Every parent is aware of the dangers with which the world surrounds their child and most have some sense of baptism as a means of protection. The image of the church as ark can help to clarify the role the church can play in a child's life if that child is fully "brought on board" and incorporated into the saving life of the church.

2. Exodus 14:19-31 ♦ "But the Israelites walked on dry ground through the sea"

The escape from Egypt is the event which forms the people of God. To this day, Jews and Christians look back to this moment as the one in which they were first set free from slavery and started on the way toward the promised land. Here water is death to the forces of slavery and life to God's people. What better image could there be of the sacrament of baptism than this? At the font, water is death to our enslavement to sin and freedom to serve God as a new people. We pass through the water of baptism and set out on the journey toward the kingdom God has promised.

This passage is central to the Easter Vigil which is the archetypal occasion for baptisms. It may be especially valuable to use this passage if baptisms are held at other times so as to link those times with the primal time. The parallels between this event and the crucifixion and resurrection might usefully be discussed in the homily. In both events, the powers of this world became determined to destroy the people or person in whom God was at work. On both occasions, the powers of this world seemed to have succeeded beyond any rational hope for escape. On both occasions, nonetheless, God's agents not only "escaped" but triumphed, not by their own power but by reliance on God. The people of Israel, between the army of Pharaoh and the sea, were clearly helpless. Christ, crucified and laid in a tomb, was clearly helpless. Perhaps we, too, should only come to baptism when we fully know our helplessness, for then God's power is most free to bring us salvation.

3. Deuteronomy 30:15-20 ♦ "Choose life"

a. Love comes first. This passage portrays Moses giving his final charge to the people of Israel before his death. Like a parent sending children out into the world, Moses can no longer be there to guide them but he can remind them of the choices they must make and the consequences of their choices.

Twice in this passage (vv. 16, 20) there is a sequence of verbs in which love comes first: "loving...walking...keeping" and "loving...obeying...cleaving." Baptism has to do with a familial relationship in which we obey God *because* we love God. Love comes first, and love is absorbed before any formal teaching or obedience is possible. The rules a family establishes for children will not always be easily understood, but because they are set in a framework of love, they will often be accepted nonetheless. And even when obedience is not accepted but compelled, the relationship will not be broken if love comes first. Those who know they are loved will try to understand the will of the one who loves them and follow it for love alone.

b. The passage also speaks of choice. This will be seen in different ways depending on whether the one to be baptized is a child or an adult.

An adult seems to make a free choice but, in fact, much has happened that led to that choice. It is normally out of an experience of being loved that one chooses to behave in a particular way. What we call *choice* is really a *response*, and the response we make is to God's choosing of us. An anonymous hymn says, "I sought the Lord, and afterward I knew / He moved my soul to seek him, seeking me...I find, I walk, I love, but O the whole / Of love is but my answer, Lord, to thee..." The people of God could respond to the choice between life and death Moses set before them only because God had already poured out life on them. They had been set free from slavery and fed with manna because God chose to love them. Therefore they could now be asked to respond and choose. An adult standing at the font has an experience of life in which God has been at work: love has been experienced in family and friends and the church community. Therefore they can respond by offering back to God the life God has given. Now they can "cross over Jordan" and come into God's presence and begin to live out an intentional and freely chosen relationship of love.

A child being baptized seems to have no choice. Rather the choice is made by parents on the child's behalf. But human choice is always a response to our experience and the baptism of infants brings the child into a place where the experience of God's love can lead gradually to understanding and acceptance and response. No child chooses human parents either, but the love children experience from their parents (in a heathly family) creates a lifelong bond. In a healthy family, a growing child never consciously chooses to accept the family he or she is given. They simply grow more mature in their response to love and there is no "moment of decision" in which they decide to be part of that family. In the same way, growth in the church should be a natural process of increasing maturity. "Moments of decision" become necessary when the process of growth has been disrupted in some way. Unfortunately, the process of growth in our relationship with God is often disrupted and needs often to be restored and renewed. The parents and godparents take on a major responsibility for attempting to prevent any such disruption by seeing that the process of growth is given every encouragement and opportunity within the life of the church. The child's choosing of life over death should be a natural and almost unconscious maturing response to God's choice of him or her as mediated through family and friends and the Christian community.

4. Joshua 24:14-24 ♦ "Choose this day whom you will serve"

This passage is similar in many ways to Deuteronomy 30 above. The same theme of *choice* can be developed.

a. Another major theme in this passage is the "putting away" of "foreign gods" and it could be helpful to explore what that means in our day. Joshua speaks of the gods served by other people in the land the Hebrew people passed through and in the land in which they now live. It is no longer possible (if it ever was) to see our country as a "Christian country." Our friends and neighbors have "different standards" and these are often not consistent with Christian faith. Most of us compromise our own standards so frequently that we are unaware of it. "Cheating" on income taxes and spouses is taken for granted: we have certain "human" needs which we assume must be met. Everyone else does it; why shouldn't we?

God calls us to a greater simplicity of life than most of us are ready to accept. One God is much simpler than many; one pattern of life is much simpler than constant compromise. There is enormous freedom in the simplicity of life to which God calls us. Baptism is a passage through water into a new country. Why would we go to all the trouble of that passage if we wanted to stay where we were? Why would we emigrate to a new country and then try to make the new country like the old? The gods of the land are very much at home here and hard to identify, but with God's grace and the help of the church we can learn to identify them more easily and set them aside. The result is simplicity and freedom.

b. *"...You cannot serve the Lord,..."* (v. 19). Having asked the people to choose, Joshua tells them that what they have chosen is impossible. Of course, he is right. God is a holy God and we are far from holy. This passage stands at the start of "Phase II," of the history of God's people. In the first phase they were set free and fed in the wilderness. They experienced love and came into the promised land seeking God. In "Phase II," beginning here, they realize the truth of what Joshua tells them. In spite of their response and their efforts, they "cannot serve the Lord" and fulfill God's commands. Therefore, "Phase III," the gift of God's love and grace in Jesus Christ becomes necessary. In a similar way, we come into the church in response to God's love and then experience failure when we try to live Christian lives by our own strength. Baptism does not complete our conversion but sets us in the place where we can find forgiveness and renewal. Baptism without continuing church membership and prayer and Bible study and sacraments would be like crossing the Jordan and then going back to live in the desert! We cannot serve God by our own strength and apart from God. Baptism opens up to us all the resources of God's love.

5. II Kings 5:1-15a ♦ "So he went down and immersed himself...in the Jordan"

This lesson is chosen for its "typological" significance.[3] Nevertheless, this passage does speak eloquently to the way God works in the world. God's

---

[3] See the discussion of "types" in the introduction to this section.

will is the good of human beings and God heals and restores those who are come out of all nations into God's kingdom.

There is a homily in Naaman's scorn of the Jordan and his servants' sensible suggestion that if you would be willing to do some big thing to be cured, you might at least try the small thing the prophet asks. Baptism is, of itself, a very small and simple thing. If our lives seem "out of joint" and lacking some critical element, can we imagine that a little water and a few words of prayer will make the difference? There will always be those who measure by human standards and who imagine God is at work only when great events take place or when human emotions are deeply stirred. Perhaps this is why, for some people, a "moment of decision" when one knows oneself to be born again is so important. But a God who works only in great and obvious ways would be a God not often involved in our lives. The God who created the universe is at work in all of it always, and the simple elements of water, bread, and wine are means by which God is able to work in the common materials and common events of our lives.

6. Isaiah 43:1-3a, 6b-7 ♦ "I have called you by name, you are mine"

a. "...He who created you,..." (v.1). God is known first of all as creator. Primitive human beings saw in the sun and stars evidence of a power beyond their own. We, whose knowledge of creation ranges from subatomic particles to black holes and spiral nebulae, know far more vividly what it means to speak of God as creator. Likewise, those who told the story of the loss of Eden knew less than we about the human failure to exercise responsible stewardship of creation. The biblical understanding of God as creator and redeemer comes as answer and promise to this knowledge of human failure. The purpose of baptism, seen in this light, is to begin the process of re-creation: to offer back to God this fallen world in confidence that God can redeem and make new what we inevitably corrupt. No newborn infant can escape the stain of human sin, but the God who created particles and galaxies beyond our reach can work in the newborn infant to re-create God's handiwork.

b. "...When you pass through the waters, I will be with you;..." (v.2). The water of baptism is a double symbol: a means of death and a means of life. The same waters that were death to the Egyptians were life to the Hebrews. We come to God needing both death and life: death to human sin and life through God's grace. It is important to stress the radical nature of what happens at baptism. This is not simply a little water to wash away a few imperfections. This is a flood in which we are drowned, in which we die and are buried, so that we can be raised with Christ to new life.

c. "...Rivers,...will not overwhelm you;..." (v.2b). The rivers of the Middle East are not placid streams meandering through quiet English meadows but wadis which can suddenly bring violent torrents down from the highlands. Flocks and herds can be swept away by rivers that were not there moments ago.

The rivers and floods of the modern world are different but just as sudden and terrifying. Men and women with well-paying and demanding jobs can find themselves unemployed overnight as a result of "corporate restructuring." Marriages dissolve, airplanes crash, a heart attack strikes. Life may go smoothly for years, but we have no security in the world we have made for ourselves. Nor does God promise to absolve us of the consequences. Our world will not be changed unless we face the consequences and find better ways to structure our society. God's people are promised, however, that they will be not be "overwhelmed." God will not "let you be tested above your strength" (I Corinthians 10:13). Julian of Norwich wrote, "He said not: 'Thou shalt not be tempested, thou shalt not be travailed, thou shalt not be diseased'; but he said: 'Thou shalt not be overcome.'"[4] In baptism we are placed in God's hands, and God's hands will not let us go.

d. *"I have called you by name...everyone who is called by my name"* (vv. 1, 7). Baptism is not primarily a naming ceremony, but it involves a radical change in who we are. Human beings have always instinctively felt that a change in status required a change of name. Native Americans gave new names to new members of the tribe; the religious orders give new names to those who take the vows; so, because it is the most radical change of status we can be given, baptism requires a new name because we become new people. Secondly, the new name is evidence of God's personal relationship to us. God knows us each by name. But the passage also says we are "called by (God's) name." As members of God's family, members of Christ's body, we are to take the name of God and be known as God's people. After baptism, we are no longer our own selves. We are honored with God's own name. It is because we are made members of Christ's body that we are appropriately known as "Christians." That we should be counted worthy of this name is the most radical evidence of God's claim on our lives. It is also evidence of God's power working in us: that power is able to make us worthy representatives of God's redeeming love.

7. Isaiah 44:1-15 ♦ "You are my witnesses! Is there any god besides me?"

a. The author of this passage describes in vivid language the contrast between two likenesses of God: the pagan image, and the living human being. As the carpenter chooses a piece of wood or the artisan a lump of metal to shape into an image, so God chooses us and forms us by water and the Holy Spirit. The second chapter of Genesis describes God molding the first human image of dust of the earth. That image, through Adam's fall, became marred and all but lost. In the birth of Christ, God restored the image and gave us one human life which reflected perfectly who God is. Baptism, by incorporating us into Christ, begins the process of restoring the image of God in the human race. God begins the work of sculpting us. Compare

---

[4] Julian of Norwich, *Revelations of Divine Love,* (edited by Roger Hudleston) p. 141.

God's sculpting of us with the pagan carpenter's sculpting of an image. Isaiah is full of scorn for those who bow down before carved wood, but we appropriately humble ourselves before each other knowing Christ to be present in each member of his body. Indeed, we appropriately humble ourselves in service even to those who do not know Christ because even there the image of God is not wholly lost, is potentially present, and can be restored.

b. Isaiah also sets out a second contrast: between the false gods represented by the image-maker and God himself. God asks "Who is like me?" (Isaiah 44:7) and the question answers itself. God alone has acted from the beginning to carry out a purpose and to choose witnesses. If we know God's glory, the absurdity of the image-maker is obvious. Yet the temptation remains for human beings to worship false gods, the gods of power, success, possessions. We still are too easily tempted to shape these as gods and give ourselves to them.

In baptism we renounce false gods and place ourselves in the hands of the living God so that we may be shaped in God's image and bear witness to God's creative power.

8. Jeremiah 31:31-34 ♦ "I will put my law within them, and I will write it on their hearts"

We often speak of baptism in family terms: "we bring this child into God's family." That may be a good analogy in human terms, but God wants us as more than family. Jeremiah spoke at a time when it must have seemed as if all God's love for Israel had borne no fruit; when it must have seemed that God had given up on Israel. Israel had been defeated and its leaders carried into exile. So Jeremiah contrasts the past, failed relationship with God's intended relationship with the nation in the future. In the past, God had been a "husband" to Israel. God had known Israel as a husband knows a wife. But that is not enough. A marriage covenant between husband and wife, though no human relationship is more intimate, is still a matter of external relationships. Husband and wife need to discuss, to plan, to come to a common mind. But now God says, "I will put my law within...and write it upon (your) hearts." Baptism creates just such a covenant by imparting the gift of God's Spirit. When that is accomplished, we need no outward law and no advice from others because the Spirit within us directs us. We will know God's Spirit within ourselves and follow the leading of that Spirit. Jeremiah gives us a vision of that day and baptism is the first step toward the fulfilling of that vision.

Imagine a world in which no father or mother needed to say to a child, "Do this," because the spirit of the parents was so deeply present in the child that their will was naturally the freely chosen will of the child! Such a world might seem desirable to parents but, since their will is not always the best, it would not, in fact, be an ideal world. If, on the other hand, each of us were so deeply imbued with God's Spirit that we naturally and freely chose to respond to the Spirit's leading, that world would be the kingdom of God.

9. Ezekiel 36:24-28 ♦ "A new heart I will give you, and a new spirit I will put within you"

The prophet Ezekiel spoke in the time of exile and imagined from that perspective what a new, restored Israel might be like. It was one of the rare occasions in human history when it was possible to begin again rather than try to modify an existing structure. Ezekiel imagines not just a restored country but a renewed humanity with a new heart and new spirit. But for all the daring imagination of his vision, it remains limited by the past. Yes, there will be a new heart and spirit, but the result will be only a more careful observance of the law.

On an individual basis, baptism also provides the opportunity to begin anew. Parents and godparents may well envision a child who grows up in a new way, preserved from the failures of the past and enabled to create a new and ideal human life. So God does indeed put a new spirit in us and open up the possibility of a new world of new people. But our vision also is limited and we continue to try to build the kingdom with laws rather than rely completely on God's Spirit. Nevertheless the promise does not simply remain an unattained vision. Through baptism Christians begin to experience this promise and glimpse the final reality and the assurance that it will be ours. Each baptism brings us one step closer to the fulfillment of this promise.

B. New Testament Epistle Texts and Commentary

1. Acts 16:25-34 ♦ "He and his entire family were baptized without delay"

The Philippian jailer would have been at home in the contemporary world. He knew a world in which "number one" was the priority and there was no mercy for those who failed. The jailer whose charges escaped might well be put to death for his failure. Thus, when an earthquake shook the prison, opening the doors, he had reason to fear for his life. Suddenly, in that crisis, he was confronted with St. Paul and Silas and a pattern of behavior he had never experienced before. Here were people whose first priority was not self. When they had an opportunity to escape their first concern was to reassure the jailer that they were still there. Beaten and jailed, their concern was still for others. This exposure to a radically different way of life led the jailer and all his family to baptism. We come to baptism because we have seen Christian lives and, because we are baptized, others also will be exposed to the transforming power of Christian love.

2. Romans 6:3-11 (or 6:3-5) ♦ "Buried with him by baptism into death"

a. *"...Our old self was crucified with him so that the sinful body might be destroyed, and we might no longer be enslaved to sin...."* (v.6). The phrase "analysis paralysis" may sum up the difference between St. Paul's approach to sin and our own. We are very aware of the impact of environment and family training and psychological pressures and prefer to deal with causes rather than results. We should, of course, use all the tools at our command to produce better adjusted citizens. But that is a slow and painful way to make the world better and not likely to succeed any time soon. St. Paul was probably unaware of the psychological causes of sin; he knew only that sin is a part of the human condition in this world and that our lives are weighed down and enslaved by sin. Wouldn't you like to be free of the tendency to lose your temper, to be jealous of others, to lust, to covet, to deceive? St. Paul has a radical solution: kill the body that does these things and get a new one. Baptism, in St. Paul's view, has to do with dying with Christ and being buried with him in order to share his life and his freedom from sin. That's what happens to us when we are baptized. The old body doesn't die easily. It will still take every opportunity to enslave us again. But after baptism, that body begins to die, the life of Christ begins to take hold, and God sees us and judges us in terms of our future, not our past. The final solution to sin is death and resurrection.

b. *"...If we have died with Christ, we believe that we shall also live with him..."* (v.8). There is a juggler in Ingmar Bergman's movie, *The Seventh Seal,* who says that his infant son will grow up to do "the one impossible trick...to make one of the balls stand absolutely still in the air."[5] We have such aspirations for our children. But whatever the child being baptized may accomplish, we are also aware at some level that we have brought a child to birth who will someday die. To avoid death forever is more impossible than to make a ball stand still in midair. The purpose of life is, however, not to avoid death but to fulfill our potential, and our potential, the Bible tells us, is to be like God. How do we become like God? By joining our lives with that of Jesus who was more like God than anyone who ever lived. And this is the purpose of baptism. St. Paul tells us that in baptism we are buried with Christ in order to live with him. Death no longer has power over him, nor does it have power over those who belong to him. The child being baptized will, in fact, accomplish the one impossible trick. He or she will, indeed, live forever because in baptism we share Christ's victory over death.

---

[5] Malmstrom, Lars, and Kushner, David, *Four Screenplays of Ingmar Bergman,* p. 106.

3. Romans 8:14-17 (or 8:11-17) ♦ "We are children of God, and if children, then heirs"

a. *"For all who are led by the Spirit of God are children of God....if in fact we suffer with him..."* (vv.14, 17). Verse 14 has an openness and inclusiveness about it which might lead to the question why baptism is needed. If all who act in a "Christian spirit" are children of God, what more is needed? But St. Paul goes on to say that we are "children of God...[and] heirs of God...if in fact we suffer with him [Christ]" (vv.16, 17). Being led by the Spirit is the beginning, not the end, of God's working in us. Most people give some evidence of God's working in their lives, but the world "most people" make is obviously far from God. Natural human goodness needs to be disciplined and developed. Baptism places us in the community where such discipline and development is available. Such development will also place us at odds with the world and face us with the need to suffer if we are to be obedient to God. The water of baptism is a symbol of death and reminds us that we need to die to this world in order to come to the fullness of life God has promised.

b. *"...a spirit of adoption..."* (v.15). One of the best results of the whole debate over abortion between the pro-choice and pro-life movements has been a renewed emphasis on the importance of alternatives. Some women will not want to choose abortion, yet they know they cannot provide for the child themselves. Therefore means of adoption should be available and the pro-life movement, at its best, has understood this and encouraged it. There are always prospective parents who want a child and can provide a better home.

Few parents at the time of baptism will see themselves in such a position, but the fact is that at baptism we bring a newborn child to God and say, "I cannot provide for this child as completely as I would like to do. Therefore I give this child to you and ask you to adopt it as your own." No human parent can provide all that a child requires. No human parent will have the understanding and patience to respond to all of a child's needs in infancy or as they begin school or during the teenage years—or even when they leave home to begin lives of their own. With no opportunity for rehearsal and all too little experience to guide us, we do the best we can, but the wiser we are, the more fully we realize how often we cannot provide what is needed. The wiser we are, the more we know how much we need the wisdom and strength which only God can give.

The first English Prayer Book at the moment of baptism said, "Then the Minister shall take the child in his arms..." But it never said to give the child back. This omission is thought to have been deliberate. In baptism, we give the child to God and God keeps that child, adopting it as a member of the Christian church, God's family. God not only knows better than we what the child's needs are and is able to provide them, but God can also overcome our failures and use them to the child's advantage. If we truly love our children, we will want to offer them for adoption as children of God.

c. *"...Abba! Father!..."* (v.15). Baptism can be seen as an adoption ceremony through which we are adopted into God's family (see above). But baptism can also be seen as the initiation of a process through which we, having been put out for adoption, come at last to recognize our true parentage. Some adopted children, having grown up, feel a great need to find their biological parents. In the same way, many people brought up without a knowledge of God begin to search, when they have grown up, for the God in whose creative power their lives began. Most human beings feel a need for someone beyond their human family to whom they can say "Father." While there is much controversy at the moment about referring to God with language that is gender-inclusive, the important point is surely that the God revealed in Scripture is one with whom a personal relationship, as of a child to a parent, is possible. The God of the Bible is a personal God, that is, a God whose being includes all that we think of as personal in human terms. Our God is One to whom we can speak, who cares about us, who loves us and wants our love. In teaching the Lord's Prayer, Jesus taught his disciples to think of God in these terms.

Remember also the saying, "God has no grandchildren." Parents can bring their children to their own parents and provide opportunity to build a relationship between their children and their parents. But this is always a "grandparental" relationship which, for all its warmth and importance, is never as immediate or vital as that between parent and child. That is not the relationship parents should try to encourage between their children and God. At first, all children know God secondhand, through their parents, but finally children must come to such a knowledge of God that they know themselves to be God's children, not grandchildren, with such a personal relationship that terms of address like "Abba! Father!" are natural and right.[6] When we reach that stage, St. Paul says, it is evidence that we are God's children ourselves.

4. I Corinthians 12:12-13 ♦ "We were all baptized into one body"

a. *"...many members...one body,..."* (v.12). The birth of a child means more than an addition to a family, it means a redefinition of roles within the family. "Husband" and "wife" become also "father" and "mother" and each couple needs to work out for themselves what that means. So, too, in the church, the baptism of a child redefines relationships. As children are added some church members become nursery attendants, church school teachers, friends, role models and guides. The image of a body with various members

---

[6] "In a true family, children learn that there is one God. They learn it first from their parents, and from the disciplined and thoughtful obedience parents and children alike pay to the same God. Parents who force on a child an obedience they are not willing to accept equally for themselves are committing one of the deepest offences of family life, for they are giving to their child a false view of the one God who rules over all life and in whose will is our peace." *Lambeth Conference 1958*, 2.152.

is, perhaps, St. Paul's most effective analogy for the church and an important one to re-examine. We play various roles in the "gathered church" and various roles as witnesses in the world. Being a Christian is not one thing, easily learned and carried out. It may be a role in the church as usher or church school teacher which we enjoy, but it may also mean agonizing decisions in our work and patience with a spouse's alcoholism or a child's teenage rebelliousness. But playing these parts need not be a lonely matter between ourselves and God: ideally, we should find support and guidance within the church from other members of the body playing other roles. The children being baptized will grow into this body and find roles to play in a children's choir, as acolytes, in a youth group and they will find that they can work with others to enrich the life of the church and serve God in God's world. Each member has a role to play to create and enhance the unity of Christ's body the church.

b. "...*We were all baptized into one body—Jews or Greeks, slaves or free...*" (v.13). As the world grows smaller and international travel easier, it becomes less and less possible to find a country which is ethnically united. Enormous tensions are building up in Europe, Africa, and Asia over linguistic and cultural differences between "natives" and "immigrants." Nor have the American countries which often pride themselves on their "melting pot" character solved all the problems which result. The Christian church began in a world just as diverse. St. Paul was always aware of the gulf between those of Jewish and Gentile heritage, and those of different economic status who had been brought together by the gospel of Christ. He makes it clear that these differences are secondary to our unity in the church. The significance of that claim is only fully appreciated if we are able to recognize and value our own ethnic and cultural heritage. It is one thing to build a church out of people of Saxon and Angle and Celtic and Norman origin whose tribal distinctions are lost in the distant past. It is quite another thing to bring together Arab and Irish, Korean and Russian. Linguistic differences may even require separate services for those of different languages. But congregations are often self-selected from very narrowly defined economic and cultural groups so that the members fail to reflect and experience and value the gifts which can be brought together in one church. An infant baptism, taking place before differences have been learned, allows our primal unity as human beings to be stressed. The growth in Christ that begins at baptism must be a growth into unity and the church must be that place where the diversity of the world is brought together into the unity of God's purpose.

5. II Corinthians 5:17-20 ♦ "If anyone is in Christ, there is a new creation"

The two key terms in this passage are "a new creation" and "reconciliation." The New Testament speaks constantly of the "newness" of life in Christ and the contrast between life in Christ and life in the world. What makes our life new? One specific answer is "reconciliation." In a family, reconciliation is a constant necessity. Parents have different goals. Children quarrel. In the larger society there are constant conflicts of interest groups. In the world, nations come into conflict over their differing needs and ambitions. By contrast, the Bible presents a vision of a world in which swords can be safely beaten into plowshares and in which love is the controlling emotion.

How do we get from here to there? From the beginning, the Bible makes it clear that something radical must take place. The story of Noah's ark shows us (among other things) that even a nearly total destruction of human life will make no difference if the people who step out of the ark are no different from the ones who embarked, even if those who embarked were the eight best people in the world. Good people are not good enough.

Reconciliation begins with God's action in Christ in which the old humanity is put to death and a new humanity, raised from the dead, is offered to us in baptism. As we, in Christ, die to sin and rise to a new life, human divisions are also put to death and the shared life of Christ becomes real. This is God's promise. The need for it is all too evident. The offer of it in baptism is a gift to be accepted with hope and joy.

6. Galatians 5:16-25 ♦ "The fruit of the Spirit is love"

"Live by the Spirit, I say, and do not gratify the desires of the flesh...." (v.16). St. Paul's contrast between the works of the flesh and the fruit of the Spirit is rather stark, and harsher than we might be comfortable with on the happy occasion of a baby's baptism. But perhaps that's exactly the time we need to be reminded that raising a child is not just a matter of medical advice and good nutrition; we will also be engaged in a battle for the child's soul. Patience, for example, is on St. Paul's list of virtues. No hungry infant understands the concept of patience. Patience has to be taught. On the other hand, no one teaches a child anger and envy. Those are built in. St. Paul's point is that "the works of the flesh" are a given; they come with being a fallen human being. But "the fruits of the Spirit" have to be acquired. Parents can teach these virtues, but finally the virtues need to be as interior and instinctive as the works of the flesh were before. Finally, these virtues become part of us only by the work of the Holy Spirit within us. Baptism begins the process of remaking our human nature both from without and within. The child is set in the Body of Christ and the Spirit is set in the child. Parents and godparents and other Christians work from outside to set an example and teach. And the Holy Spirit works from within, remolding our innermost nature.

7. I Peter 2:4-10 ♦ "you are a chosen race, a royal priesthood"

a. *"...you are a chosen race,..."* (v.9). The Bible comes back again and again to the theme of a "chosen people" and something in our contemporary culture finds that difficult to deal with. It seems unfair that God should choose some and not others. We worry about the others and how God will deal with them. The best solution may be to think of it in terms of someone who has just won the lottery or who has just received a proposal of marriage. In that ecstatic moment, do we worry about all the others who have not won and not been chosen? So, too, God's choosing of us is a matter of such great joy that the only appropriate response is gratitude and praise. God can deal with the others (if there are "others" from God's perspective); our only need is to accept God's choice of us, the "amazing grace" that singles us out and calls us into the kingdom.

This passage forms a logical pair with the passages from Deuteronomy and Joshua (above) which stress the choice we must make. As indicated there, our choice is a response to God's choice.

b. "...*a royal priesthood,...* " (v.9). It is becoming common nowadays for the service of baptism to include an anointing with oil and it is once again common for members of the congregation to be asked to bring the bread and wine to the altar in an offertory procession. Often the parents or godparents are invited to be the ones who bring the bread and wine forward. Few Christians think of themselves as "royal" or as "priests" but the anointing and the offering indicate exactly that. As members of Christ's body, we share his royalty and his priesthood.

Royalty comes first. The human race was given "dominion" over all creation (Genesis 1:28). The human race, for better or worse, rules the world. Failure to exercise good stewardship of the environment has led some to question the idea of dominion, but it is our exercise of it that is wrong not the fact of it. The solution to our failure is not abdication, but responsible rule. Kings in Old Testament times (and certain priests) were anointed ("Messiah," the Hebrew word for "King" means "the anointed one"). So, today, the infant is anointed and made a part of Christ's royal body.

Because we have this royal role, we must also be priests. The role of a priest is to make offering on behalf of others. The human race is that part of the created order endowed with sufficient (almost sufficient?) intelligence to respond to the creator. The church is that body of people who are called to offer back to God all that God has given us. There may be an individual selected as "priest" to lead the congregation in its offering, but the whole church is a "a royal priesthood" and the various roles played by lay people in the service are an expression of the "priesthood of all believers." Most dramatically, the role of lay people in the "offertory procession" makes that point.

In baptism, the newborn Christian is given a royal and priestly nature. With the help of parents and godparents, they must grow to understand these roles and act on them not only in the liturgy but in the world.

c. "...*a holy nation, God's own people,...* " (v.9). Baptism has to do with membership. We are incorporated into what is from one perspective a body, from another perspective a family, and from still another perspective a nation. The human being is a social animal, but our fall from God has destroyed our instinctive sense of belonging and commonality. Therefore God gives us a sense of our corporateness in the church. And that new corporate identity is derived from God. God's church belongs to God, therefore it must be like God, it must be "holy." Note the "holiness code" in Leviticus 19 which begins with the summons, "You must be holy, for I the Lord your God am holy," which is echoed in the Sermon on the Mount (Matthew 5:48), "You ...must be perfect, as your heavenly Father is perfect." God is not satisfied with moral improvement; God requires a new being which can come only from God. The church into which we are baptized is called to be "a holy nation" in the midst of the nations, making God known and transforming the world as yeast transforms a loaf.

d. *"in order that you may proclaim the mighty acts..."* Baptism is a gift, but gifts are seldom kept secret. Even the smallest child, after opening a present, will go show it to someone else saying, "Look what I got!" It's a human instinct. We can't help telling others the good things that have happened to us. And what could arouse that instinct more than baptism? Here in one short verse we are given a summary of gifts so overwhelming that we can never again be the same. God, the creator of the universe, loves us and calls us. Can you imagine not telling others? The first Christians were instinctive evangelists. They knew the greatness of God's gift and couldn't help sharing the news. Nor could we, if we really knew.

C. Gospel Texts and Commentary

1. Matthew 16:24-27 ♦ "Those who lose their life for my sake will find it"

Every form of life on earth instinctively acts in such a way as to preserve the life of the species. Human beings alone instinctively seek something more. The more possessions we gain, the less we seem to be satisfied with our lives. The reason the Christian faith has commended itself to so many people over so many years is that Jesus offers his followers a life more satisfying than the one we have. There are three stages in coming to share his life: first, knowledge of it; second, a desire for it; and third, a renunciation of the life we are living now.

This passage from Matthew stands at the center of the gospel story. The disciples have been with Jesus for a period of time and he has asked them who they believe he is. Peter answers, "You are the Christ." In response, Jesus points out the next stage of the journey. If they know him and want to share his life, they must renounce their own life.

Baptism is a way of saying to God that we want God's life in place of ours. Baptism is a dying to self and an incorporation into Christ. But the old self does not die easily and the possessions we know to be unsatisfying continue to tempt us. The Christian life involves a continual renewal of our baptism: learning to die to self in order to come to the fullness of life we instinctively know we need and which God in Christ freely offers.

2. Matthew 28:16-20 ♦ "Go therefore and make disciples of all nations"

"...*When they saw him they worshiped him; but some doubted*" (v.17). St. Matthew draws a fascinating picture of an assembly of disciples gathered in Jesus' presence, some of whom are moved to worship while others are controlled by doubt. Perhaps most of us are also torn between doubt and worship, and the critical question is whether we will let our doubts control us. There are no final, infallible answers in this world. We will always have doubts. Doubts serve a valuable role in leading us to further study, but if they control us, they paralyze us.

Sometimes we imagine that we must answer all our doubts before we can commit ourselves, before we are ready to be baptized or have our children baptized. But that is to let one aspect of our being, our reason, decide for the whole of us. Others will let emotions control their decision and will commit themselves in an emotional moment without consulting their minds. Perhaps a better response would be one governed by the instinct for worship.

Worship is a response of the whole person involving body and spirit, logic and emotion. The body can keep us centered on physical existence; the spirit can be pushed aside by the needs of the body; emotions come and go; logic has its limits. Worship involves every aspect of ourselves and transcends them all.

Baptism brings us into a community formed by worship. It involves the whole of our being and recreates our whole being in the image of God. We do not worship because we fully understand, but we understand more fully because we worship.

3. Mark 1:1-11 (or 1:9-11) ♦ "Proclaiming a baptism of repentance"

a. The story of Jesus' baptism builds on numerous Old Testament references, some explicit, like the reference to Isaiah in this passage, and others implicit. The most important of these is in verse 11 where two key references are brought together. The first is the phrase "You are my Son,..." from Psalm 2, a "coronation psalm." Such psalms, extolling the king and envisioning his glory, came to be seen as messianic, prophecies of the One who would come to save God's people. The second reference, in the phrase "my chosen," is to the first of the "suffering servant" poems in Isaiah 42. These poems were not part of the messianic expectation but were quickly understood as such by the early church since they helped to make sense of the crucifixion. Jesus, they saw, was not only the expected heir of David, but also the unexpected suffering servant. These two aspects of Jesus' witness are thus brought together in the acclamation at his baptism.

These two aspects of Jesus' ministry might well be discussed in a baptismal homily since they apply not only to Jesus but to those who share his life. Baptism into the Christian life is baptism into a royal heritage with all the freedom and joy that this entails. It is also baptism into Jesus' suffering and death, the unexpected and unwanted aspect of being God's chosen. Baptism is a moment of joy, but we would deceive ourselves if we failed to recognize that we also commit ourselves to share Christ's suffering. Only as the church and its members face and accept the world's suffering can we make a difference in the lives of those who are suffering.

b. Three aspects of baptism are involved in this story: John's baptism of preparation, Jesus' baptism of solidarity, and the promised baptism of the Holy Spirit. It has been said that the Christian life begins with repentance, leads to unity, and moves on to witness and action in the world.

Repentance is the first step. We cannot turn to Christ without turning away from our past. The candidate or sponsors of an infant must first renounce evil before they can turn to Christ. It seems from the gospel that John the Baptist had only to announce that the Messiah was coming and crowds responded by confessing their sins and being baptized. They were aware of their need. Most of us know our failures. Baptism gives us a way to deal with them and we are as ready to respond as the Judeans when the offer is made.

The second step is unity with Christ. Scholars have always debated the reason for Jesus' baptism, but the simplest explanation is that it was an act of solidarity through which Jesus identified himself with us. He had come to take the burden of our sins on himself, therefore he must identify himself with us and be baptized. But his true baptism, as he spoke of it later (Luke 12:50), was the crucifixion and death through which he shared to the end the burden and pain of the human condition. As he united himself with us through his baptism, so we must unite ourselves with him through our baptism.

The third step is the living of a Christian life which we can only do by the power of the Holy Spirit. The gift of the Spirit is of such importance that most churches still provide a separate service of "confirmation" to mark that gift. Yet if baptism incorporates us into Christ's life which was lived by the Spirit, then baptism also brings us immediately into the life of the Spirit. Today the primacy of baptism and the gift of the Spirit in baptism are being strongly reasserted in most churches.

The three steps which begin our Christian life remain important. Baptism is a once-for-all event, but it sets a pattern which we must continue to live. Repentance and confession of sin remain essential until our unity with Christ is complete. Unity with Christ through prayer and sacrament must be constantly deepened and strengthened. And the gift of the Spirit to empower us remains the *sine qua non* of Christian living.

4. Mark 1:14-20 ♦ "Follow me and I will make you fish for people"

The gospels often present the calling of the disciples as a sudden call and immediate response, as if the disciples-to-be had never heard of Jesus before but dropped everything to respond immediately when Jesus called them. St. John's gospel (1:35-42) shows Simon Peter and Andrew first meeting with Jesus at the time of Jesus' baptism and going with him to Galilee. The call described by the synoptic gospels, then, was presumably somewhat later and marked the beginning of Jesus' public ministry after a period in which Jesus may have withdrawn into the desert and the disciples returned to their homes and work.

But even if, as seems likely, these disciples had already heard Jesus' teaching and talked with him so that the call was the climax of a process extending over some time, this presentation of the fishermen's action as an immediate response to an immediate event is right. However much preparation there may be (and there is always preparation required to hear the gospel) there comes a moment when we suddenly really hear as if for the first time and know that we are hearing. That is the moment when we must respond without delay. If you can say, "Wait a minute," to Jesus' invitation, you have not really heard him or else are hopelessly lost.

A Christian life should be a life that is always immediately responsive. We should come to know Jesus so well that we will instinctively know his will and do it without even pausing to think. In family crises and business decisions, we seldom have time to ponder the right thing to do. We need to respond instinctively out of a deep commitment to love and justice. Jesus calls us, also, to follow him in the middle of our work and that is the right time to respond.

5. Mark 2:1-12 ♦ "He said to the paralytic,...stand up"

This passage is obviously appropriate to an infant baptism: a child unable to seek God's grace by itself is carried into the church by friends and family. (Unfortunately, they will probably not have to fight their way through the crowds or break up the roof to get in!) But this passage may be even more appropriate to an adult baptism. It is all too easy to imagine that an adult coming to baptism has come by her own decision and made an independent choice. In fact, we are as unable to bring ourselves to Jesus as was the paralytic. We are paralyzed by past habits, by inertia, by social pressures, by our own doubts, and by many other forces, recognized and unrecognized. If at last we find ourselves walking towards the font, it is all too easy to imagine that we have done so by our own initiative. It is vital, then, to recognize the role others have played in bringing the candidate to the point of decision. There are undoubtedly others, perhaps long in the past, who have made an impact and contributed to the candidate's spiritual journey. This might well be explored in the time of preparation and acknowledged in the choice of sponsors as well as in the homily.

The sequence between forgiveness and freedom might also be an appropriate subject for the homily. We often feel that we are functioning well while in fact we are tied and limited by our separation from God and inability to recognize our need for forgiveness and love. Only when others bring us into Jesus' presence can we be set free to stand up and walk freely for the first time.

6. Mark 10:13-16 ♦ "Let the little children come to me"

a. This story has often been used as a support for the practice of infant baptism, and some scholars would argue that this story has been deliberately shaped for that purpose.

Jesus' words, "...do not stop them;..." form an exact parallel with a recurrent phrase in stories of baptism in the New Testament (Matthew 3:14, Acts 8:36, 10:47, etc.) It would seem from this that it may have been usual at baptisms to ask whether there were any reason not to baptize the candidate (as today at a wedding, we ask, "If any of you can show just cause why they may not lawfully be married, speak now..."). Jesus is never directly described as baptizing, but this story forms an exact parallel to a baptism: the children are brought, the ritual question is answered, and the blessing is given.

The importance of this story to the early church is indicated by certain strong words. "Truly," (Greek *amen*) is a word which is characteristic of Jesus in all four gospels and seems to indicate especially important sayings. The word for blessing is a stronger form of the word (*kateulogei*, not *eulogei*) and might be translated "greatly blessed." And while Jesus is asked to "touch" the children, he responds by "embracing" them. We are not to be left in doubt as to Jesus' will that children be brought and received.

b. *"...It is to such as these that the kingdom of God belongs...."* (v.14). This phrase deserves separate consideration. It is through baptism that we become members of the kingdom and Jesus here sets out a basic criterion for admission. Though we use this story with infant baptisms, it might better be used at the baptism of an adult. Children are bound to be childlike, but adults try not to be. What is it that Jesus is asking?

Obviously there is a difference between childlikeness and childishness. St. Paul criticizes the Corinthian Christians for being mere children in faith and not growing (I Cor.3:1). Christian growth involves a deepening of certain traits seen most clearly in children such as innocence, joy, and trust.

Important also is the fact that children receive gifts but cannot earn them. Entrance into the kingdom is always a gift and can never be earned. Our response to God's gift must always be one of gratitude for something beyond any possible deserving.

7. Luke 24:45-53 ♦ "Forgiveness of sins is to be proclaimed"

a. In Jesus' last meeting with his disciples St. Luke shows him first referring the disciples to the Scriptures and then emphasizing two messages to be found there: the death and resurrection of the Christ, and the proclamation to all the world of a gospel of repentance and forgiveness. Each of these three points is worth stressing.

First, the Christian faith is part of an age-old process revealed in Scripture through which God has been at work. In Scripture we find the evidence that God is able to work through death to bring life and that God stands ready always to forgive the penitent. More important, it is in Scripture that we find the Messiah described as one who must suffer and rise from the dead. It is because the disciples have not really understood the Scriptures that they have not been able to recognize Jesus. It is not that Jesus rose from the dead and therefore is the Messiah, but that, as the Messiah, he had to rise from the dead. Had they understood the Scriptures, they would have known this would happen. Knowledge of God's purpose begins with the opening of our minds to the revelation found in the Bible.

Second, the death and resurrection of Christ is the event that transforms history. When death is not the last word in one single life, the world can never be the same. The fear of death can no longer dominate our lives. The promise of eternal life gives new value and meaning to everything we do.

Third, the life of a Christian begins with penitence and forgiveness. No new life can begin until we recognize the sinfulness of the life we are living and ask God's forgiveness. But the good news of the gospel is that we have already been forgiven, that we are set free to grow to our full potential in Christ.

b. *"...You are witnesses of these things..."* (v.48). The sponsors or godparents are often referred to as "witnesses" and that is one of their roles. But they are not "witnesses" in the legal sense, attesting that an action has been performed. They are witnesses in the sense that the first disciples were: people who have known Jesus and are able to tell others about him. Sponsors in baptism are specifically charged to provide an example of Christian living: in other words, to be the kind of people in whom a growing child can see who Jesus is. And that means that sponsors must also be witnesses in another sense: they must have seen for themselves who Jesus is so that they can reflect that experience for others.

8. John 3:1-6 (or 3:1-8) ♦ "You must be born from above"

The two texts suggested below are two ways of saying the same thing. Jesus made both statements with equal solemnity and one as a rephrasing of the other. Both bring together the Jewish idea of the "kingdom of God" with language more familiar to Gentile religion and philosophy: "rebirth" and "spirit." Here, as in the Prologue to his gospel St. John is skillfully weaving together Jewish and Greek ideas. But whether one thinks in terms of rebirth or of the Kingdom of God, it is clear that a radical break with the past and a new beginning is called for. St. Paul more typically uses the terminology of death and resurrection. Whatever the language used, the words are pointing to a truth beyond words; all are equally adequate and equally inadequate.

It should be noticed also that the conversation between Jesus and Nicodemus moves quickly from the singular form, "unless *one* is born anew" in verse 3, to the plural form in verse 7, "*You* (Greek plural) must be born again." Jesus is not simply addressing Nicodemus but everyone who, like Nicodemus, trusts in tradition and learning and human achievement. Human achievement is one thing; God's gift of new birth is another.

a. *"...No one can see the kingdom of God without being born from above...."* (v.3). The evangelical tradition emphasizes the importance of being "born again" and equates it with a mature, conversion experience. But conversion begins with God's action in our lives, often unrecognized at the time, and an emphasis on the conversion experience can center too much attention on human feelings. Conversely, the sacramental viewpoint concentrates on God's action and can neglect the importance of human response. Birth into God's family, like birth in a human family, has nothing to do with our initiative. But membership in a family does require a response. Whether suddenly or gradually, we must come to understand that we are loved and respond with gratitude. A child brought to birth and then left in the hospital cannot change his or her human parentage but will never learn to value it. Nor will a child baptized and then never brought again to the church learn to value and respond to the love of God.

b. "...No one can enter the kingdom of God without being born of water and Spirit" (v.5). The reference here may be to natural birth and spiritual birth or it may be a contrast between the baptism of John and that of the church. Either way, the point can be made that human life cannot come to its fulfillment without the presence of the Spirit. Christian baptism is not "mere" water baptism—a washing and a preparation. Christian baptism is always incomplete without the gift of the Spirit as human life is incomplete if it is lived at a purely physical level.

Notice that in Greek (as in Hebrew) the word for "wind" and "spirit" are the same. So Jesus' statement in verse 8 may equally well be translated, "The Spirit breathes where it will, and you hear its voice..." Those who live at a purely physical level will respond predictably to physical stimuli. A child cries and is fed. An adult covets and seeks to gratify his or her desires. But the Spirit acts in ways not predictable in physical terms. A Francis of Assisi leaves wealth and comfort to seek physical poverty and spiritual riches. A Mother Teresa loves the unlovable. A former President sets aside time to help renovate housing for the poor. An ordinary Christian hears of another's need and finds time to make a phone call and offer help. These are not "normal" actions, but results of the unpredictable movement of the Spirit. Such is the life to which the newly baptized is exposed and which, with time and nurture, will become as natural as is self-seeking and self-fulfillment to those not "born again."

9. John 14:15-18 ♦ "If you love me, you will keep my commandments"

Love of Jesus is not simply a warm glow or being nice to people; there are commandments to keep. But what are Jesus' "commandments"? In St. John's gospel there is only one specific command: "Love one another" (15:12,17). But with the injunction to "keep my commandments" there is also a promised "Counselor...the Spirit of truth" (15:16-17). No list of specific commandments can embody the "Spirit of truth" but that Spirit will require specific actions of us at specific times. Love involves obedience but the specifics of that obedience cannot be known in advance. Readiness to obey the Spirit requires, in turn, prayer and Bible study and a disciplined turning to God so that when the moment comes, we will be prepared and responsive.

10. John 15:1-11 "I am the vine, you are the branches"

a. Like St. Paul's analogy of the body and its members (I Corinthians 12), the analogy of the vine and the branches stresses our dependence on Christ for the life we have as Christians. St. John uses this analogy to make at least four points. First, we are dependent on Jesus, "the true vine," for our life. Baptism, we might say, grafts us onto the vine from which we can draw life. The figure of the vine may also have eucharistic allusions and remind us of the sacrament in which that life is constantly renewed. This life is a shared life in which there are many branches on the one vine. Secondly, the richest production of fruit involves pruning. The Christian life is not always easy, but the pruning process results in more abundant life. Thirdly, to be separated from the vine is death. Note that the gospel says it is we who fail to abide in the vine and therefore, having withered by our own action, are "gathered, thrown into the fire and burned" (v.6). And finally, the end purpose is joy. Jesus promises *his* joy, not a trivial and passing happiness but a deep and abiding joy as our lives find their fulfillment in God's purpose for us.

b. *"...That your joy may be full"* (v. 11). Does the idea still persist that religion is for the gloomy? Repeatedly in the Bible God tells us that the intention behind creation is not only God's enjoyment but ours. The English version puts it before us in words of one syllable: "that your joy may be full." Parents bring a child to birth for the joy they find in that relationship. But it is never pure joy. There is pain in childbirth and there is pain all too often thereafter: the pain of sickness, the pain of disobedience, the pain of separation. Our joy is always mixed with pain. But the purpose is joy. Joy comes when our relationship with Christ is working smoothly and we are responding almost instinctively to his will as a man and woman respond to each other in dancing. That instinctive response is the work of the Holy Spirit who is given in baptism. The Spirit begins to work within us at baptism and as we respond to that Spirit the times of instinctive response become more frequent and the times of rebellion and separation become less common. As a result our joy grows. This is what God wants more than anything else.

III. Baptismal Homilies

A. Overcoming Division

His grandfather was an Episcopalian, his parents were brought up as Roman Catholics, his mother's sister was a seminarian seeking ordination in the Presbyterian Church. He was brought back from Switzerland, where his father represented an American firm, for baptism in the Episcopal church in which his parents were married. He seemed to sum up in himself so many human divisions, and yet all had been brought together for the baptism. Unity, by the grace of God, can over-come human divisions and so the baptism of William MacLelland Guarino seemed to be an opportunity to point to the power of the God who creates and redeems and can restore unity to a world of divisions.

A short version of the text is given here but the whole passage (Isaiah 43:1-3a, 6b-7) was used in developing the homily.

"Bring my sons from afar" ♦ (Isaiah 43:6)

I doubt Isaiah knew how far away Switzerland is, but it made me look twice at this passage and think about the distances that seem to separate us and which love can still overcome. God, who created the distances, can also overcome them and bring us together for an occasion like this, can unite us across geographical distance and ecclesiastical difference in this sacrament. Baptism is, first of all, the means by which God creates unity, makes us one.

God creates. That's a fundamental theme in Isaiah. No other book of the Bible stresses creation so much. God creates unity—one world, one human race—and we divide. We divide into separate countries, separate churches, even separate families, and then God who is always one goes to work to break down our divisions and bring us together and re-create unity: one church, one world, one family, one body in Christ. And that re-creation is also called redemption. Isaiah tells us that God says, "I have redeemed you; I have called you by name, you are mine."

And perhaps the most wonderful part of all this is, that God shares that work of creation and redemption with us. You have shared in the process of creation. Here is a human life that didn't exist until you brought it to birth. The power of God is love, and by the same power of love, you have nurtured and brought to birth new life, and shared in the work of creation.

But you bring William into a world of divisions. In some ways, the geographical and ecclesiastical and national divisions are less important than the jealousy and anger and frustration and misunderstanding and selfishness that divide us even in families, that create divisions even within families, even with those we love, even within ourselves. And that's why we're here.

Creation is wonderful, but in this world we also always have to be involved in the work of re-creation, of redemption; of overcoming and bringing back and forgiving and starting again. And God shares this work with us. We come here to share in the work of redemption, to bring William into God's church because we know what lies ahead. Isaiah speaks about passing through the waters and walking through fire. Sometimes it seems like that. If William had any idea what lies ahead in kindergarten and junior high and being a teenager and going off to college and falling in love and fighting against not only a world of divisions and opposition but fighting against himself—against the divisions inside himself—passing through fire and water might seem like an understatement to him.

But we've started something here that can't be changed. "Do not fear,..." God says, "...I will be with you;...they shall not overwhelm you" (Isaiah

43:1, 2). And I'm sure he says this to parents, too: "Fear not." God our creator is also our redeemer. You are placing William in God's hands. The work of redemption has begun. And God who is able to create the Alps and the Atlantic and human love and a child called William will not let go until unity overcomes division and each of us and all the world reflects the glory of God.

B. Closer Than A Husband

Dana Manson and Tom Powers came first to talk about getting married. They had begun coming to church together and seemed to have a good understanding of the meaning of Christian marriage and Christian commitment. But Dana had not been baptized and felt it as something missing in her life. So we began a series of meetings leading to baptism as well as marriage. As Christmas approached (still months before the wedding), I asked whether she would like to be able to receive communion at Christmas with her fiancé. The response made it clear she would like it very much. So the baptism was scheduled for a Sunday afternoon in Advent when a few sponsors could be present. The suggested reading which seemed best to combine the themes of marriage and baptism was Jeremiah 31:31-34.

"This is the covenant that I will make" ♦ (Jeremiah 31:33)

I don't know whether you have thought of it this way, but baptism is a great way to prepare for a wedding. It's a lot like a wedding: you come to the church with witnesses and make vows in the presence of God and begin a new life with God's help and blessing.

This passage from Jeremiah makes the comparison in several ways. First of all, it begins with a warning: "The day is surely coming..." Jeremiah wants us to remember that life needs always to be lived in expectation. Sometimes it seems as if we are always living with the problem of getting ready for some day just around the corner. Of course, you have a wedding not very far around the corner. And before that, in Advent, we have Christmas looming ahead and the celebration of Christ's first coming. Christmas and marriage and Christ's coming all raise our expectations in a similar way. In fact, we often speak of Christ's coming in terms of a bridegroom coming to his bride. The expectation levels are similar.

Jeremiah talks about God's relationship with us in terms that might also be used of a marriage. He calls it a covenant, and he says God has been our husband. But then he says that isn't enough. It's surprising enough that God should be spoken of as our husband, but what could be closer than that? What closer relationship could you imagine?

Well, baptism like marriage begins with a physical act. A human being and God are joined together in baptism as a man and woman are joined together in marriage. But the physical unity only gradually becomes a deep and spiritual unity. Gradually, over the years, a man and woman grow into a far deeper unity than they might ever have believed is possible. They can come to the point where they not only read each other's thoughts but actually think each other's thoughts. They don't have to wonder what the other one thinks because they think the same way themselves. They become truly one, or almost truly one!

And in a very similar way, God becomes one with us through baptism. Just as we are united with another person in marriage, so we are united with another person in baptism, but here, far more powerfully, with God. As with marriage, there are wonderful moments at the very beginning, but also moments of tension and moments when we seem to be on very different tracks. But over time, the unity grows. Gradually, deep within, change takes place; our will and God's will draw together until we instinctively think God's thoughts and share them ourselves.

But there are also differences. Jeremiah says it isn't enough for God to be our husband. That's too limited. It's not enough. Unity with God is more. This service today, small and quiet in comparison with most weddings, is, in fact, the more significant and the more transforming and the more lasting. Marriage is for this life, baptism is for eternity. Marriage unites us with someone *almost* perfect (!), baptism unites us with the perfect life of God.

In that light, you might almost say, "Baptism makes marriage easy." I'm not sure anything makes marriage easy, but baptism certainly makes it easier. It brings us all the help only God can give us: the life, the strength, the love, the knowledge of God's will written on our hearts. And that's a great way to prepare for a wedding.

C. Coming Into The Family

The family that calls to "arrange a baptism" always presents a problem. Often they have had no previous contact with the church and there is no way to assess over the telephone the seriousness behind the request. But they did make the phone call and that does present an opportunity. Meeting with the family for instruction (in their home, if possible) provides opportunity to help them see the seriousness of the commitment they are undertaking and often does lead to a real commitment to follow through. The homily, likewise, provides an opportunity to work from what they know to what they need to know. The human family can be compared to God's family and their love for the newborn child, to God's love for us. John Jerome's family came to me under such circumstances and I tried to convey some very elementary aspects of the Christian faith.

"To such the kingdom of God belongs" ♦ (Mark 10:14)

We know when we have children that we have a responsibility to teach them. We need to give them an example to follow and, for better or worse, we are the example they have. There's nothing wrong with that as long as we ourselves have a good example, and that's the first reason we need to know Jesus.

But the story I read you says something else, something even more surprising. It says that children give us an example. The parents who brought their children to Jesus may have thought they were giving their children a role model, but Jesus turned things around. He took a child in his arms and said, "To such belongs the kingdom of heaven."

There are other stories that make it even clearer. Once when the disciples were arguing about who was the greatest, Jesus took a child and put the child in the middle of the crowd and said, in effect, "Be like that."

We think children learn from us. Jesus thought we need to learn from them. And what would we learn? Well, look at John Jerome. Put him down on the floor and walk away and he will die. He depends entirely on us just to live another day. And we depend on God just that much. The world exists only because God sustains it. We exist only because God holds us up minute by minute.

Children take it for granted that parents will be there and provide. And that's how it should be. But we also hope they will learn to respond to that love and return it. We take God for granted, and we should, but I'm sure God also wants us to respond to God's love for us and return it. That's one way we should be like children.

Children also learn to trust. They learn that parents can be trusted to be there. They may not always like the decisions parents make or understand them, but they know they can be trusted. Children look to parents for answers, for help, and they get them. We need to be like that in relation to God. God can be trusted, and God does have answers for questions we need answered such as "Why am I here?" and "How should I live?" God has a purpose for us and wants to show it to us. That's why God gave us the Bible and the church.

I could go on, because I think Jesus also saw a simplicity in children and an innocence and a joy that we grownups don't always have. Somehow we lose them as we grow up. But maybe we can learn them again from our own children. Maybe as your child learns from you, you can also learn from him. And maybe you can learn a relationship with God that will make it possible for you to simplify your own lives and to be more trusting and more joyful.

Jesus often used the human family as an example of God's family. You have brought your child here to be a member of God's family. So learn from him and find in God the trust and obedience and love that John Jerome will learn from you.

D. The Obstetrician's Grandchild

John Schelpert was obstetrician to a large part of the community and served his church as an usher who never missed his turn, unless of course he had to deliver a child. Though he and his family were always at the main Sunday service, the first grandchild was baptized on a Sunday afternoon to make it possible for family members to gather from Boston and Philadelphia. My choice of a text was obvious.

"Unless one is born anew, he cannot see the kingdom of God"
♦ **(John 3:3)**

You can probably guess why I chose to read this portion of Scripture!

Jesus said, "You must be born again." Nicodemus thought this was impossible and he had a lot less technical information on the subject than we do.

Most times, for most people, being born once is trauma enough. But Jesus said, "You must be born again." We'd better take this metaphor and look at it.

Birth in a human family involves first of all weakness and need. A newborn child is perhaps the most dependent form of life there is. You know that! A newborn colt is standing and running in a matter of hours. A newborn child may take a year or more even to toddle.

We can't survive alone. We can't survive at all without an enormous outpouring of energy by others. We have to be fed and carried and nurtured and supported for years. In fact, we never do become truly independent. We never do.

Apply that then to our birth into Christian life and think of how much nurture we may need. We need the church and the sacraments and the Bible and prayer. We need all the love and care and support we can get. Growing up isn't easy. But growth is what we are offered.

Baptism is lots of things: it's a relationship with God, life in Christ, commitment to others, a gift of strength, death and resurrection. But, like every new birth, it's the start of a process of growth in love and in the things of the spirit.

For a child, that growth is nurtured first of all by parents who, just naturally, teach a child love by loving her. For all of us, love is learned from others, received from others, returned to others. But that's never enough. None of us can love a child or other person enough. We never can give all the love that others need, and we never get as much love as we need.

What we need is *God's* love: a love adequate to our need, a love to surround us and sustain us and feed us and challenge us in a way none of us can ever adequately do for anyone else however much we love them.

And that's why we come here. As naturally as we go to a good doctor for our physical needs, we turn to God for our spiritual needs. As naturally as we place ourselves and those we love in a doctor's hands for the skills a doctor has, we place ourselves and those we love in God's hands to receive the life and love and strength that God alone can give.

E. Following Through

The baby's father had been an acolyte; his grandfather had served on the Vestry. The grandparents, active church members, were present at the font. Baptism under these circumstances seems an opportunity to reinforce beliefs and practices already accepted by providing reasons for them and pointing to Jesus' own words.

"That which is born of the flesh is flesh, and that which is born of the Spirit is spirit" ♦ **(John 3:6)**

Baptism is a new beginning. That's pretty obvious; but maybe not as obvious as it ought to be.

Baptism is a birth, and birth has consequences. There's a lifelong responsibility that can't be given up. Grandparents know this, don't they? You give birth to a child and that's not the end of it. First there's a brief round of congratulations, and then, then comes all the rest: midnight feedings, diapers, doctors, shopping, cooking, clothing. And then come schooling and chauffeuring, teacher's meetings, and afterschool sports. Then come SAT's and college tuition; then, marriage expenses; then, grandchildren. It's an endless chain. You take up a responsibility and you can't ever put it down, nor would you want to, would you?

Of course, there are people who do put down this responsibility. We read in the newspapers about those who abuse and neglect their children. These things are disastrous, immoral, and not easy for us to imagine. No responsible person would bring a child to birth and not follow through.

Baptism is exactly parallel to natural childbirth. After baptism, far too often, we see the evidence of child abuse, that is, a birth into God's family without any follow-up: no teaching to pray, no grace at meals, no Bible reading in the home, etc. This is also child abuse and neglect. But we see it all the time.

The point is, the child born into the human family needs more than what even the best-intentioned family can give. Good schools and nice lawns are not enough, unless we see ourselves as purely physical beings. If we are more, if we have a spiritual nature, that too must be nourished. God alone can provide that food. And God offers all the love and nurture and nourishment we need if only we do our part. Our job is to build on the new birth, new relationship, that begins here today. We must follow through with the same nurture and care of an immortal life that we would almost automatically give to a mortal one.

"You must be born again," Jesus says. Each one of us must be born again into the life of the spirit. Each one of us must continue to grow in that life. Either we grow in it or we die to it.

Today is the beginning. All the joy of God's kingdom lies ahead.

F. The Baptismal Garment

Baptismal dresses seem to be an endangered custom and certainly there is no need for a family to invest in an expensive white dress that will be worn only once. Some families, however, like Peyton's family, have heirloom dresses handed down for generations. And when the garment is important to the family, it provides a natural metaphor, a biblical metaphor, for the meaning of the baptismal event.

"As many of you as were baptized into Christ have clothed yourself with Christ" ♦ **(Galatians 3:27)**

What does it mean to "clothe yourself with Christ"? It means, I believe, that we start a process by which Peyton becomes someone else. Gradually, over a lifetime, she is meant to become Christ: not Jesus walking around in a white robe and sandals, but Christ, the love of God incarnate in a modern woman of the late twentieth century and early twenty-first century.

What does it mean to be a Christian? Some people think it's a matter of law and keeping rules, obeying the Ten Commandments. When she's small, that may be a good start. But keeping rules makes for a limited view of life.

Some people think it's a matter of the Spirit and spiritual things. But the Spirit comes and goes and there's more to life than the spiritual as all of us know.

No, Christianity is a matter of the whole of life: all the time, body and spirit, the whole of life. That's what begins with baptism.

Clothing yourself with Christ isn't like putting on a baptismal dress. This child will grow out of that dress just as everyone else did who has worn it. Christ is a garment to grow into. Never in this life will we fill out to his dimensions. But we can grow toward that size and begin to discover something of the richness of life that only God can give. And that will demand all we are willing to give. And to that end we need to work together to help Peyton discover the richness and fullness of the life she's now beginning. She needs to learn to pray and take part in the sacraments and become part of the community, the church, in which Christ is known and worshipped.

This is what we're beginning today, and this is something to celebrate. And there will be much more to celebrate as Peyton continues to grow with our help and God's help and begins to fulfill what is promised by this beginning.

G. Coronation

Stewart and Karen Bevan love music and have many musical friends. They waited a long time for their first child and, when it came, they wanted to share the joy of the baptism with their friends. Many of their friends, however, were members of choirs in other churches on Sunday morning and could only come if the baptism were scheduled for Sunday afternoon. But by no means was the result a quiet and private affair; friends and family constituted a sizeable congregation and several hymns were chosen as well as an organ prelude and postlude. As the plans went forward, someone remarked that it seemed as if we were planning not a baptism but a coronation. Indeed, we were!

"But you are a chosen race, a royal priesthood, a holy nation, God's own people, that you may declare the wonderful deeds of him who called you out of darkness into his marvelous light" ♦ (1 Peter 2:9)

Does it seem a little odd that we would put on a service like this for a child too young to have any idea of what's happening? Someone said to me that it seems more like a coronation than a baptism. I like that. It is a coronation. The first reading tells us why. It says, "You are a royal priesthood..." In the words of the hymn we are "kings and priests to God." Therefore we need to be both crowned and ordained.

More than that, this service is a marriage. The church is the bride of Christ and those who are baptized are joined in that marriage. And it's a burial and a resurrection. In baptism we are buried with Christ and raised to everlasting life.

So there's every reason you can imagine to celebrate with all the music and ceremony at our command. This is a baptism, a marriage, a burial, a resurrection, a coronation. But there isn't time to talk about all these things. Let's just stick with the theme of coronation and let me make three quick points.

First, kings are born, not made. Kingship, generally, is inherited, not acquired. It's not the coronation that matters so much as it is being born into a royal family. And that's baptism. It's birth in a royal family, the family of Jesus the King.

Second, kingship isn't earned, it's a gift. Unlike the presidency which is theoretically earned by experience and qualifications and marketing skills, in which you are supposed to demonstrate that you already are presidential, kingship often is passed on to a child who has nothing to offer but royal blood. The child has no experience, no education, no ability; nothing but an image of royalty into which to grow, to be trained for, to become.

Most kings in history, it seems to me, have not, in fact, grown into the demands of the role. They haven't learned the craft or fulfilled their potential. That's why there aren't very many kings any more. Christians, too, don't always grow up to fulfill their potential in spite of the promises made by parents and godparents but what a gift it is, and what a challenge for us to help the newborn king become the royal figure God intends him to be. We can't give the child all the gifts he needs, only God can do that. But all of us do have a part to play in the training process by which Andrew learns who he is by God's gift: he is the child of God and an inheritor of the kingdom of heaven.

Third, kingship involves a kingdom and ruling a kingdom. This is God's earth, but God gives us rule over it. We haven't done very well with that stewardship, but in the baptismal promises we remind ourselves that we are called to work for justice and peace for all people. We have a vision of a kingdom and our job is, with God's help, to make that vision a reality.

All this for a child not yet a year old! You might say, "It's too much to handle." If not for God, it would be. But we are never asked to do more than we can do with God's help. The marvelous part of it is that God not only sets all this in front of us but also makes it possible. God's grace, God's gift, makes it possible. The incredible, marvelous part of it is that God loves us enough to call us to such a destiny and that God gives us the grace to achieve it.

So how could we help celebrating not only today but every day, not only Andrew but all of us? How could we help celebrating the love of God and the gifts of God who calls us to reign with Christ and with all the saints in the royal kingdom of heaven?

PART TWO

Holy Matrimony

I. The Marriage Homily

"God is love" is undoubtedly the briefest and most appealing summary of the meaning of the Christian faith. And if the Christian faith can be summed up in three words, what better time could there be to expound that faith than at the celebration of a marriage? Here we would have two human beings intent on exploring the meaning and mystery of love and a congregation of their friends and family eager to support them in their exploration. When else is a preacher so likely to have a congregation hanging on every word and eager to apply it? And what could be easier for the preacher than to communicate the essence of those three simple words that lie at the heart of the Christian faith? Experience, however, suggests that it may not be all that easy.

In the first place, the simple expression, "God is love," like new-fallen snow, sparkles radiantly in the sunlight, but quickly turns to mush under our feet. Some truths, like pie crust (to change the metaphor), are not improved by handling. "Love" is a concept which seems to flow more from the heart than the head. The head can't come to terms with the heart and the heart has no terms the head can understand.

The plain fact is that some truths are not primarily intellectual, not capable of being analyzed usefully. Nor are all human beings motivated primarily by careful logic and rigorous systematic analysis. The church has produced brilliant intellectuals through the centuries who have hardly converted anyone and, at the same time, seen waves of converts brought in by preaching which "merely" warmed the heart.

Marriage brings us face to face with one of the most fundamental paradoxes of human life: we can explore and analyze the farthest reaches of the universe but cannot adequately understand or express our own motivation. We are called to respond to a creator who gave us mental abilities beyond those of all the rest of creation but who can be fully known only by love.

Words fail us, and yet words are essential. "I love you" is plainly insufficient as a summary of our deepest feelings. We can say it a million times and yet, if there is no kiss, no embrace, we will have failed totally to express ourselves. At the same time, if we only embrace and never give words to our feelings, never say those three meager yet vital words, we will hardly have done more than animals.

Love without words turns quickly to mush. Love with inadequate words, words without mental connection, is sticky syrup, delightful, perhaps, to the naive and unsophisticated taste, but cloying to the mature and ultimately sickening even to the childish.

Words are necessary, and the discriminating and careful use of words can guide and channel emotions which otherwise may run out of control. "Love" in contemporary English has come to cover a multitude of sins. We use that one word to express the relationship of husband and wife, parent and child, master and dog, tourist and New York State; to discuss both geography and pornography. We use it as a synonym for every emotion from affection to passion. No wonder marriages fail and God is unknown. We have bankrupted the language and left ourselves with no redeemable medium of exchange.

Two thousand years ago, the common language of the Mediterranean world was Greek and the Greek language had been sharpened by the philosophers until it could make distinctions which we have forgotten or never known. As the Eskimo's language is said to be rich in terms for snow and that of the gauchos in terms for the colors of a horse, so Greek could distinguish kinds of love. There was *philos* for friendship, *storgos* for affection, *eros* for sexual passion, *caritas* for benefaction, and *agape* for the conjugal relationship of husband and wife. The New Testament writers chose *agape*, a word rarely found except in biblical Greek before the second or third century of the Christian era, to describe God's love for God's people as they had known it in Jesus Christ. It seems probable that they were guided in their choice by a similar use in the Old Testament of *yadah*, sexual knowledge, to describe God's relationship with Israel. Adam "knew" Eve, we are told, and she conceived (Genesis 4:1). "You only," God said to Israel, "have I *known* of all the families of the earth" (Amos 3:2).

The love Christians speak of is, then, a kind of knowledge which contains on the one hand the most profound spiritual significance and, on the other hand, is indescribable, perhaps even in some sense unknowable, apart from our bodies and their physical relationships. Again and again, the biblical writers fall back on marriage as the fullest metaphor of God's love for God's people. Marriage, says the **Book of Common Prayer**, "signifies to us the mystery of the union between Christ and his church" (p. 423) for the church is the "body of Christ" (I Corinthians 12:27) and also the "bride of Christ" (Revelation 21:2, 9). Those who are married are one body as Christ and the church are one.

No, it is never easy, but yet what better place could there be, if all this is true, than the homily at a Christian marriage to expound the basic truths of the faith and to ground each new marriage in a love deeper than any human exchange? Words cannot fully express what each bride and groom have begun to know, but neither can their knowledge reach its full potential without words of guidance, words to inform and clarify and strengthen their unutterable knowledge.

And what should that homily do? What it clearly cannot do is provide an intellectually satisfying analysis of the nature of love. Not only are words inadequate, but the congregation and the caterer have limited patience. Worse yet, it is often difficult if not impossible to arrange a convenient way for the bride and groom to be seated and few of us are accustomed to listening to long dissertations while standing. It is clearly no time for a full-length sermon.

What can be done in the time available? At the very least, the homily can suggest relationships. It can, as every sermon and homily should, ground the universal in the particular. It can find words to indicate that the love of John and Mary is a reflection in some small part of the love of God for God's people, that in coming to know each other's love, they will come to know God's love, that whatever is lasting and true in their experience is lasting and true because it is God's gift.

The marriage homily, like the homily at a baptism or funeral, is grounded in the Scripture, the sacrament, and the circumstances of the individuals involved. These, in various proportions, are brought together so that both couple and congregation are shown something of God's love in relation to particular people and events. Sermons, like it or not, are remembered for the illustrations, and the whole craft of preaching has to do with so illustrating God's truth that that truth is remembered as easily as the illustration.

The marriage service itself provides rich material for the homily. The eucharist, the family banquet of the people of God, is becoming, once again, a normal part of the ceremony so that the couple can share their first meal as husband and wife at God's table. In a society which puts greater demands on a marriage than have ever been made before, it is also appropriate that the new couple be strengthened at the outset by the gifts of grace which only God can give. We are often reminded of the fact that the eucharist can be understood in terms of a family meal but not so often reminded that the family meal can be understood in terms of eucharist. It might make a real difference if married couples were helped to see that the family table is a place where God is present and that the shared meal, also, is a material expression of God's love.

Within the liturgy there are other movements which can proclaim basic Christian themes. Although Cranmer's **Book of Common Prayer** assumes the church as the setting for the marriage, it provides no direction about the entrance. The marriage procession with ushers, bridesmaids, and the bride on her father's arm, seems to be a more recent development. More recently, as efforts have been made to express the equal standing of bride and groom, it has become not unusual to have a procession in which the groom is accompanied to the front of the church by his attendants and parents and the bride by hers. Such a development brings the marriage service into parallel with the baptismal and burial liturgies. At a marriage, too, we are brought to the church by others. We are part of a living body, sustained by the common life, insufficient of ourselves. And marriage, like baptism and burial, is a death to one life and entrance into a new life and new experience of God's love. But even if the groom is accompanied to the front of the church only by his best man while all eyes are on the bridal procession coming from the back, the fact remains that we are brought to the church by others and that marriage, like the Christian faith itself, involves dying to self in order to live for others.

Like the eucharistic meal and the procession, the kiss of peace and the offertory are elements of liturgy which can express central elements of a Christian theology of marriage and be used to illustrate points in the homily. Since love cannot be expressed in words alone it is important to let the liturgy also express it. If the kiss of peace is a usual part of the Sunday liturgy, it will take on new significance when exchanged at a wedding. If the bride and groom move out from the altar to exchange the peace, kissing or embracing family and friends, the exchange becomes a dramatic illustration of the way in which love radiates out to include others and binds them together. If the offertory procession, including bread and wine, is a usual part of the Sunday liturgy so that the offertory illustrates the offering to God of all we have done with the gifts we are given, it will be appropriate to include it in the marriage liturgy also and let the bride and groom bring the bread and wine to the altar as a symbolic offering. Perhaps the marriage setting will make it more clear than a Sunday liturgy can do that the procession is an offering not simply of gifts but of lives. The bride and groom offer not only bread and wine, they offer their bodies to be consecrated to God's service. As Christ is present in the offered gifts when they are consecrated, so he is to be present in their bodies, united by his love and blessed for God's purpose.

The personal element in the homily should be easiest to interweave at a marriage. At a baptism, the child to be baptized is obviously unknown and still without any fully developed personality. The parents are often newcomers to the congregation, little known even to the pastor who has met with them to prepare for the service. At a funeral, the one who has died may have been a familiar member of the congregation for many years, but death is often sudden and never planned (except secretly by a suicide). Marriage, on the other hand, is normally planned long in advance and the pastor will usually have six months to a year in which to engage in counselling and become well acquainted with the bride and groom. The pastor will have the opportunity to discuss with the couple the lessons to be used at the wedding and the reasons for their choices. It is often possible to say in the homily, "You chose this reading because..." or, "When you chose this reading, you said..." and to ground the homily directly in their own thinking and ideas.

The only hazard in this is that it may be tempting to connect the homily to an interest or occupation of one partner which excludes the other (since one may have been longer known to the pastor) or to develop a discussion which the priest has held with the bride and groom through the months of counseling which excludes the congregation. But the marriage homily should speak to the congregation as well as the couple. They, in fact, may be better able to hear and respond than the bride and groom.

At an ordination, the sermon often ends with a direct exhortation to the ordinand. Ordination has often been compared to marriage, but marriage also is a kind of ordination, a calling into a new and dedicated relationship requiring special gifts of grace. Just as the ordination sermon often ends with a personal exhortation to the ordinand so also the marriage homily can be appropriately addressed primarily to the couple to be married. Through this word, God speaks directly to them. God knows them by the names given to them in baptism and calls them by those names now as they respond to their new vocation. Others will listen and learn and are not to be excluded, but the homily is first of all for them. It is God's word to them as they die to the selves they have been and begin to live in another.

II. The Readings at a Marriage

There are very few direct references to marriage in the Bible. Those that do occur make us aware of the drastic changes that have taken place in this central institution of human life; there is little to inspire or challenge us directly. The Old Testament references to marriage reflect a world in which the relationship between a man and a woman was usually arranged by others for the benefit of family or tribe. Marriage was an economic and political relationship for the procreation of children, the sharing of burdens, and the orderly transmission of property. We hear of a "marriage alliance" (I Kings 3:1) and of women being "given in marriage" in return for certain gifts or to cement a relationship between families and nations (Genesis 34:8-10, 41:45, etc.)

This practice does not change significantly in the New Testament where we still hear of being "given in marriage" (Matthew 22:30). Indeed, the parables of a marriage feast speak only of a king who "made a marriage for his son" and never refer to a bride at all. The epistle to the Hebrews does tell us that marriage should be "held in honor" (Hebrews 13:4), and Jesus told his disciples that divorce is not in keeping with God's purpose in creation. St. Paul provides some instruction about the marital relationship which is useful. But St. Paul, of course, assumes a world in which marital roles are clearly defined by economic circumstances. Further direct instruction is simply not provided.

This did not change in the beginning of the Christian era. Down to the Middle Ages, in fact, marriage was seldom formalized except for older sons and heirs. Others might live together but, if no significant property rights were involved, no ceremonial blessing of the relationship was thought to be necessary.

Perhaps, then, it is only in our own time that it has been possible to think of marriage primarily in terms of romantic love, a sharing of interests, and an ongoing friendship. Indeed, the very developments which seem so often to threaten the very institution of marriage and family, can be seen as enabling more marriages to reach their full potential. Anglican bishops at the Lambeth Conference of 1958 spoke of this possibility in words which still seem both prophetic and challenging:

> Perplexing though the choices in contemporary marriage are, it must also be said that the new freedom of sexuality in marriage in our time is also, and equally, a gate to a new depth and joy in personal relation-

ships between husband and wife. At a time when so much in our culture tends to depersonalize life—to erode and dissolve the old, clear, outlines of human personality—Christians may well give thanks for the chance given us to establish, in marriage, a new level of intimate, loving interdependence between husband and wife and parents and children, freed from some of the old disciplines of fear."[1]

At the same time, just as this potential has become available to us, the economic and political pressures that held marriages together are being dissolved. It is no longer *necessary* to stay married; indeed, this generation has invented the "prenuptial agreement" to make it clear that economic consequences are either limited or ruled out.

The bishops at Lambeth almost forty years ago knew little of these developments, but they knew the dangers as well as the potential for good and they knew the hard work required to realize the promise:

"It must be said at once that this will not happen automatically. It will happen only when we deliberately choose it, and pay the cost of it in self-discipline, in courtesy towards one another within the marital tie, and in willingness to receive and give the fullest possible communication of love, physically as well as in every other way."[2]

We have, furthermore, created a society in which the whole weight of maintaining a relationship is thrown on the couple themselves. Once, they would have been part of a stable community in which many of their emotional needs would have been met by friends and family members who had known them all their lives. Now, a couple marries, and often rents an apartment in a city, where they are surrounded by strangers and work with colleagues who may never have met their partner. After the first child is born, they may move to a small house in a suburb, surrounded by a new set of strangers. As the family grows and they aspire to a larger home, they move again. If they are able, they may buy or rent a summer place where they are surrounded by a different set of strangers. Then, perhaps, the company reassigns them to another area with new relationships to form as old ones wither away. Under such circumstances, all the pressures of work and friendship must be borne by the two who form the core of the nuclear family. No wonder "nuclear explosions" are so common.

It is hardly surprising to find that the Bible, reflecting a very different society, has little to say directly to these needs. Yet the issues raised are precisely those at the center of the biblical message: love, faithfulness, forgiveness, re-creation. Marriage, the Bible says, is ideally like God's relationship with God's people. If there are no human examples of Christian marriage in the Bible, there is the Bible itself, the record of God's love and

---

[1] *The Lambeth Conference 1958*, 2.150.
[2] Idem.

faithfulness and forgiveness and re-creating power. Finally, it is God alone from whom we must learn what marriage can be.

When we look in the Bible, then, for lessons to read at a wedding, we cannot expect to find many passages about human marriage for our instruction. What few passages there are will need to be interpreted for our day. We will, however, find countless passages speaking of God's love and faithfulness. The Old Testament itself is the story of the love and marriage between God and Israel. The prophets often spoke of the relationship specifically in terms of a marriage. Their language ("whoring after other gods") is sometimes too colorful for use at a marriage service, but when they speak of faithfulness and forgiveness it is always relevant to marriage because it is the marriage of God and Israel they are discussing.

When we come to the New Testament, there is a continuation of the same theme, though attention shifts from Israel to the single figure of Jesus Christ. As the normal result of a marriage is a child in whom the love of the father and mother is incarnate, so God's love for Israel leads to the birth of Jesus, in whom God's love for us is incarnate. Jesus incarnates God's love for Israel. In his body the unity God seeks between God and the human race is accomplished. God's initiative finds its opportunity in the obedient willingness of one human being. Human love and faithfulness are inadequate, but human responsiveness to God's love is sufficient for God's purpose.

The readings for a marriage, then, should be seen in this light. They are not examples of human marriage or even, necessarily, teaching about human marriage. They are the story of God's relationship with Israel and the church, the model toward which all human marriages are called.

A. Old Testament Texts and Commentary

1. Genesis 1:26-28 (26-28, 31a) ♦ "Male and female he created them"

a. "*...In the image of God he created them,...*" (v.27). We know God first of all as creator; everything around us is a reflection of God's power and purpose. But the Bible says of human beings that they are made in the "image of God." We are not simply evidence of God's creative ability, we are evidence of the very nature of God. It is not unusual for a man or woman in love to worship the one they love, and that is appropriate because they have seen something of God in the other. Of course, they get over that first enthusiasm, and they should. The other person is not God! Love for another can either block the knowledge of God or lead one on to a deeper knowledge. But it is in fact God we are learning to love in the other. A certain awe, a certain worshipfulness in marriage is a valuable asset.

b. *"...Male and female he created them...."* (v.27). Human life being so familiar to us, we take it for granted that there should be male and female within the species. But there are other patterns available. Some fruit trees are self-pollinating and amoebas replicate by division. In other worlds, presumably still other patterns would be possible. But God chose to create two kinds of humanity who would come together in a marital union which, at least according to the **Book of Common Prayer** "is intended by God for their mutual joy." God, we are asked to believe, created male and female for the joy that human beings would derive from sexual union. If so, it is strange that we commonly hold so joyless an image of God and that there is so strong a tendency in the Christian heritage to think of marriage as, at best, a "necessary evil." If, then, the emerging view of marriage as reflecting the nature of God and God's purpose in creation is correct, it will obviously take time to assimilate that understanding and develop the necessary structures, both ideological and institutional, to support it. The marriage homily can be an invaluable tool toward this end. We need to repeat as frequently as possible how central the marriage of male and female is to God's purpose and how much our growth in knowledge and love of God depends on our proper understanding and use of marriage.

2. Genesis 2:4-9, 15-24 (or 18-24) ♦ "Therefore a man leaves his father and his mother and clings to his wife, and they become one flesh"

When the woman is introduced as a "helper" (v.20), she should not be thought of as an "aide de camp" or kitchen assistant.[3] Elsewhere the Bible speaks of God as our help (Psalms 33:20; 70:5) and the same Hebrew word is used. God is our helper and if we are to be like God, made in his image, we are to be helpers to each other. The good news of the gospel is that God is not merely a creator and remote power, but a God who comes to our help. St. Paul, furthermore, speaks of how Jesus renounced power and position to empty himself out and die for us (Philippians 2:4-8). At the center of the marriage relationship there needs to be the same kind of self-sacrifice and emptying out of self for the sake of the other. We were each created for the sake of the other, not for our own sake.

It is also worth noting that it is the man who is found to be incomplete without the woman, not vice versa, and that it is the man who is said to leave his family for his wife's sake, and not vice versa. There is no basis in these texts for any idea of dominant and subordinate roles in marriage.

3. Ecclesiastes 3:1-11 ♦ "For everything there is a season"

Why is this reading frequently requested for weddings? It says there is a time to dance and a time to love, but it also says there is a time to weep, a

---

[3] Samuel Terrien suggests that the meaning of the Hebrew word is closer to "savior." *Till the Heart Sings*, pp. 10-11.

time to hate, and a time to refrain from embracing, This reading is also frequently requested for funerals. It seems probable that this reading casts a spell which has more to do with its rhythms than its reason.

Nonetheless, there is a striking resemblance between the balanced rhythms of this passage and the marriage vow itself, which asks a commitment "for better for worse, for richer for poorer, in sickness and in health." Better and worse are not put forward as equally possible alternatives, allotted by fate, but as both being part of the expectation with which one enters into marriage. The marriage ceremony is an occasion of joy, but marriage itself, over the long span of years, necessarily encompasses occasions of pain and sorrow and suffering.

The place of suffering in God's plan remains always to some degree a mystery, but observation does show us that pain and suffering can strengthen character. A marriage which encompasses pain will arrive at a deeper joy and a stronger marriage. If marriage did not include "for worse," the "for better" would not be as good. The balances of life are not merely an averaging out. They broaden our experience and deepen our faith. We learn from suffering how far God will go with us—and how deeply our partner is committed to us. One of the worst aspects of easy divorce is that we can so easily walk away from the very tests that would strengthen our marriage.

"Everything," Ecclesiastes says, is "suitable for its time" (v.11). The whole range of experience, bitter and sweet, has a place in God's plan. Real love can encompass it all and be deepened by it. These are good things to ponder at the outset of a marriage.

4. Song of Solomon 2:10-13; 8:6-7 ♦ "Many waters cannot quench love"

"The Song of Songs is an enigma," says the ***Interpreter's Bible***.[4] Other contemporary commentaries express similar bewilderment. But while there are many aspects of the book that scholars cannot explain, such as its original purpose, which passages should be assigned to which speaker, and so on, the primary purpose is clear enough to the ordinary reader so that this passage is frequently chosen for weddings. A bride and groom have no difficulty in understanding that this is a poem about the joy and delight of the love with which they are familiar.

The Song of Songs may have its roots in Canaanite liturgy or secular songs, but Jewish and Christian interpreters through the centuries have understood it as an allegorical expression of God's love for God's people. When this passage is chosen, the homilist has the opportunity to point out very directly the relationship between human love and divine love. Most couples, however far they have drifted from the church, instinctively seek out the church for their marriage. Some may be looking only for a more impres-

---

[4] *The Interpreter's Bible*, Vol. 5, p.98.

sive setting than the backyard or a hotel ballroom, but most are responding even subconsciously to the knowledge that love is of God, that their love for each other is not unrelated to God's love for them. The fact that language as "secular" and erotic as that of the Song of Songs has found a place in the Bible is evidence that God's love is recognized as present in human love and that human love is, indeed, a rich and valuable foretaste of the divine love. This passage might well be paired with chapter 5 of Ephesians in which the relationship between husband and wife is seen as a type of God's love for the church. The pastor who succeeds in impressing on a newly married couple the fact that their love for each other is of a piece with God's love for God's people and that in knowing each other they have come to a deeper knowledge of God has conveyed a central teaching of Scripture and set in place a lasting foundation for their growth in the faith.

5. Jeremiah 31:31-32a, 33-34a ♦ "I will make a new covenant with the house of Israel"

Jeremiah spoke at a turning point in Jewish history. The kingdom of David was crumbling and, by the time of Jeremiah's death, had disappeared. The leaders of Israel had been carried into exile and the future seemed to be without hope. In this period, Jeremiah looked forward to a new and better kingdom in which the old law written on stone would be replaced by a new law written "on their hearts" (v.33).

The homilist may be familiar enough with the lives of the couple being married to draw some parallels with this passage. What likelihood is there that one or both could go to work in a place where the employer would say, "We have no rules or requirements here. Just show up when you feel like it and do what you feel like doing"? In the world of business, that isn't likely to work. There have to be rules and procedures that are spelled out. On the other hand, what would happen to a marriage if one partner were to say to the other, "Let's get everything in writing. You'll go off to work at seven and be home at six. We'll eat at seven and go to bed at ten. You'll take care of the laundry. I'll do the lawn. Now just sign here."

The beginning of God's relationship with Israel is marked by the giving of a law, the Ten Commandments. No better summary of human responsibilities has ever existed. But Jeremiah saw clearly the gap that exists between laws carved in stone and the response in human lives. Therefore he believed God must write the law directly on human hearts.

Christians believe that the life of Jesus presents the fulfillment of that vision in a life in which God's will and human action were no longer separated. In this new covenant the law is fulfilled by being perfectly expressed in human action.

Christian marriage, then, is like a covenant within a covenant. Christians who have already entered into a covenant with God based on love, enter into a covenant with one other human being in which the free and loving response of the heart must be sufficient.

Will such a covenant be sufficient? All other human relationships rely on law because of the experience of human failure. Even marriage, in time past, has been reinforced by legal sanctions. But we now live in an age which has removed those sanctions and love alone is left. If we relied on our own love, our own resources, it would not be enough. Within the larger covenant, upheld as Christians are by God's grace, the marriage covenant of love can find the strength it needs. Jeremiah's vision becomes real each time two Christians set out together relying on God's love in their hearts.

6. Tobit 8:5b-8 ♦ "That we grow old together"

a. This passage comes from the Apocrypha, books which were excluded from the Bible of the Reformation churches and placed in a separate section by Anglicans. Many couples will, therefore, be unable to locate the passage in their Bibles, and those who do may not be drawn to it because of the reference to lust. The chief value of the passage may lie in the example it gives of a couple ending their day by praying together—and this activity is not obvious in the passage. Nevertheless, a homily could use this text to speak of the value of praying together and the importance of bringing before God together the concerns, the joys, and the failures of the day. A marriage which begins at the altar in prayer can be renewed daily by such a discipline. Those who adopt such a custom can expect not only to grow old together and find mercy, but to find more love than they have ever imagined.

b. Both partners in a marriage inevitably grow older, but to grow old *together* is not inevitable. The tendency in a marriage is for partners to develop in different directions. If one stays home with children while the other works outside the home, one may develop certain business-related skills while the other is developing new human sensitivities. If one is involved with people and the other with systems, the growth may be very different. To grow old *together* requires sensitivity and self-awareness and may benefit from the perspective of a third party who can see the changes and tensions that a couple may not be able to see themselves. More important to common growth is a common source of life. God's presence at the center of the marriage provides the unifying force in growing together while so many societal pressures tend to pull a marriage apart. Finally, the proper aging of a marriage depends, indeed, on "finding mercy." What human ability is unlikely to achieve, God is able to bring about in spite of our failures.

B. New Testament Epistle Texts and Commentary

1. Romans 12:1-2, 9-13 ♦ "Let love be genuine"

a. *"...Therefore,..."* (v.1). All of St. Paul's epistles are divided into two parts.

The first part sets forth what God has done for us and the second part deals with consequences. The epistle to the Romans follows the same pattern. Because God has done this for us, "therefore" we must live in a certain way. What has God done for us? God has loved us, called us, chosen us, died for us, offered us grace and life in the church and sacraments.

Christian marriage is built on this same "therefore." Because God has chosen us and loved us, we are able to choose and love each other. But marriage is not built on human "therefores." We cannot hold each other to a bargain in which I love you because you love me. To do that is to look to the other partner as the source of love, but God is the only unfailing source of love. To look elsewhere is, inevitably, to be disappointed. To look to God is to find a constant renewal and strengthening of our human love.

b. *"...Do not be conformed to this world,..."* (v.2). St. Paul begins the second part of this epistle with what amounts to a prescription for Christian living. Notice that Christian living has to do with the right use of the body. St. Paul points not to the satisfaction of bodily desires as the goal of marriage, but to the offering of the body to God for God's purposes. "Spiritual worship" is not something separate from the material body, but rather the offering to God of our whole selves. The key phrase is in verse 2: "Do not be conformed to this world,..." or, as the J.B. Phillips paraphrase puts it, "Do not let the world around you squeeze you into its mold." A couple beginning a marriage will have the opportunity to create a pattern of life different from the one in which they were brought up and different from what other couples may take for granted. The pattern St. Paul commends is not self-centered but centered in others. It has to do with hope, patience, and prayer. It involves contributing to the needs of others and practicing hospitality. The love a Christian couple finds in marriage is given to be shared with others and, in being shared, it continues to grow.

2. I Corinthians 13:1-13 (or 12:31-13:8a) ♦ "The greatest of these is love"

No passage is more often used at weddings than this, yet somehow there is always something new to say about it in a homily. The words become familiar and that makes the homilist's task both harder and easier. It is easier because the passage is already known. It is harder because the congregation may feel that they already know all it has to say.

It can be effective to add the end of the 12th chapter, so making clear that St. Paul is not merely describing love but commending a way of life, a "more excellent way." Describing love is not enough, it has to be lived. Anyone in love knows that. They will say, "I can't tell you. You'll have to meet him/her."

It can also be effective to end the reading at verse 8 with the words "Love never ends," though this eliminates the powerful final verse.

a. St. Paul begins by comparing love to a variety of other wonderful gifts (vv.1-3), saying that none of them is of any value apart from love. Indeed, he says that the individual who has these gifts is "nothing" without love. At the time of marriage, the bride or groom may well feel that they are "nothing" without the other. Will they still feel that way when the company asks them to make sacrifices for their career or when time has passed and other interests and pressures compete with the marriage for priority?

Perhaps it would be a useful exercise to evaluate the individuals who command the world's attention in newspapers and movies, sports and politics. Do they seem wonderful or important? But without love their accomplishments have only a human dimension and, therefore, no lasting value. Many of them, sadly, are nothing in God's sight. Those who do not accept God's love and share it with others have, in the end, received and given nothing that endures and are, indeed, nothing. Love alone creates anything that endures. That's the value system on which marriage depends.

b. *Love is a verb* (vv.4-8). In these five verses there are sixteen words used to describe love and all of them (in Greek) are verbs. English lacks the right words to translate this passage, but the fact that verbs are used is significant. Note also that more than half the verbs are negative. Love acts in certain ways and not in others. It is a matter of choosing this way and not that. Love requires intelligence and reflection, but first of all love is a way of acting. We can talk about Jesus' teaching, but it was his actions that made the difference. Actions always speak louder than words. Saying "I love you" is important, but demonstrating it is more important.

c. The first two verbs on the list have to do with *being patient and kind* (v.4). Love is many things, warm feelings and excitement and joy, but at the end of the day patience is more important. How can two people work together unless they have patience? One will always be better at something than the other. One member of a couple will be slower to understand. One will be stronger, the other will be more emotional. Patience is what makes it all come out right. This virtue might be illustrated by the marriage ceremony itself where, so often, the bride comes down the aisle a little late. The groom and congregation are patient, but will they always be? Remember, the bride has reasons to be late. Not least of these is courtesy to friends who may have trouble finding the church. Does the groom understand this? And is the bride patient with him when he is impatient and wants to be on the way before she is ready? Patience on both sides is required.

d. Love *"does not insist on its own way;..."* (v.5). Here, too, the marriage service itself may provide illustrations. The service and celebration will often be the result of compromise. Two families with different customs and preferences are coming together and the finding of common ground is not always easy. Ideally each gives a little for the sake of unity. It's hard to be married in two churches and have a reception in two hotels. Somehow compromises have to be made. Perhaps it's useful to remember that if "God is love," it is true to say "God does not insist on God's own way." On the other hand, human beings who did insist on their own way crucified Jesus. But love still prevailed. Love has that power: it can allow itself to be crucified and still be triumphant.

e. *Love "bears...believes...hopes...endures all things...."* (v.7). These words offer no fulfillment or realization. Love (remember that Love is another name for God) calls for suffering and endurance and has only hope and belief to offer. Nothing in this passage tells us that love is happy or joyful or successful or any such thing. Why then does this passage commend itself to us? Isn't the answer love itself? If we have love, we can endure and bear and hope all things because we have the one thing that matters. The value of love is not so much in the joy it does in fact bring but in its ability to endure the bad days and still go on. Any couple can get through the good days, but only those with love can survive the bad. If you marry for happiness, it won't always be there and you will be disappointed. But the point is that love is always there and, if one marries for love (remember that Love is another name for God), that love can never be lost.

f. *"...Love never ends...."* (v.8). If love never ends, why do marriages? Perhaps we look for love in the wrong place. God is love, and surely God has no end either in space or time. God fills all things. But the human heart is the one place in the universe with the power to bar God's entrance. If we block God out, then, in our hearts, love does end. Why would we block love out? We do it only because we are too busy and too self-concerned. Love requires a partner. Often the arrival on the scene of a partner to love breaks through our tendency toward self-centeredness for a while, but the old tendency often falls back into place and love is once more in exile. Yet love has not ended. Only our openness to love has ended. Repentance and forgiveness can always reopen the channels and let love back in. Can we say these things in a marriage homily? Perhaps we can, if the marriage is set in the context of a eucharist where the power of forgiveness is so strongly emphasized. Perhaps a lighter touch can be added by pointing out that everything else ends: the marriage service, the homily (!), the reception, the honeymoon, yet love is still there.

g. *"...When I became an adult, I put an end to childish ways...."* (v.11). Don't misunderstand. St. Paul is not contradicting Jesus who said the kingdom of heaven is for those who are childlike. St. Paul is comparing our present knowledge and understanding with what we will have in heaven. Here "we see...dimly...Now I know only in part;...." (v.12). Our knowledge and understanding are still childlike — and need to be childlike if we are to enter into a marriage with the trust and simplicity that marriage requires. Those being married may feel very grown up, and that can be disastrous. St. Paul is saying that we are all still children. Jesus would add that we need to be. Those being married might be reminded that they are still children in their parent's eyes and that they can afford to be a little silly, a little childish, and never try to be "all grown up" with the stiffness and lack of ability to grow that that implies. We are all God's children and God loves us as we are. Those being married certainly love each other as they are.

There was a wonderful cartoon in the days when the King James Version was standard that showed a roomful of scattered toys and a harassed looking man picking them up. Under it was the quotation, "When I became a man, I put away childish things." That will happen soon enough. Those being married should not grow up so soon and so fast that they miss the chance to enjoy the kind of childhood that every marriage needs.

h. *"...Faith, hope, and love abide,... and the greatest of these is love"* (v.13) This is so wonderfully satisfying a statement to hear at a marriage that we may hardly notice how faith is made secondary. We are accustomed to speak of our faith as being at the center of our relationship with God and so it is, but it is not God. Love is the nature of God but faith is simply our relationship to God. In the same way, we may think of hope as the last survivor of Pandora's box, the one virtue we can always rely on. St. Paul does, indeed, imply that faith and hope, like love, will always remain when everything else is gone. But faith and hope are the less important members of this great trilogy. Faith and hope both point ahead and deal with the unfulfilled and incomplete. But love is now. Love has to do with fulfillment.

3. Ephesians 3:14-19 ♦ "The love of Christ that surpasses knowledge"

a. When we "give our heart" to another, what does the heart contain? This passage suggests that the heart is first of all a dwelling place for Christ. Marriage, then, becomes an exchange of love in which Christ is both given and received. Indeed, the passage suggests that only if we are "rooted and grounded" in love will we be able to comprehend the full measure of existence. So marriage begins and ends with the love of God. Human love comes from God and returns to God. If this is so, then the source of love is outside ourselves and, in our failures and limitations, we need to turn to God rather than look to our own resources. To come to church to be married is to acknowledge this need. Our marriages will continue to find strength if we continue to acknowledge this need and turn to God for the help God alone can give.

b. *"...And to know the love of Christ that surpasses knowledge,..."* (v.19). This phrase is one more example of how marriage helps us to understand God's love and God's love helps us to understand marriage. God's love is a mystery beyond human understanding, so how can we speak, as St. Paul does here, of knowing the unknowable? Those who are married will come to understand. However much we know of another person, there is always an element of the unknown and unknowable in that relationship. And it is also true that we know the other person in a way that we could never communicate to others or put into words. Love is itself a way of knowing, but love also makes us aware of the element of mystery. To love another person deeply is to know something beyond knowing, as the love of God opens up to us a knowledge beyond understanding.

4. Ephesians 5:1-2, 21-33 (or 5:2a, 25-32) ♦ "Live in love, as Christ loved us"

This strange and important passage begins with a general exhortation to "be imitators of God" and "live in love," skips a long exhortation on fornication and debauchery (which might be very appropriate and would certainly get people's attention), and concludes with an analogy between marriage and the church which would certainly need to be explained if used.

a. *"Therefore be imitators of God as beloved children..."* (v.1). Children inevitably copy their parents. Often we are unaware of how deep the influence is until some specific incident makes us aware that our instinctive response was the same we had often heard from our parents. A young woman, telling a friend about an incident with her small child said, "I opened my mouth and out came my mother!" Christians are those who recognize the limitations of any human model and turn to Jesus for a more perfect example. In him we see the love of God perfectly expressed. And as children learn subconsciously from parental examples, so Christians learn subconsciously by placing themselves in a Christian environment, by participating in a Christian congregation, by prayer and Bible study that place us in Christ's presence. As children imitate their parents, so we learn love by imitating God in Christ. Marriage, in particular, needs that constant example of a love greater than our own to renew and deepen the love God has given us for each other.

b. *"...Live in love..."* (v.2). The NRSV translates the meaning but loses the vividness of the Greek verb *peripateo*—"walk" in love. Love is not an abstract, philosophical ideal but a matter of "walking." Love is real when it controls our daily behavior, shapes all our actions. Those in love may speak of "walking on air," but marriage requires that the air of love surround us as we walk, that we breathe it in and express it in all our actions. Real love is seen by the way we act when we wake up late and have to rush to work without breakfast, when we spend the day in a house with cranky children, when we come home tired to find a dozen chores that should have been done the day before. Our own resources may not be adequate to such occasions. We survive them by developing a reliance on God's surrounding love which holds us up when our own strength fails.

c. *"Be subject to one another out of reverence for Christ. Wives, be subject to your husbands as you are to the Lord. For the husband is the head of the wife just as Christ is the head of the church, the body of which he is the Savior. Just as the church is subject to Christ, so also wives ought to be, in everything, to their husbands. Husbands, love your wives, just as Christ loved the church and gave himself up for her,..."* (vv.21-25).

However difficult some phrases of this passage may be to modern ears, it sets an astounding, and still revolutionary, standard for human relationships: mutual subordination. In an age when male dominance was taken for granted, it set a woman's relationship to a man in parallel to the church's relationship with Christ, and balanced the woman's obedience with the man's self-sacrificing love.

The first English *Book of Common Prayer* of 1549 made a distinction between the man's vows to the woman and the woman's vows to the man in that the woman said, "to love, honor, *and obey.*" But in giving the (single) ring to the woman, the man said, "With this ring I thee wed, with my body I thee worship..." So the woman was to obey the man but the man was to worship the woman, and who wins in that exchange? Perhaps status in that society was not equal, but an ideal was created in which both partners, in a way unique to their sex, were to give themselves fully to the other.

We live in a world confused about sexual identity and looking to science for answers. There are some things we can learn from such studies that are useful. There are indications that men on the whole (but not always) have better spatial abilities while women have better verbal abilities, that women on the whole (but not always) react to stress more emotionally and recover more quickly. But as a society, we are so intent on asserting the equality of the sexes that we cannot yet find adequate ways to verbalize or recognize sexual difference. Nor is it easy to suggest how it might be done. Whatever distinctions scientific studies have observed between the sexes are not universal; they may be true 80% of the time, but not 100%. Women can bear children and men cannot; beyond that nothing is certain! Nonetheless, any working marriage will tend to differentiate roles, though not necessarily along lines indicated by one's sex. One partner, for example, may do most of the cooking, another most of the finances; one will do most of the gardening and another most of the home repairs. Two people can't work at the same sink at the same time. A Christian marriage would be one in which each partner willingly subordinates his or her own interests to the overriding needs of the other. To insist on certain rights is destructive while to seek the other's good first is life-giving.

This passage sets up a relationship in which the wife looks to the husband as the church looks to Christ. Christians could hardly see that as a demeaning relationship to be avoided. At the same time the husband is commanded to love his wife as Christ loved the church and gave himself up for her. That is hardly a relationship of control and domination.

We will have to find our own ways to live out this teaching in our own world and with our own personalities, but it remains a valid, demanding, and revolutionary framework for the marriage relationship.

d. *"...This is a great mystery, and I am applying it to Christ and the church,..."* (v.32). It is hard to tell, when reading this passage carefully, whether the author's primary interest is in the relationship between male and female in marriage or between Christ and the members of the church. The opening exhortation in the marriage service in the *Book of Common Prayer* says of marriage that "...it signifies to us the mystery of the union between Christ and his church...." Evidently the church has always taught that we can learn about marriage by looking at the church and learn about the church by looking at marriage. Human love can help us to understand God's love but God's love challenges our human love to grow beyond our ordinary horizons.

A couple about to be married will know an intensity of human love that may enable them to hear the words "God is love" with new appreciation. They are less likely to appreciate the fact that their love has limits and needs to be set in a loving community to be challenged and deepened and reinforced. But they have instinctively come to the church to be married in the presence of a larger community and they can be guided to see how important it is to keep their marriage centered in that place and presence.

5. Colossians 3:12-17 ♦ "Clothe yourselves with love"

a. This passage begins with a list of virtues not easy to come by and not very often seen (vv.12-13), but it does go on to tell us where to find them: "...As the Lord has forgiven you, so you also must forgive...." (v.13). Because the Lord comes to us in "...kindness, humility, meekness, and patience" (v.12) and has given us these gifts, we also can give them to others.

b. "...Love...binds everything together..." (v.14). Love is the cement that creates every relationship. And love is to clothe us. Love doesn't just well up within us. It isn't evoked as a response to the lovableness of the other. Rather God offers it to us, and we can put it on or not as we choose. Too often we think of love as something that happens to us and, if it stops happening, we assume we are helpless to maintain it. But the fact is that we choose to love or not to love and we can also choose to renew a love that has stopped happening. It may be that it has stopped happening because of something we have failed to do. Adults should be able to shape their lives, not be helpless victims of emotional urges.

c. *Peace* (v.15) in the Bible is not simply an absence of warfare—that wouldn't be much of an ideal for marriage! Peace is a creative relationship, a rich harmony to which each contributes for the benefit of both. In T.S. Eliot's play, "Murder in the Cathedral," Thomas à Becket preaches a sermon just before his martyrdom in which he cites Jesus' words, "Peace I leave with you, my peace I give unto you," and asks,

> Did he mean peace as we think of it: the kingdom of England at peace with its neighbours, the barons at peace with the King, the householder counting over his peaceful gains, the swept hearth, his best wine for a friend at the table, his wife singing to the children? Those men His disciples knew no such things: they went forth to journey afar, to suffer by land and sea, to know torture, imprisonment, disappointment, to suffer death by martyrdom. What then did he mean?[5]

---

5 Eliot, T. S., *The Complete Poems and Plays*, p.199.

Peace, Eliot suggests, is something more profound than mere lack of hostilities or comfortable ease. Peace, indeed, may be found in the midst of suffering. Peace may be the acceptance of suffering for the sake of another. An image of marriage that includes that vision of peace would save much division and strife.

d. The picture in verses 16-17 is one of Christian life in general, not married life as such, but marriage, too, begins in worship and praise of God. A marriage centered on self has only human resources to draw on. A marriage centered in praise of God begins with joy and is constantly renewed by grace.

6. I John 4:7-16 (or 4:7-12) ♦ "...those who abide in love, abide in God"

a. *"...God is love...."* (v.8). Simple formulas are dangerous, and this equation, dealing as it does with the ultimate power in the universe, is the most dangerous formula ever devised. The problem is that we do not know God but we think we know about love. This equation seems to suggest that we know who God is and can drag God down to the level of our knowledge of love. A civilization as confused as ours about the nature of love cannot come to know God by studying love. On the contrary, we can only learn what love really is by studying God. As this passage also says, the love of God is revealed, "made manifest," in the life of Jesus. So knowing about love means knowing about Jesus. Love, to be complete, needs to be guided by his life. It must, above all, involve total self-sacrifice, the giving of oneself for others.

Notice also that the formula cannot be reversed. We cannot say, "Love is God," because that would define God in terms of our knowledge of love. We tend to do that anyway with disastrous results. We reduce God to the level of our knowledge.

To say "God is love" is to say that love is a mystery ultimately beyond our knowledge but, if we want to know more, we must turn to God in worship and service to do so.

b. *"...God is love...."* (v.8). A second aspect of this formula is the revelation that the ultimate meaning of life is found in relationship, not singleness. Singleness is not the ultimate truth either about God or about humanity. William James identified religion as "the feelings, acts, and experiences of individual men in their solitude."[6] This is true only if "solitude" is actually used to establish a relationship with God. But that would not be true solitude, because no one can be alone who is with God.

This formula tells us that human beings are made for relationship; that we are incomplete by ourselves. This is not to say that marriage is required. Many great saints were not married, but they gave themselves to relationship either with God alone or, more often, with God in others. It is to say that marriage can be a means of growing in knowledge of God. As we learn the joy of the marriage relationship and learn to give ourselves more fully to an-

---

[6] James, William, *The Varieties of Religious Experience*, Lecture 2.

other, we do come to understand more fully who God is and what God's love for us means.

This formula tells us that the ultimate relationship is with God. A love which is wholly bound up in another human being is destructive because it cuts us off from the source and center of love.

This formula tells us that God is by nature relational: God's unity is no more ultimate than God's triune being. The relationships we develop with other human beings have a parallel in the relationship of Father, Son, and Spirit and need to be shaped by that pattern. As God's being is triune, our relationships also need to be triune. A married couple cannot find completion simply in each other. The dual relationship of marriage needs to be completed in one direction by God's presence and in the other direction by children or other human relationships. Love is not solitary, nor dual, but multidimensional. True love does not simply reflect back and forth between two, but is always reaching out in new directions. True love is not reflection but radiation.

C. Gospel Texts and Commentary

1. Matthew 5:1-10 ♦ "Blessed are the poor in spirit"

The Sermon on the Mount has often been seen as the simplest and clearest summary of Jesus' teaching and the Beatitudes may be the best known part of that sermon. Each line could be explored at great length to understand all its dimensions and the promise "they will see God" (v.8) embodies the highest aspiration of the greatest mystics and saints. The Beatitudes are not, of course, specifically directed at a married couple. They are, rather, a statement on Christian living which applies to all Christians. A couple facing the challenge of establishing their marriage in a non-supportive society may have even more reason than others to look again at these ideals and learn from them.

a. *"Blessed"* is a word used so often that it is hard to establish its meaning. Some modern translations say "happy" and that throws a useful light on the subject. "Blessed" seems to have religious significance while "happy" may be more secular in its connotations. "Blessed" seems to imply God's gift while "happy" may seem to come from within. Happiness is an elusive goal but the Beatitudes direct us away from ourselves and toward God for its attainment. They also point to self-emptying and selflessness—never more needed than in marriage.

b. *"...The poor in spirit,..."* (v.3) is paraphrased "those who know their need of God" in the Jerusalem Bible and that may be a helpful focus for marriage. The children's counting rhyme which (in one version) says, "One for the money, two for the show, three to get married..." may make the same point. A marriage based on the love of two people for each other is like a long bridge with no supporting tower. Those who know their need of God and turn to God for support will have the strength and resilience every marriage needs for the long haul.

c. *"...They will see God...."* (v.8) is the ultimate promise given to God's people. A couple in love may think there is no higher happiness than to see each other and that is a good first step away from the sin of self-centeredness. But even though love and marriage are God's gift, they are not an end in themselves. Though we find a higher level of happiness (blessedness) in love of another person, even that love cannot fulfill all our need. It is dangerous to look to any other human being to complete our happiness. Most broken marriages are the result of such disappointment. But if we are drawn on from love for another to love for God, then our deepest needs can be satisfied, we will not ask of our partners what they cannot give, and our marriage will have the strength it needs in God, our true goal.

2. Matthew 5:13-16 ♦ "Let your light shine before others"

a. *"You are the salt of the earth;..."* (v.13). There was a day when salt was seen purely as something good. Now we know that salt can also be dangerous. We need a certain amount of salt in our diet, but in large amounts it can lead to heart disease and even death. So being hailed as "the salt of the earth" is a dubious blessing. Perhaps there is value in saying to a newly married couple that they can, in truth, have too much of each other. Our world lacks the extended families and stable communities which once balanced the marriage relationship with a host of others. The "nuclear family" is thrown in on itself and tends, like the nucleus of the atom, to explode under pressure with devastating effects. Salt piled up is useless, it needs to be spread widely to give the most benefit. The couple is surrounded by friends on the wedding day, but will those friends be there in the coming weeks and months and years? To be "the salt of the earth," a couple needs to keep their marriage at the center of a wide network of relationships, flavoring the lives of others and sharing the love God has given them.

b. *"...You are the light of the world...."* (v.14). To see this text illustrated, go to a wedding. Marriage takes two happy people, puts them in the center of a gathering of family and friends, and lets their joy radiate out so everyone is affected by it. But is it fair to expect that that can continue? Can a couple continue to light up other lives?

It may be helpful to balance this text with John 8:12 in which Jesus says, "I am the light of the world." Jesus can say "You are the light of the world" to his followers because they have a source of light in him. The joy that illuminates a marriage is God's gift. The ability to continue to shine is also God's gift. And if it requires discipline and self-sacrifice to continue to receive that gift, think how much expenditure went into making the joy of the wedding. A year's planning and a good part of a year's income often goes into the brief joy of the marriage events. If we are willing to make that expenditure, how much more willing should we be to give God the time in prayer and study and service that will enable our lives to continue to be enlightened by God's light and other lives to be enlightened by that light in us?

3. Matthew 7:21, 24-29 (or 7:21,24-25) ♦ "Like a wise man who built his house on rock"

This is the final passage in the Sermon on the Mount and provides a kind of summation: to "hear these words" and act on them (v.24) is to build on rock. "Hearing" and "acting" are, therefore, critical. Marriage is not a matter of instincts, but of guidance and response to that guidance. God who created us knows how our lives should be shaped, and security and stability in marriage (as in all human life) are found in God's word.

The reference to a wise man building on rock may be difficult to use in an era of "inclusiveness," and the passage is seldom chosen for that reason. Some modern paraphrases speak of a wise person, but that is still difficult as a marriage metaphor since we are looking at a couple, not an individual.

Nevertheless, the rock metaphor is a basic one in the Bible and the church and can provide a useful metaphor for marriage. Marriage is not made strong by the quality of the relationship between husband and wife but by the relationship they establish with God. God is the foundation; we are the building. Rock walls built on sand will last no longer than cardboard. But a seemingly frail house built on rock will stand because of its foundation. Rocks, it might also be noted, are for building on; they should not be strewn in someone's path or used as missiles.

4. Matthew 19:3-6 ♦ "Therefore what God has joined together, let no one separate"

This passage is parallel to Mark 10:6-9 and almost identical. It is suggested as a reading for weddings because it is the one place in which Jesus speaks specifically about the purpose of marriage. The trouble is that it comes here in a negative context, in a discussion of divorce. In a society in which divorce is so common, however, it may be well to have that connection clearly made. Divorce is contrary to God's will because God's will is that male and female become one flesh and inseparable. Jesus responds to the question about divorce by going behind the Mosaic permission to ask God's purpose in creation. Whatever concessions may be made by Moses or other lawgivers to human weakness, God's original purpose is clear.

"...[God] made them male and female,..." (v.4). In creation, there were, presumably, alternatives. God might have created a sexless humanity or enabled human beings to reproduce in some other way as amoebas do. But

God made human beings who need each other to survive both as individuals and as a species and then gave that dependency such a potential for love and joy that in it can be learned something of God's ultimate purpose.

What reorientation of human thinking is so profound as this? Apart from revelation, marriage could be seen as simply a physical necessity with no spiritual significance. Even within the church, the blessing of a marriage is often seen as simply ecclesiastical acceptance of a biological situation which is irrelevant (or even contrary) to the divine purpose. It seems very hard for human beings, flesh and blood as we are, to believe that the creator really cares about the material world God made. Yet the Bible consistently shows us a God content to be revealed through and in creation. The climax of this story comes in the incarnation—God revealed in human flesh. This passage, consistent with the whole thrust of God's revelation, tells us that human marriage is fundamental to God's purpose. In human flesh we are to learn about love and self-giving and to be given a foretaste of the joy of the kingdom.

5. Matthew 22:35-40 ♦ "Which commandment in the law is the greatest?"

It's interesting to note that Jesus selected two commandments from the Law of Moses, love God and love your neighbor, as the summation of God's will for us. Nothing is said about loving your spouse! Should Jesus have added a third commandment? In view of the divorce rate, one might think so. When we read this passage at a marriage we are, so to speak, putting marriage "in its place." We are remembering that however intense the marriage relationship may be, it is really only a variation on the theme of loving your neighbor. We are commanded to love God and those human beings whose lives touch ours in any way. Love of a spouse is just loving one particular neighbor in a more intimate way — and it comes second to love of God. That does not demean the marriage relationship. It is simply a reminder that God is the source of our love and that our love for each other is always less than God's love for us.

6. Mark 10:6-9, 13-16 ♦ "Therefore what God has joined together, let no one separate"

This passage has been carved out of its context in a strange way. The first part is a parallel of Matthew 19:3-6 (above) and its context, like that of the Matthean parallel, is a discussion of divorce. But in this reading from Mark the references to divorce, found in verses 2-4 and 11-12, have been cut out. Presumably the subject of divorce is out of keeping with the joy of a wedding. But, as suggested above, the reality of divorce is such in our society that it may be worth pondering even at a wedding.

a. This passage gives recognition to the fact that marriage is not a matter of two people working out their own lives, but a matter of two people in society whose lives are shaped by many others and whose marriage is upheld or endangered by others.

Some marriage services today provide for a specific expression of support from the congregation: "Will all of you witnessing these vows do all in your power to support these two persons in their marriage? (Answer) We will." A wedding homily might well be addressed to the congregation whose members have taken on this responsibility. Certainly a newly married couple whose friends are supportive will find it easier than one whose friends are critical, negative, and interfering. One of the few explicit commands Jesus gave us was to avoid dividing those God has joined. In a society plagued by divorce, that is a command to be taken with utmost seriousness. God's will is unity. God is bringing a new couple together in pursuit of that goal. Insofar as their friends or family work against their marriage, they are working against God.

b. *"People were bringing little children..."* (v.13). At first glance this passage seems to have been added merely to make a longer reading. What connection is there between Jesus' words about divorce and his blessing of children? The fact that in both Matthew and Mark the blessing of the children follows immediately on the words about divorce may suggest some relationship between the two passages. In any event, it would certainly not be inappropriate to think about family and children at the time of marriage. Mark (not Matthew) connects Jesus' blessing of the children with teaching about the kingdom of God. To enter the kingdom one must be like a child. This teaching is surely relevant to marriage. Those who marry need to be reminded of Jesus' teaching about the kingdom. The qualities of life that fit us for the kingdom, are the same qualities needed to make marriage succeed. Again and again, Jesus pointed to childlikeness as an ideal. Trust, simplicity, openness, ability to grow and change are all characteristics of children which are also much needed in marriage. A bride and groom often do have a childlike sense of wonder in their relationship to each other and their discovery of the joy of loving and being loved. That quality needs to be preserved and extended. A bride and groom need to begin their married life like children, without prejudice or ingrained habit, but with an openness to new ways. Adults assume much on the basis of experience, but a bride and groom (ideally) come without experience and have the opportunity to learn together, to make a new life by mutual consent.

It's easy to see verses 13-16 as an irrelevant addition, but that misses the opportunity to come to the heart of Christian discipleship and find there the essence of marriage as well.

7. Luke 24:13-35 ♦ "He had been made known to them in the breaking of the bread"

a. This passage, of course, makes no direct reference to marriage, but few of the other suggested texts do either. What it does speak of is the way Christ is known to his disciples in the simple things of life, at the table, in a meal, in the sharing of food. It speaks of the way we are often blind to Christ's presence.

b. The passage might also be used to comment on the difference between the ways men and women understand and respond to Christ. (Such generalizations are always dangerous since there are exceptions to every rule.) The women in the story see and know but are not believed. The men need to be led by a longer process of reasoning to the point at which they can finally see. Both kinds of response have value. There is need for a quick and intuitive grasp of a situation and need also for a slower more reasoned approach. The men and women who followed Jesus all had a vital role to play. The witness of both groups is important. A man and a woman in marriage will respond differently to different challenges, and to the role of faith in their lives. Each needs to be sensitive to the wisdom of the other and learn from the other where they themselves may be blind.

c. If the marriage service includes a celebration of the eucharist, this text comes alive. The disciples came to know that Christ was alive at a table in the breaking of bread. In the breaking of bread, despair was turned to joy. It was nothing they said to each other that made the difference, but the recognition of Christ's presence. That presence, recognized at the marriage itself and sought again and again in the years that follow, can in the same way turn despair to joy and bring new life where all human hope has vanished.

8. John 2:1-11 ♦ "There was a wedding in Cana of Galilee"

How could Jesus be present at a wedding and not "steal the show" from the bride and bridegroom? Yet John shows Jesus apparently sitting on the sidelines while the celebration went on and quietly contributing to the joy of the occasion. The story is packed with symbolism, but it would seem better to concentrate on the "big picture"—Jesus as wedding guest, as part of every Christian marriage, transforming the marriage, filling it with joy, yet doing so in a manner almost unnoticed. Jesus takes the simple materials we offer and provides an abundance beyond anything we ask or expect.

9. John 15:9-12 ♦ "This is my commandment, that you love one another"

"...*If you keep my commandments, you will abide in my love, just as I have kept my Father's commandments and abide in his love....*" (v.10). The connection between "commandments" and "love" is probably unexpected in our society and worth thinking about. We might hear it as saying, "I will love you, if you do what I tell you." But that is a prescription for disaster. We cannot remake another person in our image in order to love them.

The point to note is that Jesus asks us to keep his commandments "as I have kept my Father's commandments" (v.10). But we never hear of Jesus feeling threatened by his Father's commands. Rather, he spoke of doing God's will as "my food" (John 4:34). It was responding to God's will that sustained him.

Think of God's commands as a dance in which the partners are, in a sense, limited by the other's moves. To fail to respond would be disaster.

But responding easily, smoothly, instinctively, is a joy to do and beautiful to watch. So a married couple will learn to respond to each other's movements as Jesus responded to God. Such obedience, responsiveness, creates love and joy and true freedom.

10. John 15:12-16 ♦ "No one has greater love than this"

This passage starts off with two apparent impossibilities: 1) we are commanded to love, and 2) we are told that we should love each other as much as God in Christ loves us.

a. A bride and groom come to be married because they "can't help loving" each other, not because someone commanded them to. In fact, if they had been ordered to get married by someone else, the marriage could be annulled. It is an essential aspect of marriage that it be freely chosen.

But the laws of God, like the laws of physics, are statements of how things are. Whether we like the laws of physics is irrelevant. We obey some of them, like the law of gravity, because we have no choice. And as we discover more about the laws of physics, we are able to live fuller, richer lives. God's laws are like that. There are times and places when we love because our instincts compel us to love. But love is a law of nature. The more we understand it and base our lives on it, the richer our lives become. What begins as instinct, grows easily at first, but later there may be times when instinct and inclination are not enough. There may be times when we will need to recognize a law of love and submit to it when we would rather not. There are times when we would rather not obey a number of laws: traffic laws, income tax laws, and so on. But obeying them enables society to function and makes our own lives safer and fuller as well. So the commandment to love has a value in an imperfect world, guiding us when our own guidance system isn't working and reinforcing our wills when our wills are weak.

b. As for the commandment to love each other as Christ loves us, the point is quality, not quantity. We cannot love as much as Christ loves us, but we can love in the way that he loves. Jesus speaks here of willingness to die for another as the greatest love, and so he died for us. The example is one of self-sacrifice. Love is giving, not getting. Those who give up on a marriage because they no longer "find it fulfilling," never understood love in the first place. God must find human beings more than slightly "unfulfilling." But that is not the point. God loves us purely and simply for the sake of loving us. We derive far more from it than God ever could. Our love will be like God's if we give more than we get and never think of measuring.

11. John 17:20-26 (or 17:20-23) ♦ "That they all may be one"

Jesus' prayer at the Last Supper centers on the deepest aspects of the relationship between human beings and God. For that reason it has much to say about marriage. God's will is unity and the perfect example for human unity is found, Jesus says here, in the relationship between Father and Son in the Trinity. As the Father is in the Son and the Son in the Father, so those God calls are to be in God and to know God in themselves.

a. Is it possible to set out the doctrine of the Trinity as a model for human marriage? Can the bride and groom recognize the presence of the other in themselves and their presence in the other and know it so deeply that, as with God, the unity is as fundamental as the distinction? If a couple chooses this passage and if they have had time to discuss it with the pastor beforehand, it may well be that some profound teaching can be done and that something of that teaching can indeed be communicated in the marriage homily.

b. At a simpler level, if the marriage takes place in the context of the eucharist, it may be possible to draw relationships between Jesus' prayer at the Last Supper for his disciples' unity and the special intention of the nuptial eucharist for the unity of husband and wife. Jesus prayed for his disciples and fed them with his own life. So at the marriage, through prayer and communion, we seek the unity of two of Jesus' disciples.

c. Perhaps, also, there is a point to be made concerning the context of this prayer. The prayer takes place at a critical turning point in the disciples' relationship with Jesus. His presence and guidance will be with them now in new ways and they will have to learn to seek his strength in new ways. So, too, the newly married couple is at a critical turning point. Like the disciples, God has brought them together and now sends them out to make their way in the world The family and friends who have been their strength and support will step back and they will have to turn to each other. More important, they, like the disciples, will need to find Jesus' presence in prayer and communion. The purpose of the nuptial eucharist is to center the new marriage in the strength and life for which Jesus prayed and to ask that the same unity which is at the heart of the Godhead may be at the heart of their marriage.

III. Marriage Homilies

A. Hollywood Wedding

Sarah Todd and John Garretson grew up in the same community but had moved to Hollywood when they became engaged. Neither was really a part of the film making community. Sarah, a church member and former choir member, was involved in art. John, brought up in the Christian Science tradition, was a musician and played with small jazz combos. The homily built implicitly on that interest in music and explicitly on the Hollywood residence. I dislike taking the liturgy for a text instead of the Bible, but the words "I will" are powerful and important and it seemed better not to complicate the structure of the homily with a biblical theme that might have appeared subordinate.

"I will."

This is my first Hollywood wedding (and maybe my last!), so I want to take the opportunity to say something about Hollywood weddings and real weddings.

A few minutes ago I asked you each a question and you each answered, "I will." I've never seen a Hollywood wedding, on television or in the movies, where they said that. In Hollywood weddings, they always seem to say, "I do." I think that's significant. I think it makes a difference.

Here today, you aren't so much doing something as willing something. Now that we live in a world where Christian marriage isn't just taken for granted and there are all kinds of marriages and relationships, that difference may be even clearer than it used to be.

Christian marriage is something willed. It involves a commitment to an unknown future, a deep commitment of the will, not just a passing impulse. It isn't a matter of today "I do" and tomorrow "I don't." Most Hollywood weddings seem to be "I do" weddings, or at least that's their reputation. More and more weddings everywhere seem to be "I do" weddings, and more and more weddings fail. So the question is, how can we will one thing and continue to will it? It isn't easy.

What it comes down to, I believe, is really a matter of being human, of becoming human. Machines do things, but only human beings will them. And the goal is to blend two wills, two human wills, into something larger and fuller and more complete. It's when we treat each other as objects, as things, as machines that do or don't, that work for us or get traded in, that we have trouble. It's when we take the time to be human, to treat each other as persons, when we *will*, that a new dimension of life and love opens up.

Of course, that's why marriage manuals and all that sort of thing are not much use. That's all about how to *do*, not how to *will*. What we need is not a guide to doing but a support in willing. What we really need is another will beyond our own, a will that knows us and respects us and loves us and so can support and strengthen our wills to accomplish what we intend. And this is why, toward the end of the service, there's a prayer that asks that your wills be united in God's will. That's what makes the difference.

A friend of mine and I are working on recorder lessons with the same teacher and we've begun working together on some duets. It's been interesting to see what happens. The teacher works with us and we try some pieces with all three of us playing together. We start off well enough but then either my friend or I misses a note—wrong fingering, wrong timing, wrong line perhaps—and if we two were alone, that would do it. We'd be stopped right there. But with the teacher playing with us and one or the other hanging in there, the other can get back on track, pick up the beat, and carry on. We often make it through only because of that strong third party holding us together and keeping us going.

I think Christian marriage is something like that. We need a sustaining will, a third party, to help carry us so we can make mistakes and not have a total disaster. There's still that sustaining strength to rely on. In the same way, the two wills that make a marriage are held up, held together, sustained, by a third will. We are not alone. We don't depend entirely on our own resources.

Nothing in a Christian marriage matters more than that three-way relationship, third will, third person. And you won't know God overnight any more than you'll know each other in a few days or a few weeks or even a few years. But over time, with three wills united, you can build the kind of marriage that is seldom seen in Hollywood or anywhere else these days; a marriage that lasts not just for three reels but for a lifetime and beyond. Your family and friends are here today to ask God to be with you in a marriage without a Hollywood ending; a marriage with no ending at all. That's the marriage God wants you to have. With God's help, you will.

B. In The Beginning

The opportunity to discuss the text with the congregation before writing the sermon is a rare one, but marriage often provides it. The couple chooses the texts and when they come to discuss final details of the service, there is a chance to ask why they made those choices, what the texts said to them. Sometimes, of course, the reply is not very helpful. But other times the reply can shape the homily that is to be prepared and can almost take precedence over the text. That was what happened when Ralph Carlson and Nancy Grove were asked why they had chosen a passage from Genesis. "We wanted to begin at the beginning," they said with a chuckle. So it was from their own words that the homily was built.

"These are the generations of the heavens and the earth when they were created" ♦ **(Genesis 2:4)**

I don't know whether you remember this, but weeks ago, when you gave me the list of readings for this service, you told me the first reading would be from Genesis because, you said, "We want to begin at the beginning." That's exactly what you're doing today and it's well worth thinking a little more about what that means.

First, of course, you *are* at the beginning. As of today you are a new person that has not existed before. You are no longer Ralph and Nancy but RalphandNancy, one person in Christ sharing one life, a life that is not "his" and "hers" but yours together, belonging to neither of you but belonging to both of you.

Now, a newborn person has no experience, no maturity, no wisdom. All of that comes later. And with a newborn child, we make allowances. We know maturity only comes with time. But we seem to expect more of a newly married couple, and I wonder why we should. It takes time to learn living. It takes time to learn marriage. And we ought to be allowed to start at the beginning and take one small step at a time. We all make mistakes. You will make mistakes. But at the beginning we should expect that and make allowances. Concentrate on the first steps, one at a time. A good marriage, like all good things, comes with time.

But in another sense, you are not the beginning. It may feel that way, but you aren't. God is the beginning. All things begin with God. A marriage that begins at the beginning begins with God, as yours is doing here today. And that means many things. It means strength. It means joy. It means right priorities and right relationships. If God, from the beginning, is first in your life, things are in the right order. If not, not.

And, perhaps most important, God at the beginning means forgiveness, which is another way of saying "new beginnings." With God's forgiveness, you can always begin again. And nowhere is that more important than in marriage, where failures hurt most and love is needed most, if beginnings are to lengthen into continuings and mature into completions and come at last to triumphant endings. And all of these bring us back at every step of the way to the same God who is our beginning and our destiny, our source and our goal.

The love we know in marriage begins in God and ends in God. And that may be recognized or unrecognized, but it is always there. I pray that your love will recognize its source and its goal and that your love will always - today and tomorrow and every day - begin at that beginning and bring you at last to that end.

C. Everything Beautiful

No list of readings I have seen suggests the third chapter of Ecclesiastes for either weddings or funerals but it is not an uncommon or inappropriate request for both occasions. It is probably the music and poetry of it that attracts people to it rather than the sense, but the meaning, for all its despair and hopelessness, is worth considering. Sheila Hanna had been through a painful divorce, raised two children by herself, completed her education, and developed a very successful day care program when she came to marry Ed Fitzgerald. They were both old enough and experienced enough to know that there is indeed "a time for every purpose under heaven." I was, in a real sense, preaching to the converted.

"He has made everything suitable for its time; moreover he has put a sense of past and future into their minds" ♦ (Ecclesiastes 3:11)

No one, I think, ever tried harder to understand the meaning and purpose of life than the author of Ecclesiastes. No one tried harder or was more sure he had failed. And of course he had failed. He wanted to understand it all, and he couldn't. Nor can we. But few people ever saw the mystery of life so clearly or wrote about it so beautifully.

"For everything there is a season, and a time for every matter under heaven: a time to be born, and a time to die;...a time to weep, and a time to laugh;...a time to embrace, and a time to refrain from embracing;...a time to love, and a time to hate; a time for war and a time for peace...." He ends it all with a marvelous summary less often quoted: "He has made everything suitable for its time; moreover he put a sense of past and future into their minds, yet they cannot find out what God has done from the beginning to the end."

In a few minutes, we'll embrace all those contrasts in the marriage vows that say, "for better for worse, for richer for poorer, in sickness and in health,..." You can almost hear the same mind at work in the balancing out of the phrases. A good marriage is one prepared for it all and ready to embrace it all. A good marriage is one that knows life is not all sunshine, and knows that we wouldn't enjoy it if it were.

There are religions that are escapist. Sometimes people even use Christianity as an escape from reality. But they ought not to, because Christianity is the world's most realistic religion. It centers on another balance: Good Friday and Easter, death and resurrection. It begins with a life that embraced laughter and tears, success and failure, peace and conflict, life and death.

There are religions that are dualistic, that see life as a matter of continuous conflict between good and evil, unresolved polarities. But that also misses the point.

God has made "everything suitable for its time" (v.11). Everything we face has a use and value. Not only that, but the worse times give depth and added value to the good times, and the times of trial give us a strength that comes no other way.

It seems as if there is more to life than we can absorb in any one way or two or three. Laughter and love and embracing and peace are wonderful, but even they are somehow incomplete. There's something more, the whole span of past and future, sometimes called eternity, which God has put in our minds, yet which we cannot fully understand. We want it and yearn for it, but we can't get our minds around it. We find part of it here, part of it there, like the colors broken by a prism.

This life is like that. We only see the beauty in the parts. If you brought it all together at one time and place, blended all the colors in one, the light would dazzle and blind us. So, instead, we are asked to know and love God in the broken pieces of life and, perhaps, by doing that, to bring them back to God, bring them back into one.

All of this may seem terribly theoretical and philosophical and there is nothing theoretical about marriage. But marriage does have its seasons, all of them potentially beautiful and all of them, taken together, a foretaste of eternity. I think that's the secret: to value it all and by God's grace to learn and grow in every season, and so to find in the times and seasons of your love for each other more and more of the eternity of God's love for you.

D. The Ocean Of Love

Christine Lalumia met Pepin Clout while studying in England and eventually, after a good deal of commuting, brought him back to America to be married. Then they returned to England to live. Her family was, if anything, more aware than the couple themselves of the tension involved in stretching close family ties between two distant countries. That was one factor in the homily. A second factor was the text from the Song of Solomon. The third and providential factor was the way the weather contributed its own emphasis to the metaphor of water and floods. Not only had there been recent floods in Mexico and Texas because of a hurricane, but the wedding day itself was rainy.

"Many waters cannot quench love, neither can floods drown it. If one offered for love all the wealth of his house, it would be utterly scorned" ♦ **(Song of Solomon 8:7)**

Chris and Pepin, you picked the right text for today: "Many waters cannot quench love!" And it's not just the weather, of course, that makes that text appropriate. You are the living evidence that all the waters of the ocean can't quench love.

You have come together over distances that would have stopped most people. They would have stopped you, I'm sure, except for love. It will continue to be that way. You two will live in England or America or Australia or Mongolia, perhaps, but wherever you live, you will still be linked by love to others in this country and England and you and your family will be crossing oceans year after year because of those bonds. As you do, I hope you will remember the text with which it all began. Look down at the ocean below as you fly back and forth to renew your family ties and remember, "Many waters cannot quench love, neither can the floods drown it."

Why not? Why can't water drown love? Many waters can drown people and have in the last few days in Mexico and Texas. People can drown; why not love?

The answer is obvious, isn't it? People are physical and love is not. Yes, love is expressed in a physical way but love itself is not a physical thing. It's really amazing to find this text in the Song of Songs because that book is in some ways the least "spiritual" book of the Bible. No other book of the Bible has so much to say about the physical aspects of love, yet this book also knows that love is much more than physical. The physical can express love but not drown it.

"Many waters cannot quench love," but there *are* waters that can threaten it, and that can, indeed, kill a marriage if not love itself, if that marriage is not deeply rooted in the love of God. There are tears in a marriage, of course, floods of tears, and they *can* drown a marriage that has no depth of love. But that's not what tears are for. The water-floods in a marriage, like Noah's flood in the Bible, can be a means of cleansing and renewal and salvation. They can wash out the evils of selfishness and re-center our priorities and re-establish communications. The danger of a flood can get our attention and help us ask what we really value. But floods cannot drown what God values nor drown the love that begins with God and that knows God as the source of all we are and all the joy we have. The right amount of water can make a garden grow.

"Many waters cannot quench love," and your love has already proven that, and has proved it again today. I pray that your love will continue to demonstrate this truth day by day and year by year as you grow in knowledge and love of each other and of the God who calls you through the floods of life to the unquenchable fire of God's eternal love.

E. Gifts Of Healing And Love

Deirdre McSweeney and James Tyson were in medical school when they were married and planning careers as doctors. They studied carefully the suggested readings and looked at the context as well as the content. They asked for the familiar thirteenth Chapter of I Corinthians but realized that the passage made better sense if it included the end of Chapter 12. They were also struck by the references there to gifts of healing.

"Now you are the body of Christ and individually members of it. And God has appointed in the church first apostles, second prophets, third teachers, then deeds of power, then gifts of healing, forms of assistance, forms of leadership, various kinds of tongues. Are all apostles? Are all prophets? Are all teachers? Do all work miracles? Do all possess gifts of healing? Do all speak in tongues? Do all interpret? But strive for the greater gifts. And I will show you a still more excellent way" ✦ **(I Corinthians 12:27-31)**

Let me point out to everyone here that James and Deirdre did something unusual in the lesson we just read from the familiar thirteenth chapter of I Corinthians. Almost everyone, it seems, asks for Chapter 13 at a wedding, but you added on four verses from Chapter 12. You took a passage about love and added a passage about gifts. You wanted especially to add the reference to gifts of healing. It's a good change you made. It's a point I hope you'll always remember.

Healing is a gift. Like any other gift, it needs also to be developed. It needs, as you know, hard work and long years of study. But it begins with a gift, something God gave you. Someone without that gift might study and work just as hard, but never become a good doctor. Someone with that gift who failed to study and work hard, would also never become a good doctor.

God gives you the gift and your job is to develop it and then to use it for the sake of others. Maybe that's obvious to you. Healing is a profession and you work at it in a disciplined way. But love, too, is a gift and yet somehow we assume that love will take care of itself. The song says "All you need is love." And that's true, but it makes it sound too easy.

Why do we do that? Any gift carries a responsibility with it. It takes work. It takes discipline. It takes years of study and years of growth. There's no other way to develop a gift and reach its full potential. Why do we imagine that love is different and needs no work, no discipline, no study?

You know already how rewarding it is when you go to the bedside of another human being and bring healing in their need. You will learn how rewarding it is when you can go to the side of another human being and bring love.

James and Deirdre: you have been given gifts of healing and gifts of love.

Use them both. Develop them both. Don't neglect either one. Give your best effort to let them both grow in you so that you can share those gifts with others as God has shared them with you.

F. Love In a Mine Field

This is a homily that was written for a particular wedding of a particular couple. Undoubtedly the shape and content of the homily developed out of my conversations with them, but the theme now seems of so general an applicability that I have omitted their names. Sometimes what was said to one needs to be said to all.

"[Love] does not insist on its own way" ♦ (I Corinthians 13:5)

I read an article on marriage recently that used a rather striking metaphor. It said, "In marriage we are tiptoeing through a mine field to the promised land." That's not, perhaps, very reassuring, but we might as well be realistic. Marriage these days is an adventure for the foolish or the faithful, and maybe you need some elements of both.

As I thought about that metaphor, it occurred to me that I could try to identify some of the mines in the mine field. The longer I thought about it, the more it seemed possible that the mines may be planted in us as much as outside us. And the antidotes (if you have antidotes to a land mine!) may be planted inside us as well.

For example, is it only coincidence that the more we know about psychiatry and human sexual behavior, and the more marriage counselors there are, the more divorces there are? It may be a chicken and egg situation and I don't know which came first, but some things don't bear too much study. If you keep checking the soufflé, you'll never make a good one. If you keep digging up a plant to check the roots, the plant will have trouble growing. If you keep worrying about your marriage, you'll keep finding things to worry about.

I think our society builds up assumptions that may be like land mines planted inside us. We assume we ought to be able to make a marriage work if we just work at it hard enough, and then each normal tension becomes a matter for deep concern and major analysis - and incipient disaster.

Perhaps we need to defuse some of the expectations our society plants and plant some others instead. There is, for example, an assumption in the gospel that a man and a woman become one flesh, inseparable. Might it not give us a better start to make the assumption that we are indeed inseparable and that the normal problems of life can be taken in stride, confident that the basic unity is secure and indestructible?

But how can you assume that? I think the answer to that is also in the gospel: "What God has joined together let no one separate" (Matthew 19:6). The point here surely is who makes a marriage? Human beings *can* try to make a marriage, but it would have the same security as every human accomplishment: the security of a coal mine in Pennsylvania, an office building in Bucharest, a suburban home in Lewisboro, a bank loan to New York

City.[7] That's human security. But a Christian marriage is God's doing. God makes it. It depends on God. We depend on God. That's the fixed center and reference point. Jesus' parable about the man who built his house on sand and the one who built his house on rock says it all. If we go through marriage centering on ourselves, building on our own resources, we've created our own hazard. Christian marriage is centered on God.

I hear so often that the problem with a marriage is the other person's unwillingness to do something the first person wants done. "I've got my rights," is the refrain. I get very tired of hearing about rights. The first reading says, "Love does not insist on its own way." Marriage has to do with giving up rights and giving ourselves in love. And that's what the Christian faith is all about too. Marriage is the attempt to find our life by losing it in someone else. Christianity is the attempt to find our true lives by losing them in the love of God. And if we set out to lose our lives, a mine field has no perils for us. We weren't trying to save our lives anyway or our rights or our dignity or anything else. Marriage, like Christianity, has to do with losing and giving and loving.

May you, —— and ——, so give yourselves to each other in Christ that you find all God's love forever.

G. Subject To Love

No passage in the New Testament speaks as directly about Christian marriage as does Ephesians Chapter 5, yet few couples ask to have it read at their wedding because of the verse that says, "Wives be subject to your husbands." That's not something a modern couple is prepared to listen to and understand. In context, however, it's a valuable injunction to listen to, and occasionally the opportunity comes to explain it. Tom Pappas, a computer installer, and Kim Cutting, a secretary, were a typical couple in many ways, but not in their choice of Scripture. Their families, different in many ways, had given them a respect for stability and security, and Ephesians seemed to them to express that more clearly than other passages.

"Wives, be subject to your husbands, as you are to the Lord....Husbands, love your wives, just as Christ loved the church and gave himself up for her" ♦ **(Ephesians 5:24, 25)**

Not many people have the nerve to choose that reading from Ephesians in this day and age but Kim and Tom have done it and they have given us something to think about. And maybe the first thing to point out is that when St. Paul wrote those words it was not surprising at all to say, "Wives, be subject to your husbands," but it was revolutionary to say, "Husbands, love your wives." Today it's the other way around, or so we like to think.

"Husbands love your wives." It sounds fine, doesn't it? But don't stop

---

[7] The references are obviously dated but others are always available.

there. St. Paul doesn't. St. Paul goes on to say "love your wives *as Christ loved the church and gave himself up for it.*" In other words, "Husbands, you should love your wives enough to die for them." And we might reply, "Yes, of course, if it came to that, but I don't expect it to come to that." And that's the trouble. I'll die for my wife, I suppose, but not postpone my golf game on a day she's not feeling well. I'll die for my wife, if I have to some day, but not help today with the housework. But if I won't do the little things, what are the odds that I'll do the big ones?

Marriage is about dying; dying to self, dying daily to self in a thousand little ways, not usually one big one. "Little things," as the song says, "mean a lot."

In that context, comes that other verse from this passage: "Wives, be subject to your husbands." In fact, just before saying this, St. Paul has said to everyone, "Be subject to one another." All Christians should put the needs of others first. All of us. And *therefore,* because all Christians should act that way, each wife also should put her husband's needs before her own. Having said that, St. Paul goes on to say, in effect, "Husbands, be willing to die for your wives."

"Wives, be subject... Husbands, be willing to die..." If anyone wins in this equation, it's the wives, not the husbands. At least they're still alive! But it isn't a question of winning and losing, it's a question of loving others more than ourselves.

When love is new, it's easy to love the other that much. We learn a lot about love when it's new. The trick is to remember it: to remember day by day and year by year what love can be. The gift is to remember day by day that love means forgiving, means self-sacrifice, putting the other one first. That's not always easy. There are days when it's very hard. But God in Jesus Christ has done more for us than we are ever asked to do for God. He *did* die for us. He loves us that much. That's where our love comes from. That's the example we're given.

God asks us to learn from the example of Jesus; to learn from him, to follow him, to put him first in our lives. Doing this day by day and week by week and year by year you will learn at the same time to honor each other and make yourselves subject to each other and give your lives for each other. In doing that, you will find more love than you have even yet experienced, more love than you ever thought possible.

H. A Common Language

Margaret Everson grew up at Christ Church and sang in the girls' choir. She was finishing a program of graduate work in Texas. Larry Fossi was working on a small-town newspaper in Connecticut. Because of his Italian ancestry, they resolved to go to Italy for an extended honeymoon and to learn Italian. Because of their commitments, they knew they would have to live apart except for vacation times until her graduate work was complete. One year or two of such problems, they reasoned, was a small price to pay for a lifetime of happiness. They were married in

March of 1980. Less than two years later, as their separation was coming to an end, Margaret Everson was murdered by a serial killer in Texas. Her funeral took place in the same church as her marriage and the homily for both used the same text (see funeral homily G).

"Let the word of Christ dwell in you richly" ♦ (Colossians 3:16)

St. Paul is giving advice about living together, about the love and forbearance and kindness and patience without which no human relationship can grow. He says: "Let the word of Christ dwell in you richly;..." He's saying that we need to absorb God's word into our lives from the Bible and sacraments in order to nourish the gifts that make for unity.

But let me ask you to think about this in terms of words, of language— God's word and our words. Larry's been working with words, editing a newspaper. Both of you are going off for awhile to live in another country and learn another language. And you can think of marriage in those terms.

If your plan was a week in Rome and no more, you wouldn't bother much with language. You could rely on guides and interpreters and sign language and facial expressions. But you're not planning a quick trip, you're planning to stay awhile and get beneath the surface and try to enter into the experience of a different way of living, a different culture, a different understanding of life. And that requires language, not just some standard phrases, but all the nuances and shades of meaning. And that requires time and hard work and failures and frustrations as well as success.

Marriage is like that too. Lots of people enter marriage assuming that they already have a common language, but all they have is a few standard phrases. They've toured the high spots but they don't really know the country. A man and a woman who have grown up in different families have had very different experiences. Each family has its own language. Its members have learned how to live with each other and how to fight with each other. They know the deep meaning of the words the others use and how to respond. That comes of years of living together, and it can't be learned overnight.

Living in Italy, living with Meg, living with Larry, looks like a great idea. You know enough about Italy and about each other to know there's a richness there that can enrich you. But only with time; only with patience; only as you learn the language and learn to avoid the painful mistakes that tourists make because they don't really understand.

The Bible speaks of "the word of Christ," and that is a deeper dimension as well. Christ is God's word to us, and God's word to us is love. St. Paul is asking you to let the love of Christ enrich your lives and that again is a question of the source and the surface. You've made a decision to go back and look at the sources of western civilization in Italy so as to understand better who you are and where you come from. Love, too, has a source. You have begun to learn a new dimension of it in each other but so far you have only scratched the surface. Beyond the surface there's more in the one you love than many people ever discover. And beyond yourselves there's a source of love. Love flows into you from God and you are asked only to open yourselves to that love and let it dwell in you richly. God invites us to embark on a journey of discovery which is not only lifelong but eternal.

Let the word of Christ, the love of God, dwell in you richly. Let Christ in you speak to your partner. Speak to Christ in the one you love. Speak as Christ, in Christ, to Christ and his word will transform your words, teach you a new language that is a deeper, richer, fuller expression of love than you can imagine or pray for.

I. Building On Rock

Building on rock is a metaphor which will probably mean more in some locations than others. In the Midwest, it might be hard to find rock to build on in the first place and be a poor choice in the second place since the possibility of a tornado cellar could be more important. In Westchester County, New York, however, and Fairfield County, Connecticut, rock is a prominent feature of the landscape and houses are often, quite literally and obviously, built on rock. That Sarah Marshall came from Bronxville in Westchester County and Taylor Gibson came from New Canaan in Fairfield County provided the needed geography to make this metaphor familiar to all concerned.

Sidestepping the reference to a "man" building on rock and concentrating on the subject of foundations, the text provided an obvious and familiar metaphor for marriage.

"Everyone then who hears these words of mine and acts on them will be like a wise man who built his house on rock" ♦ (Matthew 7:24)

There are lots of houses in Bronxville and New Canaan built on rock. If the gospel were architectural advice, we would have to give people in these parts high marks for following it.

But the gospel is not architectural advice. Its concern is for people. And there are plenty of people in these communities whose homes are not built on rock. Not just in these communities, but in every community, houses divided and houses falling are a common phenomenon. You would think that with all the resources of these communities, houses and families would be solid as rock; dependable and unshaken by tension. But it isn't so. We all know that. Maybe that's why this passage struck you as a good one to choose for your wedding. It's good to remember that we need to build on rock.

But what does that really mean? It's not architectural advice or geological advice. It's not a question of Westchester rock versus Long Island sand. It's not even financial advice like, "Buy a piece of the rock." All this we have in abundance, and it isn't enough.

Jesus is talking about people, about the way we live and the relationships we create. He's suggesting that it isn't the way we build that creates solidity, it's where we build. It isn't the way we put things together, it's the foundations we put them on. The same houses that might last forever in Westchester could be washed away on a sand bar. The same people and the same building can endure or dissolve depending on the foundations they choose.

St. Paul, in another passage, says "the rock was Christ" (I Corinthians 10:4). It's a metaphor used all through the Bible. And it points to a three-way relationship. Marriage isn't just two people and the relationship they create with each other. Christian marriage is at least two people and a rock, two people and Christ, a three-way personal relationship that has the strength and endurance no two-way relationship can ever have.

Think about that from time to time when you are looking for a place to live, when you are building or buying a home, when you are creating a family. Are you relying on your own wisdom and your own resources, or have you kept your lives centered as they are today on God's word and that foundation?

We have come here today to pray that you will choose always to build on rock in a living relationship with Christ that will bring you strength and life and joy.

J. Like a Little Child

The suggested reading from Mark (10:6-9, 13-16), in one lectionary at least, tiptoes carefully around the references to divorce and adultery and then, oddly, jumps to the subject of children and childlikeness. The skittishness about divorce and adultery is our twentieth century problem, but the linking of teaching about marriage and childlikeness is part of the gospel and, very likely, of Jesus' own thought. Most often, when a couple chooses the reading from Mark they select only 10:6-9 and omit the suggested verses 13-16 as irrelevant. The result is a ringing endorsement of lifelong marital unity but, it may be, a failure to be exposed to the full impact of Jesus' teaching. Robert Libutti and Joyce Sturner, perhaps because they were older than most couples, selected the full reading - and gave me an opportunity to explore something of its significance.

"Whoever does not receive the kingdom of God as a little child will never enter it" ♦ (Mark 10:15)

When I first looked at the gospel reading you chose for today, I thought, "Isn't that strange! Why have they included that bit about children, about becoming childlike, in the reading for weddings?" It wasn't really your idea, of course; the Prayer Book suggests it. But why? Why doesn't it give us those verses in which Jesus is speaking about marriage and then stop? Why does it go on to talk about Jesus telling us to be like children? Surely too many marriages end in divorce because people aren't sufficiently mature! Why commend childishness to anyone?

I think I see three reasons.

One reason would be adaptability. Children can pick up new patterns of behavior easily and those who are married need to do that.

My family and I moved to Japan years ago and in no time at all the younger children were speaking Japanese. For adults, that's something you pick up slowly, if at all! And then we came back and, just as quickly, the children lost that gift. But whatever hard-won ability I had, I kept. I can speak Japanese now as well as ever—which isn't saying much! Adults learn slowly and forget slowly. We get set in our ways. It's hard for us to adapt to a new country.

Marriage is like a new country. We need to be able to enter it with that same flexibility children have: take nothing for granted, be open to new ways, be ready to change, be willing to explore. You can bring two human beings together the way you might bring together Russians and Americans, Israelis and Arabs, through painful inch by inch negotiations. "I'll give you this if you give me that." Or you can do it the way young children adapt themselves to new surroundings. "I never saw that before. That's interesting. Let me try it." Marriage needs two people willing to be childlike in that respect.

A second requirement is trust.

Unfortunately, we try to train children not to trust. Children are entirely too trusting. Parents can be relied on so children assume other adults also are trustworthy. And then we have to disillusion them, teach them to trust no one else. And so we grow up prepared to doubt and question and distrust, and we may bring that attitude to marriage where we need to be even more trusting than children, trust each other completely and trust God even more completely and assume ourselves to be able to trust. In fact, we have to trust beyond reason because trustworthiness, trustability, grows out of trust. The more we trust God, the more we will know God's strength and be ready to trust. In a marriage, the more we trust each other, the more that trust will be answered with strength and joy. Children bring out the best in us because they're so trusting. We need to trust each other to bring out the best in each other.

But the third quality of childishness is an opposite. I felt instinctively that this was the wrong combination of passages for a marriage and perhaps that's because children have another characteristic—learned, I think, from us—that is absolutely destructive to a marriage, and that is an insistence on being fair. "Johnny got more than I did and that's not fair!"

Where do children get the idea that life has to be fair? Where do we get it ourselves? People long grown up will come to me and tell me that they've given up on their marriage because they have to give more than they get, because somehow their partner isn't "fair." That's really childish!

The marriages that work best are the ones where both partners set out to be as unfair as possible, where each tries as hard as possible to give more than they get, where they ask nothing and give everything, and where they never have time to notice whether they are giving back 10% or 50% or 150%. Those are the marriages where both in fact receive 100% and more, because God supplies more than they could ever ask.

I think we all have the idea today that a working marriage requires great skill and wisdom and maturity, and that's why it seems so strange to find the gospel talking about becoming as little children. But with that one exception, I think it's tremendously wise.

Be childlike. Be adaptable. Be trusting. Don't worry about what's fair. When it comes to that, ask God to help you grow. But for the rest, ask for help to be childlike. Ask God to help you understand that the more we give, the more we are able to receive. Ask God to help you receive so much that you will be able to give to each other love and joy and strength beyond anything you can imagine.

K. The Comprehensive Exam

The counseling process, as I have said, should provide a good knowledge of the couple being married and enable the homilist to shape material accordingly. In this case the couple lived too far away for me to do the counseling and it had been done by another priest. But I did have a certain advantage all the same since the bride was my daughter! She was at the time a graduate student working on a doctorate in English literature and so was her fiance. That helped set the tone of the homily. The readings from I Corinthians 13 and John 15 were supplemented by a reading from Henry David Thoreau. The challenge was to weave them all together into one homily.

"Abide in my love" ♦ (John 15:9)

Think of this as an exam. Think of marriage as the ultimate comprehensive exam with questions involving everything you ever read, everything you ever learned, everything you ever could have learned and could never have learned, requiring that you integrate information from English and history, biology and psychology, economics, and political science: every aspect of human knowledge. And while there is no time limit on the whole exam, each separate question is asked with no warning and has to be answered at once.

But the strangest part of it is that they give you tenure first and then start the exam.

First the commitment is made: "until we are parted by death." Few universities will go that far when they make appointments. First comes the commitment, then the questions. From the human point of view, this is backwards. No university hires without first asking questions. No customer buys without first examining the product. And some people think you can try out marriage the same way. Maybe you can; but not Christian marriage, not the union of three in one. Because this is not a human institution and it isn't lived by human rules or human logic. With human institutions we have to worry: have we read the right books, have we got the right skills, how will it all turn out, what if I fail? But we just heard in St. Paul's letter that we don't have to worry about these things because "love never fails." So here you have the tenure first, then the questions, because the result is already assured. There can be no failure.

There can be no failure! How do I have the nerve to stand here at the end of the summer of 1987 and say that? Don't I read the papers? Have I never met the other half of the human race? Don't I know that love fails all the time? Don't I know reality? Yes, I'm talking about reality. I'm talking about the deepest reality, not our bumbling human imitations.

What's real about a world where nothing stays the same, where nothing is fixed and secure, where we worry about image, not integrity, and no one expects anyone to keep a promise for ever? What's real about a world like that?

Love is what we're talking about, real love. Real love never fails. But you won't find that in each other or any other human being. The mistake we make is to look for that kind of reality, that kind of integrity, that kind of commitment, that kind of love, in another human being. And why do we do that when the wreckage is all around us? Why do we continue to look for perfect love where perfect love has never been found?

Gordon Allport once said, "The truest statement that can be made of a normal person is that he [she] never feels that he [she] can love or be loved enough." There is in each of us an inexhaustible need to give and an inexhaustible need to receive. But there is no inexhaustible giver or receiver in ourselves. "Abide in me," Jesus said in the gospel reading. In him our love can rest and be complete.

You come here today to be joined in a three-way relationship because you have found in each other a love you never knew there could be, and that love has a source, and that love has a name. We begin to know that love in fathers and mothers and sisters and brothers. We explore it further in an ever-growing circle of friends. We find it even in strangers. You have found it in unbelievable richness in one particular human being to whom today you make an ultimate commitment. But even that is only the incomplete evidence of something infinitely greater because neither of you is the source. "The sun itself," Thoreau says, "is but a morning star."[8]

Libby and Mark, you are in the early stages of a lifelong exploration of the mystery and power of language and the mystery and power of love. And the Word is God, and God is love.

God shows us love to draw us back to God. We can't help being drawn. God's love, mediated, draws us here. But don't stop here. Edna St. Vincent Millay said "This world is an inn on a thoroughfare."[9] Someone else has said, "It is the inns on the through roads that are the best maintained."[10] And maybe, since I like to paraphrase things, I could paraphrase that this way: "The marriage that continues on is the marriage that has a source and a goal beyond itself."

May your love increasingly know that source and finally reach that goal.

---

[8] Thoreau, Henry David, *Walden and Civil Disobedience,* p. 221.
[9] Barrett, George W. and Casserley, J. V. Langmead, *Dialogue on Destiny,* p.84.
[10] Ibid.

L. Global Relationships

Alice Wheeler, like so many brides, grew up in the parish and met her fiance elsewhere—in Switzerland on a skiing holiday. She was an American living in England. He was an Australian living in Sydney. They planned to be married in Alice's home parish in suburban New York. Before that date they would, of course, be together only a few times in England, Australia, the States, and elsewhere, so there seemed to be no possibility of the normal counseling relationship. How do you do premarital counseling on an intercontinental basis? They were well educated and articulate. We decided to try premarital counseling by mail. Obviously there is a loss of immediacy and freedom in that kind of exchange, but sometimes we reveal ourselves more and learn more about each other when we put it in writing. They worked hard at the project and the collected letters make an interesting document. At the end, there was a face to face session a few days before the marriage. In view of the long correspondence, it seemed best to use the homily simply to say some basic and simple things and, because Peter was in a strange country, to illustrate the homily with an Australian flavor.

"This is my commandment, that you love one another as I have loved you" ♦ (John 15:12)

Peter and Alice, you've set an impossible agenda. I hope you know that. You've chosen a reading that requires the impossible. Jesus said, "This is my commandment, that you love one another as I have loved you." That asks a lot of beginners. It's as if I were watching a tennis match between Lew Hoad and Rod Laver and one of them were to hand me the racquet and say, "Now you do that." It's as if I were watching a yacht race in Perth Harbour and they were to bring me a yacht and say, "Now you do that." I'd like to, of course. I'd like to try. But let's not imagine I could.

Where would you start?

Let me say just three things about God's love that are worth remembering. These are guidelines, basic tips for beginners.

The first thing we know about God's love is, it's practical. God didn't just love us at a distance or just in a spiritual way. God came into the world in the life of Jesus and used a physical body to show us love. God didn't just say, "I love you." God did something about it. God came to us in Jesus. He helped. He healed. He did the practical things that needed doing. God's love is practical.

Second, God's love is total, unlimited. God didn't say, "I'll do this and that, and that's all." God never said, "I'll do this if you'll do that." God set no limits. And when that meant dying for us, God in Christ did that. God gave everything including life itself. Nothing was held back whatever the cost. God's love is complete.

And third, God's love is God's love. It begins with God. It finds its source in God. I don't get the impression that Jesus loved Peter and James and John and Mary and Martha because they were just so loveable. He loved them because he loved God, and God's love poured through him to others. His love began with God, not with a warm feeling about human beings.

So, here's the racquet. Let's see you play a set. Where would you begin?

We begin, of course, with God. However much we love each other, we still need help. We still need to turn to God again and again for help because our love won't be strong enough or wise enough. That means prayer and Bible study and the support of the church and its sacraments. The source of love is outside ourselves. We need to turn towards the source.

And we can work on removing limits. People tell me they'll only go so far, that they have their rights. That's not love. That's selfishness. Love is giving, not receiving. Anything else is a bonus. We can try not to set limits, to give all we have and still look for more to give.

And first and last, we can be practical. Look for ways to help. Use your head and your hands as well as your heart. I knew a man once who was talking about divorce because his wife had left a pair of dirty socks on the bedroom floor for a week. He left them there to see how long it would be before she picked them up. I suggested he pick them up himself. It could have saved their marriage. But no, that was *her* job. That's the whole thing in a nutshell: the mentality that sets limits, that isn't practical, that depends on human love, not God's.

When Jesus says, "Love one another as I have loved you," he sets an impossible standard but we can try to move that way. Be practical. Set no limits. Look to God for help. That's what God's love is like. I pray that your love for each other will be like God's love for you.

PART THREE

Burial

I. The Funeral Homily

One Sunday in the early 1960's a family I knew decided to go for a drive. They had recently moved from England to America believing that they could make a better life for themselves in this country. They had begun to feel at home in the New World and, hoping to enjoy a leisurely afternoon with their family, set off in their car with two of their three daughters in the back seat, while a brother and sister-in-law followed in their own car.

As they drove along a suburban parkway another car came toward them driven by an elderly man returning from a celebration of his birthday. He had celebrated well but not wisely and, as he approached the cars of the family I knew, he lost control of his car which wandered across the center divide and crashed into them head on. The wife was killed outright and the husband died ten days later.

We had, as I remember it, two funerals at the church. At the first there was no homily; homilies at funerals were uncommon in the Episcopal church in those days and, in any event, I think we were all too stunned for words. But when the second funeral was held there was a need to say something. How can God be good in a world where such things happen? What can faith say to us in the face of such tragedy?

When I was ordained, it was not the custom in the Episcopal church to preach at funerals. There might have been some choice of lessons and psalms, but a sermon or homily was seldom included. In those days if other words than prayers and Bible passages were spoken at a funeral (as they often were in non-liturgical churches), those words were generally in the form of a eulogy. These, at their best, were a way of commending certain Christian virtues to others, but all too often they took the form of biographical summaries and reminiscences. The liturgical churches, on the other hand, had a Burial Office to read and the eucharist to celebrate and that was thought to be enough. In one sense, of course, it is enough. What is there to do at the time of death except to hear again from the Bible God's promise of life, to place ourselves and those we love in God's hands through prayer, and to be united with those we love in Christ through the offering up of the eucharist? Surely that is enough.

And yet it is not enough. It is axiomatic to the Christian faith that God calls us to share in the work of creation. We are given skills and asked to use them in God's service. We have been given minds and the gift of speech and asked to speak God's creative Word. Word and sacrament stand together at the center of the church's life and both are shaped and mediated by human minds and art. Human beings make and choose the prayers, vestments, and

107

ceremonies in which the sacrament is clothed. So, too, the sermon is the Word of God clothed in human phrases.

No doubt we would like to have, especially in times of trauma, a "pure word of God" speaking to us, unmediated and undiminished by any human agency. Perhaps, in an ideal world, there would be a service or sermon already "given" so that we would need only to open a book and read, so that we would need only to go through a prescribed ceremony and be sure that we had said and done all that God asks and all that God's people might need. In such a world, the inadequacy of human words and ceremonies would not be allowed to come between ourselves and God.

At one time or another in the history of the church, Christians have proscribed almost every form of human expression as an unwelcome barrier between the human soul and its maker. So organs and vestments and candles and crosses have all been proscribed as vain inventions, and reformers have shied away from the eucharist while traditionalists have shied away from preaching. But the inadequacy of human skills is no reason to abstain from their use. If music and ceremony can become barriers through unfamiliarity on the one hand and over-familiarity on the other, so also preaching can fail and the preacher become a barrier to the expression of God's word.

Yet the sermon, like music, ceremony, and symbol, can also be a powerful means by which to express the presence of a loving God. The spoken word can be, perhaps especially at the time of death, trivial and irrelevant. It can draw attention to the preacher or the one who has died rather than the creator. But the spoken word can also communicate the power of a loving God in a uniquely immediate and personal way. The preacher's calling is to be an instrument to that end: to speak God's word to the needs of particular people at a particular time. In the time of death, that calling is of the utmost importance.

There comes a time when we have to say something. There comes a time when we are unavoidably faced with the mystery of life and death and, however inadequate our understanding may be, we have to speak. But what should we say, and how should we say it?

In the church today there is obviously no consensus. With the renaissance of biblical studies in the liturgical churches has come a revival of preaching as well. Brief sermons are no longer unusual at weekday services and early services on Sunday. Preaching is once again a normal part of the funeral and wedding service. But that preaching at funerals is often governed by the expectation created elsewhere of a eulogy rather than a proclamation of the gospel. It is common to use this special opportunity to remind the congregation of the virtues of the deceased. Such a message can be re-assuring. It may help the mourners feel that the person they have loved was indeed a special person and that their feelings of loss are appropriate and shared by others. The "eulogy" has a long and honored tradition in the Christian church and it is obvious that it plays an important part in the bereavement process.

On the other hand, for the preacher to attempt to speak well of every person who has died places him or her in an ultimately untenable position. How, finally, can one human being "speak well" of every other human being? Some will be unknown to us and, even though friends and family may provide ample briefing and documents, it remains difficult to speak "second hand," to testify to the character of someone we have not really known. Beyond that, of course, there are, unfortunately, human beings of whom little good is known. Even family and friends may have little to say in response to the injunction *de mortuis, nil nisi bonum:* "speak nothing of the dead, if not good."

I remember going once to visit a parish family after reading in the paper that the father's body had been found filled with bullets in a car on the waterfront. I had known that he was involved in illegal activity and it seemed that others also had been all too familiar with his manner of life. I arrived in the apartment to find his sister sitting with the family and crying out hysterically, "He was good! He was good!" "We all know what he was like," I said, "but right now we need to be calm and help his family." That also was before the day when Episcopalians normally preached at funerals but, had it been the custom, even his sister might have found it hard to provide corroborative detail to expand on her three word eulogy.

But if there is little to be said for some individuals, is it right to speak well of others and not of them? There are some whose virtues are evident and easily extolled and others whose virtues are less evident but equally real. Should the preacher be in the business of comparing and judging, whether explicitly or implicitly? Should the congregation be able to go away saying, "That was a good eulogy, but the one for Bill Smith last month was better"? Judgment, the Bible tells us, is best left to God. It may be that we have no intention of judging or comparing, but how can we avoid the appearance, at least, that we have in fact done exactly that? God, we are told is "no respecter of persons." If a standard part of the funeral service is a discourse by the preacher on the particular virtues and accomplishments of the departed, does it not seem to deal partially with those God treats impartially?

To go even further, are we not faced here with the age-old distinction between works and grace? It was an oddity for many years that Protestants, whose whole *raison d'être* was to proclaim that salvation is by faith alone and not by works, were more prone than other Christians to behave at funerals as though works were what really mattered. Nowadays it seems as if the practice of the eulogy is spreading without any reference to theology. Whatever the theology of the particular church may once have been, when death comes, faith seems to become a secondary consideration while a recital of works becomes a central part of the final ceremonies. Again and again, when the media cover a funeral, what is reported tends to be a eulogy, not the prayers, not the action of the liturgy, and seldom if ever a proclamation of the mercy of God and the resurrection of Christ. We may say, of course, that this is merely honoring the family's wishes or providing comfort to those who mourn, but surely it also proclaims to all in attendance, Christian and non-Christian alike, that the true theology of the church today is that we are saved by our works, for this is the only part of the service which is noted by the media and remembered when all is said and done.

The word "eulogy," it should be noted, means "good word" (from the Greek *eu-logos*) and has almost the same meaning as the word "gospel." Gospel (from the Anglo-Saxon "God's spell") also means "good word" or "God's word." The Greek word for gospel used in the New Testament (*eu-angellion*) is closely related and also means "good message." Custom, however, has determined that the good words of a eulogy are centered on a human being and the good words of a sermon or homily are centered on God.

What sort of good words are most likely to be helpful at the time of death? There will, in fact, be many good words said about the deceased and it is appropriate that there should be. Family and friends will gather and will talk about the one they have loved, recalling past events, personality traits, and all the characteristics that made that one person special to them and memorable. We need to put into words what we feel about other people and we will find ways to do that, whatever form the funeral service may take. But that will take place inevitably on an informal basis and without need for rehearsal or plan; it need not be part of the formal service.

If, nonetheless, some kind of eulogy seems to be required, a member of the family or a friend can usually be found who will speak briefly at the beginning of the service. The eulogy then serves as an introduction, a simple reminder of the person whose life touched so many others. If the service has begun in the ancient way with the bringing in of the coffin, and if a member of the family or congregation then comes forward to speak, both movements can be seen as an offering. Rather than the central and dominating phase of the funeral service, the eulogy becomes part of the preparation after which we can move on to hear God's word read and proclaimed so that our offering is placed in the greater light of God's gift. If the eucharist is celebrated, an even greater exchange becomes evident: we offer a particular life to God; the life of God is offered to us in return. And that offering is not by way of substitution for what we have lost, but inclusion; it encompasses living and dead in the unifying power of the new and risen life of Christ.

In the first **Book of Common Prayer** of 1549, Thomas Cranmer gave instruction that baptisms were to be held "upon Sondayes and other holy dayes, when the most numbre of people may come together...(so that) euery manne presente maye be put in remembraunce of his owne...Baptisme." No such instruction was given concerning burial, nor was the burial service filled, like the baptism and marriage services, with exhortations, nor was any homily suggested. Presumably Cranmer felt, and with some reason, that death was its own instruction. Death was seen as a universal event, the response to which could always be the same.

Until recent years, the **Book of Common Prayer** made no direct reference to the individual at all. From the opening words of Scripture, through the Psalms, the reading, and prayers, there was no place to insert so much as an individual name. Clearly the emphasis was intended to be on God and on the survivors. The funeral was an occasion for remembering our mortality and for proclaiming God's purpose. Overreacting to the medieval church's teaching of purgatory and indulgences, there was only one brief prayer for the one who had died. Just as it was intended that in the baptismal service "euery manne presente maye be put in remembraunce of his own ...Baptisme," so it was intended that in the burial service each person present should be put in mind of his or her own death. No wonder Anglican services had the reputation of being "cold"!

Now, in a less divided time, we should be able to strike a better balance. Indeed, the involvement of the congregation in the service and the opening of ears to the gospel, should encourage us to look for ways of linking the gospel to the particularity of an individual life, yet always keeping the gospel, not the individual, at the center. The Christian gospel is a proclamation of grace, not of individual accomplishment. It is a proclamation that Christ has triumphed over death and that in his victory—in his victory alone—we also triumph. At the end of life we have nothing to plead except the death of Christ for us. No works, no merit avail, but grace through faith alone. That is the heart of the good news. Without that gospel, we are indeed like "those without hope"; with it, rich and poor, saint and sinner, stand in equal hope of inheriting a kingdom. And where can that be proclaimed so effectively, where does it need so particularly to be heard, as at the time when we come before God to offer our prayers for one who was baptized into Christ's death in order to share in his resurrection? The comfort available to us is the power of that triumph and if it is not proclaimed, we have surely been false comforters.

The telephone rings in the middle of the night to tell you that John Smith has died. Perhaps he had been ill for a long time and death was a merciful release. Perhaps death was sudden and unexpected. But whatever the circumstances, the moment of death almost always comes suddenly and unprepared. The finality of it is not something that can be taken easily in stride. Some few individuals (more in recent years but still all too few) will have written down requests by which they want the survivors to be guided in arranging the funeral service. In most cases, the family and their pastor will be working without much guidance and in a very limited span of time.

From the perspective of the clergy, there is no other kind of preaching quite like that to be done at a funeral. In the first place, time is short. Normally, there is a span of seven days between sermons. Normally, there is time to plan ahead, to think of themes to develop, to do research on texts. Normally, time can be set aside each week for sermon preparation. But the funeral homily must be prepared with none of these advantages. Time is limited; there may be as much as three or four days, but even then the funeral has to be fitted into a schedule already crowded. The family will need pastoral care and have first priority. Other responsibilities, even if postponed, will still require some attention; even postponing them takes time. And the family may not be able to decide on Bible readings quickly. Often a first meeting to discuss possibilities will lead to decisions made only on the day before the funeral. Sometimes family members are reluctant to make decisions until a particular member of the family can come from a distance. So the time for preparation will be limited and not free from intrusion, and in that brief time a text must be chosen from the readings agreed on and words found to make that text live for those who need to hear of life as never before.

These are real difficulties, but they may be more than offset by a special advantage: the family members can often be brought into the planning process and help give the homily its direction. The preacher, under these circumstances, is not working alone. If family members choose carefully, they will have studied several relevant passages of Scripture and the time spent in that choice will itself be of value. The preacher, then, will be speaking to a congregation at least some of whom will be prepared to hear the word both because of the circumstances and because they have already studied the text on which the homily is based. If the homily is briefer than a Sunday sermon, it can afford to be because it needs to spend less time in trying to bring a diverse congregation into a unity of thought. Here the circumstances provide the unity and the preparatory study which one might like but seldom hope for from a Sunday congregation has already been done, at least by some of those present.

The interplay between the preacher's knowledge of scripture and knowledge of the people concerned will give the homily its fundamental thrust and shape. Illustrative material should arise naturally out of a knowledge of the individuals involved and their interests. The same question is asked in preparing a homily that is asked in preparing any sermon: how does this text speak to these people? But here the focus is sharper and more immediate. There are certain basic things that need to be said: God is good; God loves you; death is painful but Jesus has shared our pain; Christ's resurrection is the evidence that God is able to give life even to the dead; through prayer and the sacraments we share one life with the dead in Christ. Only one or two of these things can be said, of course, on any one occasion and knowledge of the individuals will determine which are most important, but these assertions, these proclamations of the gospel, are the stuff of which the funeral homily is made.

If the funeral homily is placed in a liturgical setting, that setting, too, proclaims the faith. White is frequently used now as the color of funeral vestments as a way of proclaiming the joy of the resurrection, and that is appropriate. Yet joy is not necessarily the predominant note. Sorrow and a sense of loss are also appropriate. Paul does not say "we do not sorrow" but "we do not sorrow like those without hope" (I Thessalonians 4:13). Death is still real and it still causes pain. Purple or blue vestments, symbolizing heaven or the royal robes of Christ and setting a more somber tone, are also appropriate. The eucharist is a traditional part of the burial rites in many churches and is a powerful means of turning attention from human loss to the reality of God's presence and nurturing care. The hymns chosen can speak also of God's love and a postlude can end the service on a note of triumph. All these, are a vital part of the gospel to be proclaimed.

As for the homily, there will normally, as at a baptism or wedding, be three reference points: God's word, as contained in the specific scriptural passages chosen by the family, the individual who has died, and the burial liturgy itself. The particularities of the individual are not used as material for a eulogy, but to give immediacy and relevance to the homily. If the person who died was a farmer, references to the seed that is planted and dies to produce a plant are relevant; they would seem less fitting if the individual had been an investment banker. If the person committed suicide, that is one thing; if they died at the age of 98 after a long illness, quite another. All such circumstances of death may appropriately shape the message, but the word to be spoken is finally not of the individual but of God. It is God to whom we are turning when we come to church at the time of death, and it is the power of God's love overcoming death for us that we need to hear proclaimed.

II. The Readings at a Funeral

Suitable material for funeral readings might be found in three places in the Bible: accounts of death and burial, explanations of the phenomenon of death, and expressions of God's promise of life. Most of the readings suggested in the standard lectionaries are of the third type.

There are, to begin with, few accounts of burial to be found in the Old Testament. We read that Sarah and Abraham were "buried...in the cave of Machpelah" (Genesis 23:19, 25:9) and that is a fuller account than is normally provided. The New Testament speaks at somewhat more length of the burial of Lazarus (John 11:38) and Stephen (Acts 8:2) and, of course, Jesus but, with the possible exception of the latter, there is nothing helpful as an example for others to follow.

The second chapter of Genesis with its story of the expulsion of Adam and Eve from the garden is the only significant explanation of the phenomenon of death in the Old Testament, but that explanation is too negative to be of much use at funerals. Discussions of the phenomenon of death are plentiful in the New Testament, especially in the epistles, and are frequently chosen, but the emphasis in most of them is not so much on the explanation as on God's promise of life. This is appropriate. It is not explanations we need so much as hope.

As for the promise, it appears slowly in the Old Testament, almost as a by-product of the central theme of God's purpose for Israel. Deutero-Isaiah is, perhaps, the first to see that death must at last be destroyed for God's purpose to be fulfilled. Old Testament readings for a funeral will be, for the most part, foreshadowings of something not yet fully revealed and understood. Even in the gospels the promise is not clearly seen until the end. One of the most frequently chosen passages for a funeral (John 14:1-6) makes no specific reference to death and resurrection but seems to provide hope and strength by its reassuring command, "Let not your hearts be troubled," and its poetic promise of "many mansions," "many dwelling places," or "spacious rooms."

A bereaved family, however, will not be looking for reasons and logic so much as the reassurance of familiar words and phrases, images that "speak to them" at a level almost beyond words themselves. These the Bible, itself the product of many voices and the reflection of the experience of a wide variety of individuals, provides in abundant measure.

A. Old Testament Texts and Commentary

1. Job 19:1, 23-27a (or 21-27a) ♦ "For I know that my Redeemer lives"

We are told that the music we know as the "Passion Chorale" was once a drinking song. That may be so, but today it summons up thoughts of Holy Week and Easter, not beer halls in Germany. So, too, these words from the book of Job have become transformed in meaning by the resurrection of Christ, the music of Handel, and the meditations of 2000 years of Christianity. While it is doubtful, in the light of other passages from the book of Job (e.g. 14:7-12), that the author of this book believed in any sort of resurrection (19:26 is textually corrupt), and while the "Redeemer" in this passage is the Hebrew go'el, a family member responsible, among other things, for avenging the unjust death of another member of the family, in the Christian context these words are heard as a reference to Christ and resurrection, and it is this understanding which is important when we come to plan for a funeral service. For this reason it might be better to omit the introductory words "Then Job answered": (19:1), rather than include them.

a. *"Have pity...O you my friends....Why do you, like God, pursue me,..."* (v.21-22). The role of friends at the time of death is difficult. There may be few other times when we feel so inept. Indeed, it is seldom that so much uniquely inept advice is given. There are familiar remarks, such as: "It's all for the best," "God wanted him/her back," "It's God's will." Many of these lines go back to "Job's comforters" who are notorious for their failure to provide help. Job, at this point in the drama, is preoccupied with the God-

Job relationship and is, in essence, asking his friends to stand clear and leave him to that critical dialogue. To speak to these matters in a funeral homily would not be easy, but there might be a time when it was appropriate to take the opportunity to point to this need for silence in the face of mystery and to suggest a presence that makes no demands, offers no explanations, but is content to be with the sufferer (the dying or the bereaved) in a shared waiting on God and even questioning. Somehow it is enough, finally, to know that God is God and we are created beings for whom presence and relationship matter more than reasons.

b. *"Why do you, like God, pursue me,..."* (v.22). Sometimes it seems as if an individual or family is, indeed, "pursued"; agonizing death, suicide, mental illness, and other tragedies strike one after another, while other individuals and families go happily on. Job's comforters today, as then, have ready explanations: "You have sinned," "It's God's will," "You will be rewarded in heaven." And some people, indeed, find these remarks comforting. But the truth is that the good and evil suffer alike, that we do not know God's will, and that a heavenly reward is little use in the midst of tragedy. Jesus taught that "God sends rain on the just and the unjust" (Matthew 5:45) and, if that is so, we can learn nothing of the merits of an individual by the wetness of their clothing. Insofar as God does pursue us (see Francis Thompson's famous poem, "The Hound of Heaven") it is out of love, not to inflict suffering. Suffering and tragedy can be used toward that goal, but so can love and mercy. God works in all things to win us, but the problem of evil remains. What we know, and Job did not, is that God in Christ has shared our suffering. When it seems that we are pursued by evil, we can at the least remember that Jesus' suffering and death is God's clearest answer: God shares our suffering, and, in the resurrection, God has the final word.

c. Verses 23-27 are familiar from the opening words of the Burial Office and can hardly be heard without the music of Handel's great aria coming to mind. These words and that music sing triumphantly of our knowledge of both Christ's resurrection and our own. But what does it mean to "know"? I know of the subatomic particles, the outer reaches of the universe, and the summit of Mount Everest by the testimony of trustworthy individuals who have seen for themselves and reported what they have seen. I know just as certainly of the resurrection by the testimony of great saints and ordinary Christians. The first apostles were specifically commissioned to be witnesses of the resurrection and they bore witness to the truth of the gospel by their own deaths. I am persuaded by their lives, by the power and beauty of Handel's music, by the logic of theologians, by the lives of ordinary parishioners, and by the goodness that flows from this belief. Scientific knowledge is useful but has no moral weight. Knowledge of the gospel changes my understanding of the meaning and purpose of life and, for that reason, is more certainly true.

2. Ecclesiastes 3:1-11a ♦ "For everything there is a season"

Although this is one of the most familiar and beautiful passages in the Bible, its use at a burial service requires caution. The author was clearly skeptical about the possibility of life after death and saw only that there was a rightness and beauty to everything in its time. While that appreciation is true and can be usefully proclaimed at the time of death, it is far from adequate as a proclamation of the Christian gospel. The most suggestive allusion in the passage, "he has put a sense of past and future into their minds" (v.11), is extremely difficult to translate accurately. The RSV said "he has put eternity into their minds" and there is as much to commend that translation as any other. "Eternity," for this writer, may mean only the endless succession of times and seasons rather than an implication of eternal life. Nevertheless, the passage does suggest that there can be a perspective on death as something other than tragic and that it plays a role in God's design of the universe. What that part is cannot yet be seen clearly. Death remains evil, a consequence of sin, even when extreme old age or suffering may make it seem like a friend. The author of Ecclesiastes looked for evidence that even death can be used for good and could not find it. Only the death and resurrection of Jesus Christ provides this evidence.

a. *"For everything there is a season,..."* (v.1). The balanced phrases of this passage suggest that there is a natural pattern in life of which death and mourning are a proper part. The Book of Genesis, on the other hand, tells us that death is a consequence of sin and that God did not create a world in which life and death, weeping and laughing, dancing and mourning were neatly balanced. There are, indeed, times in old age and suffering when death seems appropriate and welcome. More importantly, there are those who use their death to help others. For Christians the death of Jesus opened the way of life to us. If death seems appropriate to us, it is evidence of God's power to overcome even this evil and a cause for rejoicing as we bear witness to that power.

b. *"...A time for every matter..."* (1bff). The contrasts between birth and death, weeping and laughing, mourning and dancing, embracing and inability to embrace are evident at the time of death. Life has its rhythms. We cannot be always pondering the inevitability of death anymore than we can spend our whole time laughing. But in a world of sin, death has a place. Death may enable God to get our attention, and that is always useful. Death can make us aware of the value we place on family, friendship, and faith. Death can bring us together. Martin Luther once said, "Man and the devil use all good for evil; God uses all evil for good." Perhaps this is most evident at the time of death as God uses this inevitable evil to unite us and make us aware of life's value. So death itself becomes a gift through God's power.

c. *"...A time to weep, and a time to laugh; a time to mourn, and a time to dance;..."* (v.4). There was a time when death was seen as unmitigated evil.

It was only a time to mourn. The color of funerals was always black. There are still Italian villages where many of the women wear nothing but black since someone is almost always being mourned. But allowing death and mourning to dominate our lives would seem wrong for Christians who truly understand God's promise of life. So today at funerals we are more often reminded of the resurrection—that death is an entrance into life. The funeral vestments are often white and "alleluia" is sung. But this, also, can have its dangers. Death is still seen in Christian theology to be a consequence of sin, and it always involves separation from those we love. There may be a psychological price to pay (at the least), if we gloss over the pain of death and provide no opportunity for mourning. If, on the other hand, we allow ourselves to reveal our emotions, we will be better able to minister to those who are in pain. This text may provide a chance to say "OK" to the emotions we are too apt to hide and to put them in perspective and balance.

d. *"...A time to embrace, and a time to refrain from embracing;..."* (v.5b). The time of death is a time for both of these. It is clearly a time to embrace those we love, but it is also a time when our arms are no longer able to reach out to the one who has died. A woman dying of cancer told me that what she regretted most was that she would not see her children grow up and live their lives. I told her I was confident that she would, and she said, "Yes, but I want to hug them." Death is a very physical event in which we deal with the material reality of a dead body and a grave cut into cold earth. It is also a time when someone who has been a physical reality for us is no longer there to embrace. Part of the grief and disorientation of death is caused by the need to change our orientation from the natural and easy physical relationship which we take for granted to the "spiritual" of which we have all too little experience. The embraces of friends and family are important as we begin to experience this physical emptiness. The sacraments of the church assume new importance as they continue to provide us with a physical expression of God's love.

e. *"What gain have the workers from their toil?"* (v.9). The rewards of human labor are obviously very different for different individuals. The farmer has crops to harvest. The construction worker can look at a building he has helped build. A lawyer or executive has the satisfaction of "winning" a case or making a profit. A doctor feels a sense of accomplishment when a patient returns to health. All these may feel that their skills are well used if they have "served others." Parents and teachers and clergy will be gratified if children learn and grow and become useful citizens. Not all of these are material rewards which can be put in the bank or counted on to endure. But whatever our particular accomplishment, physicists tell us, the earth will finally fall into the sun and the sun itself will burn out and nothing will remain of this planet and human civilization. In the long run, Ecclesiastes is right to ask "what gain have the workers from their toil?" But this text needs to be balanced with a reading from I Corinthians 15 which is also recommended for burial services. "In the Lord," writes St. Paul, "your labor is not in vain" (v.58). So the question posed in Ecclesiastes can only be answered if we ask what our purposes are. If our purpose is to make monuments to ourselves (and even serving others or raising children can be for that purpose), we will ultimately fail. Nothing in this world has enduring value in itself. But if our purpose is to serve God, we will have used our material and temporal gifts to make an offering to God and so, to use Jesus' words, will have "laid up for ourselves treasure in heaven whether neither moth nor rust can corrupt" (Matthew 6:19).

f. *"He has made everything suitable for its time;..."* (v.11a). Older translations say "beautiful" rather than "suitable", but perhaps the sense is the same. Even death can be beautiful or appropriate if it is a revelation of faith and an opportunity to proclaim the power of God's love and the good news of the resurrection. God's grace can take the worst consequences of human behavior and make them useful and even beautiful. If God can do this with death, what else might not God do in the world around us and the lives of others if opportunities were created through prayer?

g. *"Moreover he has put a sense of past and future into their minds,..."* (v.11b). As noted above, this phrase may mean less than it seems. Yet even the skeptical author of Ecclesiastes was driven to look for meaning and purpose in human life and to try to find traces of a creator at work in the world. While it is doubtful that this author found anything particularly comforting, the very tenacity of his search is evidence of the need God does seem to have instilled in all humanity to look for some purpose larger than their own lives. There is, it has been said, "a God-shaped blank" in human hearts. Or, as Augustine said, "You have made us for yourself, O God, and our hearts are restless until they find rest in you."

3. Ecclesiastes 12:1-7,13-14 ♦ "all must go to their eternal home"

This seems, at first glance, a strange choice for a reading at funerals. The author had no hope of eternal life; it is uncertain that he believed in God (verses 13 and 14 are thought to be an addition by a later and more pious hand); and his picture of old age is bleak and despairing. Yet, especially paired with an appropriate New Testament reading, there are "intimations of immortality" even here.

One striking aspect of this passage is the poetic treatment of the weaknesses of old age. Verses 2-5 depict failing sight and hearing, weakened limbs, tooth decay, sleeplessness and other common afflictions of age, yet it is done through such striking and beautiful language that the regrettable becomes almost attractive. There are few better examples in literature of the human instinct for creating beauty in the midst of hopelessness. And why do we do that if it is, as the author says, "meaningless" and "vanity"?

What is there to say when someone dies after long years of increasing helplessness? This may be the appropriate passage to read. It provides an opportunity to say something about the beauty of great age: the dependency that often draws families together, the gentleness of those who have lived long, the satisfaction of being able to return the care that an elderly parent gave us. Nothing in God's world is without redemptive possibility. As the author of this passage created beauty out of failing strength, so we can learn sympathy and compassion and be enriched by them.

4. Isaiah 25:6-9 ♦ "the Lord...will make...a feast....And...he will swallow up death forever"

This ancient prophecy still speaks to us because of the concrete vividness of the language. "Fat things" may seem an unwise diet to a calorie conscious age, but a paraphrase like "rich food and well-aged wine" lacks the poetry. In fact, however calorie conscious we may be, we are still brought together by food as in no other way. Weddings and funerals alike require food because the sharing of food unites us both in sorrow and in joy. If the funeral includes a requiem celebration of the eucharist we have a foretaste of the promise of the heavenly banquet. God unites us in that feast and we celebrate Christ's victory over death as we receive Christ's life. If the funeral ends with a reception, that also will be a foretaste of the banquet at which God will at last unite us when death is defeated and the present sorrow is only a memory.

a. *"...He will swallow up death...wipe away the tears..."* (v.7-8). These verses, taken up again in Revelation 21:4, are appealing in their concreteness. Just as our bodies are buried, so death itself will be buried. And the tears we shed now will be wiped away by God himself.

b. *"We have waited...that he might save us...."* (v.9). In an age of instant everything, there is still no instant salvation. God created time and we cannot eliminate the time process. There is no instant bread because grain must be grown and harvested and dough needs time to rise. There is no instant wine because grapes must be grown and harvested and wine needs time to age. Who would give up the years it takes for a child to grow in order to produce a full grown responsible adult? God takes time with us and we must believe that that time has value. Even the often painful waiting of old age has a value. We may misuse this valuable time — old people can be abandoned — but old age can and should have worth and meaning. It can be a time of deepened relationships and caring. We need to learn to wait better, for in the waiting itself, our salvation is being fulfilled.

5. Isaiah 40:1-11 ♦ "Speak tenderly to Jerusalem"

This passage, by virtue of the great aria and choruses of Handel's "Messiah," is one of the most familiar passages in the Old Testament. Though I have not found it in any suggested list of funeral readings, its very familiarity commends it as helpful and its opening and closing emphasis on "comfort" and God's loving care makes it undoubtedly appropriate. The passage brings together two aspects of God's being which are seldom closely related yet are important themes to stress at the time of death: God's loving care and God's power.

a. It is remarkable that Isaiah, who speaks here to God's people in national and even cosmic terms, should still speak in a way that seems so individual and personal. In such phrases as "warfare ended" and "iniquity pardoned," Isaiah has the people of Israel in view, but at a funeral it is inevitable, and appropriate, to find personal significance in these words. The passage's closing picture of a shepherd with his sheep also brings out this personal note. A shepherd has care of the whole flock, but that care is expressed in individual attention to the needs of each animal. All must be fed, some must be carried, while others must be gently led. God knows the needs of each individual and provides the care that is needed.

b. The second theme, God's power, is a recurrent theme in Isaiah. The prophet delights in portraying a cosmic creator and universal God who shapes the events of history. For example, he wrote, "The grass withers, the flower fades; but the Word of our God shall stand for ever" (Isaiah 40:7). Our life in this world is brief and transient, but we belong to a God who knows no such limits and who gives to us the promise of unlimited life.

The two themes of this passage belong together. A loving God without power is of little help when our needs exceed human strength, and a powerful God who takes no personal interest in us is no help at all. The God revealed in the Bible is one who cares and is also able to help.

6. Isaiah 40:12-18 ♦ "Who has directed the Spirit of the Lord"

Here Isaiah expands on the theme of God's omnipotence stated in the first part of Chapter 40 (see above). These verses, however, stress God's wisdom. We may need instruction in wisdom and justice, but God does not. There are times in bereavement when we need to be reminded especially of this fact. It may be that death has come in a way that leads us to question God's justice and wisdom, or that leads us to affirm it. Either way, we may well be mistaken. It has been said that our perspective is like that of a moth chewing its way across an oriental rug and aware only of the color immediately before it, not the whole pattern. From such a perspective, one can hardly say of a particular event that "it is God's will" or that it is pointless evil. We do not know. But we do know two things: 1) that God's purpose is often invisible to us, and 2) that God is able to accomplish that purpose often in spite of the evil that stands in the way. In times of questioning and doubt we need to realize that we may not always understand and remember that God is able to bring good out of the most tragic human failures.

7. Isaiah 40:21-31 ♦ "Those who wait for the Lord shall renew their strength"

This passage responds to the suggestion that God does not know or care by pointing to the universe and created order. Isaiah suggests that if we have really looked at the world and understood what we see there, we would have no reason to question. He cites the stars as evidence. Who created these and who is able to name each one? Astronomers are reduced to numbering the stars and, even so, would not have numbers enough for all of them. We who know so much more about the universe than did Isaiah, know even more certainly that the stars are innumerable. But if we, who certainly could not create a single star, cannot begin to name them all, why should we imagine that we are able to judge the rightness or wrongness of the events of our own lives?

Yet, having stressed the contrast between God's wisdom and power and ours, Isaiah continues to portray God as a personal and loving God who gives us renewed strength. God is able to bring down princes and blow them away like stubble, yet God also gives new strength to the weak and new energy to the weary.

8. Isaiah 55:6-9 ♦ "Seek the Lord while he may be found"

The circumstances in which a passage is read will alter the manner in which it is heard. Therefore, certain circumstances may make this reading appropriate. It is easy, on the other hand, to imagine circumstances which would change Isaiah's gracious promise into a threatening admonition. This would be unfortunate. If someone not known for piety were to die suddenly and this passage were read at the funeral, it would probably be heard as a warning to those present to mend their ways before they share the fate of their friend.

To use this passage appropriately it would be important to understand first of all that it is a gracious promise, not a threat. These were words spoken, presumably, at the end of the time of Jewish exile in Babylon. God, who had promised to restore the Jewish people to their land, was already seen to be acting to keep that promise. Because God is seen to be working for the good of those in exile, this is a moment to be seized by those who are alienated or who have questioned God's providence. Now is the time to put aside these doubts and come home.

Can death create a mood similar to this? Yes, if the one who has died is seen to be one in whom God was at work and if the funeral is a time of thanksgiving for what God has done in this person. Then it might be a time when others were able to see for the first time how God's love can change and renew the lives of those who place themselves in God's hands. This passage could be properly described as a promise seen to be true in the funeral event and used as an invitation to those who had begun to see God's grace at work.

9. Isaiah 61:1-3 ♦ "To provide for all who mourn"

a. "*...Good news to the oppressed,...liberty to the captives,...*" This passage is a primary text for Christians. According to Luke, Jesus used these words as the text of his first sermon (Luke 4:18-19). This would indicate that Jesus believed that these words were a good summary of his vocation. Thus words which may first have been spoken to a discouraged group of former exiles longing for the fulfillment of God's promise became the text for Jesus' ministry of healing and freeing. Therefore they provide an appropriate text for a

Christian funeral. There is freedom both for the deceased and for the mourners. The deceased is set free from sickness and death; the mourners are freed from the weight of hopelessness. Human circumstances change, but our needs are always the same and the message God sends us is always the same: a message of hope and comfort. God will break down the walls of our captivity and stand with us in our time of need.

b. *"...The oil of gladness instead of mourning,..."* (v.3). This verse mentions three exchanges and then tells us the purpose for them: "to display his [God's] glory." "The chief end of man," in the words of the old Scottish Catechism, "is to glorify God...." This is a prescription not only for worship but for all of life. A life which glorifies God would be one in which God's power and goodness are evident in the joy, peace, and goodness of God's people. It's a poor advertisement for God if the people of God are always in mourning. The first Christians seem to have been noted for their joy and confidence though they faced persecutions beyond any we are ever likely to know. Though they had been slaves and people with no power or position, the Roman Empire itself was threatened by the freedom and joy which had transformed their lives. Because they knew Jesus had conquered death, they were set free of the fear of death. It was in that freedom that this prophecy from Isaiah came true. Because we share Christ's life this same freedom is ours. When a Christian dies, it should be a time when God is glorified both in reflecting on the life which has ended and in praising God for the promise of resurrection life.

10. Lamentations 3:17-26, 31-33 (or 3:22-26, 31-33) ♦ "The steadfast love of the Lord never ceases"

Patience is a widely commended virtue, but hard for time-bound human beings to acquire. We live in the moment; God works in another time frame entirely. This passage, written at a time when Jerusalem had been destroyed and all God's promises seemed all to have failed, counsels God's people to be patient: "...the Lord is good to those who wait for him,..." (v.25). Perhaps the point is that only when we wait, do we come to the time when our hopes and God's promise come together. From the perspective of those who had seen Jerusalem destroyed, that must have seemed difficult or impossible. For us, looking back, it is easy to see how God's promises have been kept again and again. Only patience carries us to the point where we can look back and see that fulfillment and the truth of the exclamation, "great is your faithfulness" (v.23).

But this passage speaks of more than patience and fulfillment. It reminds us that the fulfillment always goes beyond the promise. "New every morning" (v.23) is more than the sun coming up again on another day. God's mercy is, indeed, "new every morning". Death brings the old and familiar and loved to an end, but for the deceased there is a new beginning beyond what human minds can imagine. For the bereaved there is also a new beginning. The same God who not only restored the exiled people to Jerusalem but gave them a Messiah whose love transformed all history, can give us a new day in which we will find mercy beyond our previous experience.

11. Daniel 12:1-3 ♦ "Those who are wise shall shine like the brightness of the sky"

Daniel may be the last of the books of the Old Testament to have been written. In Daniel we begin to find an unmistakable vision of a life beyond the present. The setting of the Book of Daniel was the time of the Maccabean revolt in which people sacrificed their lives for the sake of God's law. But Daniel suggests that life does not come to an end with physical death. Somehow God's people began to believe that the love of God could only be complete if death were not the last word. The vision of this book anticipates the resurrection. So we have this vision of a dazzling future in which our dull, lackluster lives will shine with all the glittering brightness of the stars. How do we use the vision to speak to people in grief today? What we see here is the confidence of those who know God's love that the reality we presently see is less important than the future in which we hope. We who know of Jesus' resurrection can hold a far greater confidence that the God who has shown such power can assuredly transform our mortal lives into immortal glory.

12. The Wisdom of Solomon 3:1-5,9 (or 3:1-9) ♦ "But the souls of the righteous are in the hand of God"

The *Book of Common Prayer* says that the books of the Apocrypha are not to be used "to establish any doctrine." That might be a useful caveat in considering these passages from The Wisdom of Solomon. This book was written in the First Century B.C. and is heavily influenced by Greek philosophy. Thus we find in it a doctrine of the immortality of the soul rather than the resurrection of the body. Nevertheless, there are themes in these passages which are paralleled in several books of the New Testament and which could help to set human life in a useful perspective. Among the themes found in this passage are:

a. *Death as release from suffering* (vv.1-3). A parallel passage is Revelation 7:15-17. It should be noted, of course, that the New Testament has much more to say about the value of suffering, especially the value of sharing in Christ's suffering (cf. Romans 5:3-5, Hebrews 2:10, I Peter 4:12-14 *et al*). While one can be thankful for release from suffering, the emphasis should be primarily on the way God can use suffering to good purpose as in the crucifixion and in the past and present suffering of God's people. It might be noted that the sacraments of baptism, confirmation, and marriage all involve a deliberate acceptance of suffering. Baptism is a sharing of Christ's death, the confirmation rites of some churches exhort the confirmand to "endure hardship," and the marriage vow is "for better for worse." It seems that human beings need to suffer in order to grow and that greater suffering very often leads to greater growth. The meaning of suffering is, of course, an enormous subject and cannot be fully dealt with here, but the death of one who has suffered is an important opportunity for teaching on this subject.

b. *Discipline* (v.5) That the Lord disciplines those he loves is a theme that occurs in Proverbs (3:12), Hebrews (12:6-11), Revelation (3:19) and elsewhere. It is also worth remembering that God's people have been disciplined by suffering throughout their history. The Old Testament story of Israel is part of that story and the story of the church includes long chapters on this subject down to the present day. The epistle to the Hebrews goes so far as to say that Jesus himself "learned obedience through what he suffered."

c. *Testing* (v.6)—This verse is paralleled in Revelation 3:18. Perhaps the emphasis should not be so much on the testing as on the fact that such a value is placed on God's people that they can be compared to purified gold. Gold has two significant qualities: it is valuable because it is both rare and beautiful, and it has remained valuable throughout human history while other fads have come and gone. Such is the value of our lives to God.

d. *Trust and truth* (v.9)—Truth is not something to be measured objectively (like "facts") but to be learned through experience and, especially, through faith and trust. Jesus said, "I *am* the ...truth" (John 14:6 q.v.); Christianity is not based on Jesus' teaching but on Jesus. It is through knowing Jesus Christ that we come to understand the meaning and purpose of human life. The personal witness of those who have learned the truth of the gospel from a faithful walking with the Lord is of much more value than many books. This is the reason why we give thanks for the lives of such people when their lives and witness come to an end.

13. The Wisdom of Solomon 4:8,10-11,13-15 ♦ "Old age is not honored for length of time"

The first paragraph on The Wisdom of Solomon 3:1-9 (above) is also relevant here. Though God can undoubtedly act to remove people from life, it would be dangerous to assume when anyone dies young that "it was God's will." Some people find comfort in this thought and repeat it, but it does no honor to God. The apocryphal books were written at a time when God's people were stretching toward an understanding of life after death but, apart from a knowledge of and reflection on the resurrection of Jesus, they can hardly be asked to provide us with a fully developed and balanced doctrine. One valid insight in this passage is that old age is no sure sign of God's pleasure. Against the view that the good are rewarded with long life, the author cites the example of Enoch, who though he died at the relatively young age of 560, was one who "walked with God." Therefore dying young is not a sign of God's displeasure. Even those who die young are in God's hands, therefore God's purpose is not defeated by their death. Also, span of life is not the ultimate good. Young people may achieve much in a short time. This passage provides opportunity to reflect on the great good that can be accomplished in a few years and the failure of most of us to use a longer span well. But we should not blame God when a life is cut tragically short. We should rather blame ourselves for not using our time better and give God praise for what is often accomplished even in a life that seems to us tragically foreshortened.

B. New Testament Epistle Texts and Commentary

1. Romans 5:5-11 ♦ "While we still were sinners Christ died for us"

a. *"...Hope does not disappoint us,..."* (v.5). It's hard to imagine a more reassuring text for a Christian funeral. We may need, however, to begin by making a distinction between hope and wishful thinking. Often enough we "get our hopes up" and are disappointed. That is wishful thinking. Christians will not be disappointed in their hopes "because," as Paul says, "God's love has been poured into our hearts through the Holy Spirit" (v.5). Our hope is based on the experience of God's love and we can be confident that one who loves us so much will not let us hope in vain. Indeed, it is God who has raised our hopes by sending Christ into the world and raising him from the dead.

b. *"...If while we were enemies,..."* (v.10). The latter part of this passage elaborates on the first by pointing out that Christ died for us while we were still separated from God by our sins. It is hard to imagine that God would do so much for sinners. But now that Christ has died for us and taken on himself the burden of our sin, we are no longer in a such a state of separation and our confidence can be all the greater. Therefore we have reason to hope. In light of the resurrection and the subsequent evidence of the power of resurrection life at work in God's people, we have much more reason to hope than human beings might have had when God first began the process of redemption.

Wishful thinking builds castles in the air. Christian hope builds on the bedrock knowledge of what God has already done.

2. Romans 5:17-21 ♦ "One man's act of righteousness leads to...life for all"

This passage may be too "theological" to commend itself easily for use at a funeral, but it does state very clearly and simply the basis of our hope for life. There is a sermon about logic here but also one about love. Perhaps both themes can be combined in a way that speaks to both aspects of human life.

a. St. Paul sees a very simple pattern in salvation history: the first act of sin has condemned us all, and the one act of perfect obedience offers us life. What else do we need to know and be assured of at the time of death except that by Christ's death and resurrection we are able to pass through death to life? Most people probably want to be comforted at the time of death. But for those who want logic and understanding, those who ask "Why?" and want answers, this is the passage to turn to. Why is there death? Because the human race, summed up in "Adam," sought to satisfy self rather than obey God's will. Self-seeking leads to death. That is as obvious as the front page of the newspaper. That is what brings us to the church in mourning. The only possible antidote or remedy is one life of perfect obedience. No human being, stained by sin, could offer such a life. God therefore came into human life in Jesus Christ to live that life for us and offer it for us. That is our reassurance and hope. That's the logic of salvation and there will be times in the days of mourning when such logic may be helpful.

b. Beyond the logic is the language of love: words like "abundance" and "free gift" speak of a love beyond all logic and reason. There is a logic to salvation, but it is not the logic of gravity in which objects fall where they must. No human being could expect that there could be a God so loving as to reach out to all and to love each one. That is the free gift and abundance that lead Christians to sing hymns like "Amazing Grace." Most especially at the moment of death, we can't help being amazed at the love and grace that can conquer death and bring each of us the promise of eternal life.

3. Romans 6:3-9 (or 6:3-4,8-9) ♦ "Buried with him by baptism into death"

a. "...*Do you not know...*" (V.3). Christian life begins with baptism, so how could we not know that baptism is a passage through death? How could we not know that we have already died to sin and been given new life? Why is death such a trauma? Paul seems surprised—as he should be—that Christians should not have grasped this basic fact. If the burial service is carried out with full ceremony, we are reminded again and again of the fact that baptism and burial are closely parallel. We are brought to the church both times for both events. Perhaps an asperges recalls the water of baptism; perhaps the same white vestments are used. But then our thoughts were dominated by new life and the references to death were secondary. Now we are dominated by thoughts of death and the references to life may escape our notice. Then the promise of eternal life was distant and now it is reality. We were baptized to share Christ's life and through the eucharist that sharing becomes a more and more familiar reality. Now the sharing is fulfilled. Paul rehearses the facts which we once accepted in theory and sacrament and which now have become immediate.

b. "...*Death no longer has dominion over him....*" (v.9). This powerful phrase has been echoed by such great poets as John Donne and Dylan Thomas. We live in a world governed by certain facts, like the proverbial "death and taxes." These rule our lives. But Christ having been raised has altered these "facts of life" for ever. Death could not exert its authority over him, therefore those who belong to him are also set free from its control. We too must pass through death, but since we know death does not have the last word, death cannot hold us in fear and shape our lives. "Death shall have no dominion,"[1] said Dylan Thomas. "One short sleepe past, wee wake eternally, And death shall be no more," wrote John Donne; "death, thou shalt die."[2]

4. Romans 8:1-13 (or 8:1-10, or 8:1-11) ♦ "He who raised Christ from the dead will give life to your mortal bodies also"

St. Paul makes a distinction between the "flesh" (*sarx*) and the "body" (*soma*) which we need to bear in mind in dealing with this passage. St. Paul is not saying, "the body dies but the soul lives." That way lies a dangerous dualism. Elsewhere (I Corinthians 15, for example) St. Paul is clear about the raising of the body to eternal life. The distinction made here is one of life's goals and purposes, between those who "set their minds on the things of the flesh" and those who "set their minds on the things of the Spirit" (v.5). The body is important. God made it and God will raise it. But the body exists in the realm of the flesh, not the Spirit, until by baptism we move from the one to the other. Once that is done, we live in a time between the times in which the realm of the flesh still seeks to control us and make us act as if flesh were the final and only reality. St. Paul speaks to this tension, reassuring us and reminding us of the commitment we have made, saying, "You are not in the flesh; you are in the Spirit, since the Spirit of God dwells in you." We Christians have already been brought into the realm of the Spirit and of life through our baptism and that is a realm where death has no power. At the time of death we need to be reminded of this. Death has power over the flesh but not the Spirit, and we belong to the Spirit.

5. Romans 8:14-19, (31-33) 34-35, 37-39 ♦ "Who will separate us from the love of Christ?"

a. "*...All who are led by the Spirit of God...*" (v.14). Those who live by faith are subject to doubt. How can we be sure we belong to God and that God cares about us? The evidence is that we are "led by the Spirit," and that is seen most often in little things: an instinct for kindness to others, a sincere seeking for God's will, church membership, a loving family, community service. Those who cry out to God as "Abba...Father" give evidence, says St. Paul, that they belong to God. Those who see themselves as God's children are also heirs, and nothing can prevent the love of God from completing God's purpose in us.

---

[1] Thomas, Dylan, *Collected Poems, 1934-1952*, p. 62.
[2] Donne, John, *The Poems of John Donne*, Grierson, Herbert (ed.), p. 297.

b. *"...The sufferings ... are not worth comparing with the glory..."* (v.18). St. Paul was undoubtedly referring to the persecution suffered by the first Christians, but the sufferings of prolonged illness, or poverty, or other personal circumstances are equally relevant. Christians have been criticized as offering "pie in the sky" but there is no excuse for accepting injustice now on the plea of justice hereafter. The fact remains that this life often is filled with suffering which cannot be avoided, and that God has promised us a glory that outweighs any suffering we may face. It is also true that human beings often accept suffering and death for themselves for the sake of greater good for others. Avoidance of suffering is not the highest good and we seem to know that instinctively.

c. *"...The creation waits with eager longing for the revealing..."* (v.19). Human life is filled with a sense of expectancy. We are always, it sometimes seems, waiting for something just around the corner: a visit from children or grandchildren, a new job, a raise, a special event. Politicians trade on our expectations. We know life ought to be better and look for those who can make it so. Scientists work to find cures for disease. Architects work to create better housing. Urban planners work for better living conditions. All these and many others are evidence of the truth of St. Paul's words: we are waiting to see what God's kingdom will be like. Many work for that goal and wait for it. Indeed, not only human beings but *"creation* waits with eager longing" (or, as J.B. Phillips' paraphrase says, "The whole creation is on tiptoe to see the wonderful sight").[3] The creation cannot reach fulfillment until God's rule is established by "the revealing of the children of God" (v.19). Death may end our individual working and waiting, but it also opens a clearer vision of the realm we have hoped to see.

d. *"...What then are we to say about these things?..."* (v.31). "These things" are the present sufferings St. Paul has just mentioned in verses omitted here. In many circumstances, however, it will seem to be a direct reference to the death that has just taken place. What shall we say when one we love has died? The words that follow this verse in Romans 8 tell us that we can at least say, "If God gave his own Son for us, we can be confident that he will complete his purpose in us." Christ's death is not in vain. We should also remember, however, that "these things" refers back to the preceding verses (8:14-19). There we have been told how our suffering is a shared suffering, an evidence of our membership in Christ and participation in his sufferings. And we have been told that these sufferings are not worth comparing with the glory to be revealed for which all creation eagerly waits. Suffering and death can so dominate our lives at the moment that we fail to see them in context, but they are seldom the predominant aspect even of the span of our earthly life and cannot be the dominating aspect of life in Christ with its promised glory. We have, indeed, much to say to "these things."

---

[3] Phillips, J.B., *Letters to Young Churches*, p. 18.

e. *"...Who is to condemn?..."* (v.34). Most translations make it hard to hear the full power of this verse. Perhaps the NRSV is clearer than many. "Who is to judge us?" is the question. And the answer, says St. Paul, is "Christ Jesus, who died, yes, who was raised, who is at the right hand of God, who indeed intercedes for us." Others may judge us favorably or unfavorably, but finally the only judge who matters is our Lord—and that same judge died for us and intercedes on our behalf. What better news could there be than that? The justice system is "stacked" in our favor. The judge is on our side!

f. *"Who will separate us from the love of Christ?..."* (v.35). The closing verses of Romans 8 are a hymn, a powerful song. Notice that at the time of death our concern is that we are separated from one we love. St. Paul does not speak directly to that. The point that concerns him is that we cannot be separated from the love of God (v.39). Indirectly, of course, that also means we cannot be separated from each other. But however much we love each other, we need the love of God more. If God is a God worth serving at all, we cannot lose.

6. Romans 14:7-9 (or 14:7-12) ♦ "Whether we live or whether we die, we are the Lord's"

a. The lectionaries suggest using only verses 7-9, perhaps to avoid speaking of judgment. But judgment is what this passage is about so it may be better to add verses 10-12. The thought of these verses is summed up in verse 10: "We shall all stand before the judgment seat of God." St. Paul has been discussing particular issues of Christian behavior and his point is that they can only rightly be judged by the one who is our Lord. The purpose of Christ's death and resurrection, he says, is that we should belong to him and, therefore, that we are answerable to God and to God alone. However squeamish the lectionaries may be concerning judgment, the fact that there is a judgment is good news since it means that our lives are not ended by death. Judgment is good news.

b. St. Paul's line of argument also brings into focus by an indirect route the unity we have in Christ. Christ is Lord, he tells us, both of the dead and of the living. Jesus in the synoptic gospels puts the same point in almost the same way by saying that God is "God not of the dead, but of the living;..." (Mark 12:27 and parallels). Both statements make clear God's sovereignty over death and God's ability to "hold all souls in life."[5] So, then, as St. Paul says, "Whether we live or whether we die, we are the Lord's" (v.8).

7. I Corinthians 13:1-13 (or 12:31-13:8a) ♦ "The greatest of these is love"

This chapter is, of course, the quintessential marriage reading but, just as love is first in our minds when we begin a relationship, so it might well be first in our minds when a relationship comes to an end. Indeed, the statement that "love never ends" (v.8), may well transform our understanding of death itself. It should be carefully noted that the Christology of this passage is implicit, not explicit. There is no specific reference to Christ or to God. St. Paul is appealing to universally accepted values to point toward the highest value. But as these are not specifically Christian values, it is possible to draw less than fully Christian lessons from the passage, as will be noted below.

a. *"...If I hand over my body so that I may boast, but do not have love, I gain nothing...."* (v.3). Other versions usually translate "if I give my body to be burned." The difference is one letter in Greek, but the meaning either way is approximately the same: the destruction of the physical body is meaningless without love. Death, without love, is "a simple interchange of protein."[4] Conversely, if I die having given my body, my mind, and my heart in love, I am not "nothing" but something. I will have given myself to the power that moves the universe and that power will not allow my life to be extinguished and meaningless.

It might be added that we do, in love, give our bodies to be, not "burned" perhaps, but spent, burned out for others. The physical is transmuted into spiritual force. A transformation takes place so that, at the end of life, we have indeed become joined with the lives of many others. This fact gives a certain hope and meaning to the lives of many who die without faith. Love endures even when we fail to recognize who love is and respond in faith. But this is far short of faith in the resurrection. The giving of myself to others and my survival in others is only a hint of what can be when we give ourselves, spend and offer ourselves, in love to God. Then it is not simply a bit of myself that survives in others, but I myself who will live again, fully and forever, in Christ.

b. *"...Love never ends...."* (v.8). This verse in particular commends I Corinthians 13 as a passage to be read at funerals. The bereaved have come to one very real end: the physical body of one they loved is dead. But love does not die so easily. The love which was a central focus of our lives continues. The memories remain, the influence remains, the fact that we have been loved remains a vital part of what we are. This is not what is meant by resurrection, but it is part of the natural evidence God provides us with for the reality of the spiritual element in existence. If "mere" human love has so powerful and persistent an influence, then what can God's love mean when we come to know it in Christ and respond to it? It is not surprising that this great chapter on love leads on very quickly to St. Paul's powerful teaching about the resurrection in the fifteenth chapter of this same epistle.

c. *"...For now we see in a mirror, dimly, but then we will see face to face. Now I know only in part; then I will know fully, even as I have been fully known...."* (v.12). The partial quality of our knowledge is never more painfully evident

---

[4] "Love is a carrier of death — the only thing in fact, that makes death significant. Otherwise it is . . . a simple interchange of protein." Stegner, Wallace, *All the Little Live Things*, p.80.

than at the time of death. There is so much we would like to know and so little that we can say with confidence. But the details are unimportant compared to the one over-riding fact that Christ died and rose for us. Why do we want to know more? It is the nature of love to wish to know fully. To love is to seek out the fullest knowledge of the one loved. And death only intensifies that "need to know." We are frustrated by loving someone and not being able to know fully their circumstances. Someday, of course, we will know and St. Paul points that out. But St. Paul turns the phrase in a surprising way: I will know "even as I have been fully known." What matters, perhaps, is not that I will know fully, but that God fully knows me. The love which can work through death is beyond my knowing, but never beyond me. The same love which is at work in the deceased is at work in me and knows me through and through - and my need to know is therefore lessened. The child needs to know only if a parent is absent or if the child is not fully understood. When I am perfectly loved and fully known, I do not really need to know anything more than that.

d. *"...Faith, hope, and love abide,...and the greatest of these is love"* (v.13). Faith, hope, and love are obvious supports to those who are bereaved — and perhaps in that order. Faith may come first to mind: "What would I do if not for my faith?" Because we know God, we can face the worst and be strengthened by God's presence. And we have hope. The Christian faith is built on the knowledge of Jesus' resurrection and the hope we have of sharing that resurrection life. Love, however, is even more important though it may be less obvious. Few people can pass through the process of bereavement without becoming intensely aware of the love others have for them and the one who has died. The one thing we know how to do for someone bereaved is to be with them. Presence expresses love. But this is so natural and instinctive a response we may not see it so clearly as God's own way of being with us. We may not stop to realize that it is God who so surrounds us with love, who holds us in human arms. Perhaps never more than in the time of bereavement are these three virtues so strongly and evidently at work in our lives. At the moment of death, theology comes to life.

8. I Corinthians 15:12-58 (or 15:20-28,35-58, or 15:20-23 [or 20-26],35-38,42-44, 53-58 or 15:20-23,53-58) ♦ "Christ has been raised from the dead, the first fruits of those who have died"

Those who want solid meat to sustain them at the time of death will find no greater passage than this. Here St. Paul brings together "scripture, tradition, and reason" in a ringing proclamation of the truth of the resurrection and its centrality for the Christian faith. Because of the length of the passage and because some of its reasoning may not speak to contemporary listeners, some sections may be omitted without serious loss.

a. The first paragraph (vv.12-19) seems rather oddly to demonstrate the truth of the resurrection by the fact of Christian faith rather than, as we would normally expect, the truth of the faith by the fact of the resurrection. But on further consideration, is this not what we often do ourselves? What greater evidence is there, in fact, of the truth of the resurrection than the witness of transformed lives? We cannot now obtain photographic evidence of the empty tomb and the risen Christ, but every Christian congregation contains men and women whose lives have been changed by the power of the resurrection life. If the resurrection is false, how do you account for these people? The first evidence of the existence of God and the resurrection of Christ is, in this world, the witness of Christian lives. We are, as St. Paul says, "of all people most to be pitied" if the resurrection is false. The evident joy of Christian people, however, could hardly be based on deception.

b. The second paragraph (vv.20-28) paints a cosmic picture subsuming all time and eternity in three movements. All history to Christ is summed up first "in Adam" as the story of human rebelliousness and sin and death. Secondly, "in Christ" there is a restoration of life, though the restoration is not yet complete. We see in Christ's resurrection the evidence of new life which we have begun to taste but which must await his coming at "the end" to be fully shared. Still in the future lies that final kingdom in which all rebellion will be ended and those who belong to Christ will live with him. Then (it is interesting to note that the NRSV abandons the clumsy "God will be everything to everyone" of the RSV to return to the phrasing of the King James Version) "God may be all in all."

c. (vv. 29-30) In the first flush of enthusiasm, it seems that new converts, concerned for deceased relatives who had had no opportunity to be baptized, were baptized on their behalf (v.29). Although Mormons have revived the tradition and carry out massive genealogical research to be sure that all their ancestors are given access to the kingdom, the Christian church long ago concluded that God would not require baptism of those who responded to the best light they had in their time. But this is a side issue at a contemporary Christian funeral.

d. In verses 35-44 St. Paul suggests two analogies of resurrection to help us think about ideas beyond our understanding because they are beyond our experience. Everyone sees how a seed is planted and "dies" in order that a new life may begin. Everyone sees that there are different kinds of existence in the material world: that of stars and planets, of birds, of fish, of animals. Today our knowledge of the created order extends to the mysteries of subatomic particles and the transformation of mass to energy. St. Paul simply suggests, as we can do also, that a creator who can bring all this into being can surely provide us with a new way of being when this physical existence comes to an end.

e. Four great assertions climax this chapter (vv.53-58). First, we must pass through a transformation of what we are in order to become what we are meant to be. God's kingdom is not made of physical things and flesh and blood; we must become something else to take part in it. Second, "The sting of death is sin,..." (v.56). The story of the creation does not suggest that human beings were immortal before the fall (Adam and Eve were exiled to prevent their eating the fruit of the tree of life and so living forever) but rather that the pain of death is the punishment for sin. Death might be a peaceful transition were it not for sin which introduces the pain of separation. Third, we are reminded that through Christ we are given the promise of final victory. And all this leads to the final assertion, most important for self-centered and accomplishment-oriented human beings: "...in the Lord your labor is not in vain" (v.58). Not only does God care for us, God values the work we do and uses it toward the establishment of that kingdom. That, at the time of death, is good news beyond any reasonable expectation.

9. II Corinthians 1:3-5 ♦ "Our consolation is abundant through Christ"

The word "console" (or "comfort" in some translations) occurs six times in these three verses. It is a word often used in times of bereavement and a useful word to look at carefully in a homily. The Greek word *parakaleo* has to do with calling. One primary meaning of the verb is to "exhort" and "urge", and this leads to the secondary meaning of "encourage." "Encouragement," as an active word, may be more helpful to the bereaved than passive "consolation." St. Paul says in these verses that God is a "God of all encouragement" (v.3). God is a God who exhorts and urges us, who calls us forward. Death may stun and immobilize us, but what helps us most is to be shown a way forward. God provides that way. St. Paul tells us that it is "through Christ" (v.5), that we "share abundantly in encouragement" (v.7), and that is because Christ comes to call us, to encourage us to walk with him. Bereavement leaves us feeling alone. "Encouragement" comes when we have someone to walk with and help us forward. That is God's gift in our time of need.

10. II Corinthians 4:7-18 ♦ "What cannot be seen is eternal"

"...While we live, we are always being given up to death for Jesus' sake,..." (v.11). Death should not be a surprise for Christians. To be "given up to death for Jesus' sake" (v.11) means that the inevitable, daily deaths we face are given a meaning and purpose. They remind us that this life is not eternal and that we have staked our hopes on another life which can only be gained by giving this one up. Coming to take part in a funeral reminds us of who we are and what we have valued. St. Paul often listed the daily deaths he encountered as he does here: "afflicted...perplexed,...persecuted,...struck down,..." (v.9). Yet he was not "crushed;...driven to despair;... forsaken;...destroyed" (v.9) because he did not expect life to be a crescendo of hosannas. Life had not been such for Jesus and there is no reason why it should be such for his followers. But this constant affliction which never destroys us is evidence of the "transcendent power" of God. It is clear that without that power, we could not survive. The greatness of God's gift of life to us is seen more clearly because of the weakness of the "earthen vessels" (v.7)[5] in which it is contained. Death itself is the supreme clarifier of values: when we come to give thanks for the life of one we have loved, it is to be hoped that we can begin to see that life clearly, perhaps for the first time. And what we should see is not the accomplishments of the one loved but the gifts God gave which enabled them to accept their own mortality and bear witness to God's grace.

11. II Corinthians 4:16-5:10 (or 5:1-9) ✦ **"We have a building from God, a house not made with hands, eternal in the heavens"**

a. Once again (cf. commentary on Romans 14:7-12 above), the various lectionaries tend to omit the closing verses of this passage because of the references to judgment. It might be noted that the word translated as "judgment seat" in 5:10 can also be translated "throne" or "an elevated place." In context, reference to judgment is obviously being made but the word itself is not used. Nevertheless, we will say here and cross reference it elsewhere that judgment is a central biblical theme and one which can only be reassuring if it is properly understood.

Judgment has to do with value. That which is valueless or irrelevant is not judged. In a world without God, there is no judgment because there is no Creator who cares and therefore, what we do has no lasting significance. To say that we must all appear before the judgment seat of Christ is not reassuring at first glance because we will be so aware of our failures. But we will be there because all we have done makes an eternal difference. And we will be there because God loves us. We can be indifferent to other people's children's misbehavior but not to that of our own. We only judge those we care about, who make a difference in some way in our lives. So judgment is evidence of God's love and our value in God's sight.

How can we balance this idea of judgment, involving "works," with the doctrine that we are saved by faith? There is a mystery here that cannot easily be resolved. In chapter 5 St. Paul goes on to say that "...in Christ God was reconciling the world to himself, not counting their trespasses against them,..." (v.19). So what we do makes a difference and must be judged on the one hand, but on the other hand doesn't count. It would seem to be one of those places where the human perspective is inadequate and two seemingly contradictory statements are both true. We may have a glimpse of the truth in our own attitude towards our own children: what they do matters deeply and can cause us enormous pain, but the slightest evidence of contrition can "make it right." We judge them more harshly than others but forgive them more readily.

---

[5] The NRSV says "clay jars," which may be more accurate but seems to lack a certain *je ne sais quoi*.

It may be appropriate on some occasions to omit the references to judgment found in so many passages, but finally the truth needs to be told. Part of the fear of death and the grief at the time of death surely comes from a consciousness of the wasted opportunities that mark our lives and the lives of those we love. Many people are torn between a fear that death is the end and life is meaningless and a fear that death is not the end and we will be judged without mercy. The gospel (good news) is that death is not the end; there is judgment, and there is mercy. What we do does matter and before Christ's throne we will have reason to be ashamed. But we also have great hope because he died to overcome our sins.

b. *"...Our outer nature is wasting away...but what cannot be seen is eternal"* (4:16-18). The first part of this passage is a powerful reminder of the danger of a false perspective. In a world dominated by concern for material things it is easy to lose our perspective, but a moment of reflection would remind us that in a world of change it is not the material things that last. Bodies waste away and die, but truth and beauty and goodness and love remain strong.

c. *"...We have a building from God...eternal in the heavens...."* (5:1). St. Paul uses various metaphors for the transition from earthly life to heavenly but all of them try to convey an idea both of continuity and change. The tent which becomes a house is like the seed which becomes a plant (I Cor. 15). We do not cease to be what we have been but through death and resurrection we fulfill the potential which is only glimpsed here on earth.

d. *"...By faith, not by sight...."* (v.7). From the time we are infants, we should be learning how deceptive sight can be. The pretty flame can burn; the glittering knife can cut. But still we trust appearances. Some people appear more beautiful than others or stronger, but they may not be there when we need them. We do indeed learn to walk by faith, not sight—and at last we have no choice. Everything we can see will decay and die, and only those who have learned to trust in the invisible but durable qualities of faith and love will have something left at the end. And they will have everything that matters most.

12. Ephesians 3:14-19 ♦ "That you might be filled with all the fullness of God"

These words seem directly aimed at those who are bereaved. The author prays for Christians to be given the gift of inner strength (v.16)—and when are we ever as aware of the need for such strength as at a funeral? Death is a challenge to the living; it is we whose lives are the poorer, not the one who has died. We have already urged that the funeral service should not be centered on the life and accomplishments of the one who has died. Among the reasons for this is the need of the living. Eulogies may be "comforting" in a sense, but they can also be profoundly depressing as we hear chronicled the many gifts of the one we have lost. It is the living who need to be strengthened and the full resources of the church, the gospel and the sacraments are available for this.

What is the strength God gives? Notice how the imagery of this passage becomes contradictory in its richness: we are to have "Christ...dwell in [our] hearts" and, at the same time, to be "rooted and grounded in love" (v.17). So Christ is to be in us and we are to be in Christ. Likewise we are to "know the love of Christ which surpasses knowledge" (v.19). Clearly the strength God gives is beyond what language can describe, yet the contradictions of language still do present a picture of God's grace surrounding and upholding and inspiring. We are surrounded by a great ocean of love which holds up and sustains both the living and the dead, but they know fully what we know only in part.

13. Philippians 3:10-21 (or 3:10-14, 20-21 or 3:20-21) ♦ "But our citizenship is in heaven"

a. *"I press on..."* (v.12). If it is at the time of death that we feel our humanity and our insecurity most strongly, it may be helpful to notice St. Paul's own insecurity when he compares his life with the perfection to which we are called. But St. Paul is able to maintain a kind of double vision in which he sees not only his limited accomplishment and imperfection but the finality of Christ's call. One the one hand, there is much more to be done, but, on the other hand, the goal is already a given. So St. Paul can write that "I press on to make it my own" and recognize at the same time that what he aspires to is his already "because Christ Jesus has made me his own." In the same way, at the time of death we can hardly help recognizing (in the midst of tributes and encomiums) the limitations and failures of the deceased. But it is God's claim on us that matters. If God has adopted us as children in baptism, is it possible that a lifetime of failure is able to wrest our lives out of God's hands?

b. *"...But our citizenship is in heaven,..."* (v.20). This is a theme developed more fully in Hebrews 11:13-16 and would be an appropriate text for one who has served the community as well as one whose life was centered on the church and the life of the spirit. While service in the church would be an obvious result of a love of God's kingdom, service of an earthly community should also result from our knowledge of a better community. To see something better is to want it for ourselves and those we love. The vision of a "new Jerusalem" should make us dissatisfied with "Jerusalem" as it is and lead us to use that knowledge to change our human communities for the better. Knowledge of our "citizenship...in heaven" leads directly to the prayer "your kingdom come...on earth" (Matt. 6:10).

c. Having said this, it should also be said that part of our comfort at the time of death is the belief that those who have died have already obtained the promise of the kingdom. We are given a citizenship at baptism which leaves us somewhat in the position of aliens on this earth. In our world, this is a common condition. We see Hispanics in the United States, North Africans in Europe, Asians in Arab countries, and business people of every country living abroad on behalf of their corporations. The result is an amazing interchange of cultures in which the alien is affected by the country of residence and the country of residence is affected by the alien in its midst. So Christians should modify their surroundings by seeking always to reflect the peace and unity and justice of the city they belong to and have heard of and long for though it remains unseen. We "live abroad" as "goodwill ambassadors" of God's kingdom and, in death, are finally given entrance into our homeland. If the community we have lived in is the poorer for our leaving, it is the richer for all the years of our exile.

14. I Thessalonians 4:13-18 ♦ "That you may not grieve as others do"

This was probably St. Paul's first letter and he wrote it when the church was still very new and Christians very unclear about the implications of their new faith. The advantage for us is that St. Paul is speaking simply and trying to reassure Christians confused by the death of loved ones.

a. *"...That you may not grieve as others do..."* (v.13). First of all, St. Paul wants the church to know that our natural grief is transformed by hope. The church in our day lays heavy stress (perhaps too heavy) on the joy of the resurrection, using white vestments for funerals and singing Easter hymns. Such stress can be overdone and make us feel guilty for grieving. But grief is natural and, in measure, appropriate. St. Paul simply says that our grief is different from the grief of those who have no hope — because we do have a hope.

b. *"...Those who have died...."* (v.14). A footnote in the NRSV indicates that the Greek here is more accurately translated "those who have fallen asleep." It seems to have come naturally to the first Christians to speak of death as "falling asleep." Sleep comes to an end when we awaken and this provides us with an image of death and resurrection.

c. *"...Encourage one another..."* (v.18). (The word translated "encourage" here — "comfort" in the RSV and KJV — is translated "console" in II Corinthians 1:3-5. The comments on II Corinthians 1 above, are also relevant here.) Even though we have confidence and even though our grief is transformed by hope, we still do need the encouragement of a shared faith. Having laid out the basic facts we need to know, St. Paul very sensibly tells us to encourage one another with the words he has given us. We need to do that and continue doing it. The suddenness of death, the radical separation with which we are faced, leaves us stunned at first. Then we must adjust to a new life over weeks and months and even years. Friends and family will be there at the time of death and the funeral, but they need to continue to stand by for the long haul. Faith and love have some specific work to do in the bereavement process. This work is called "encouragement" and it is the gift those we love need most.

d. Because at this early stage of the church's life St. Paul seems to have expected an imminent return of Christ, the balance of the passage deals with the question of how the dead and those who "remain" will be reunited. It is not those who remain who have priority, St. Paul explains, but those who have died. So we need not grieve for them that they will be left out or come to the kingdom later than we. But this is not much of an issue 2000 years later. The details of the end of time are not what matter to us when someone we love has died (though the dramatic picture of the Lord shouting, archangels calling, and trumpets blowing still makes an impact). What matters is St. Paul's confidence and his command that we console, comfort, encourage one another.

15. II Timothy 2:8-12a ♦ "If we have died with him, we will also live with him"

Verses 11-12 seem to be part of a familiar formula, perhaps a hymn, with which the author is confident his readers will be familiar. The equation: to die with Christ is to live with him is fundamental to the Christian faith and to the Christian understanding of the whole meaning of human life. Ladislaus Boros has suggested an equally pithy summary: "Man is the being that can die into God."[6] There are, in effect, two ways to look at life: either it is a rising and falling arc like that of trees and animals and, indeed, the universe itself, with a set span of existence and no more, or it is, as the Bible suggests, the seed out of which something eternal is to grow. In this latter view, the human life span is intended as an incubation period during which the spiritual potential of human life is to be developed. This spiritual potential must at last outgrow the limits of a physical body. Then, unity with Christ becomes the means of a new and fuller existence.

What does it mean to "die with Christ"? It means, first of all, baptism in which the physical is renounced and the spiritual affirmed. It means, then, a lifelong transition from a life centered on physical priorities to one centered on spiritual priorities. It involves good stewardship since giving away our material possessions is a means of establishing proper priorities. It involves social and political behavior centered on spiritual values such as justice and peace. It involves selfless love of others. In a life so centered, as Boros puts it, "The energies of the 'external man' are not simply 'used up,' but are transformed into a certain 'inwardness'."[7] Such a "dying" is not, then, simply a negative process but the construction of something new, "hidden with Christ in God" (Colossians 3:3). That life is finally completely hidden from us by death, but we have committed ourselves to that process in confidence that it is in fact, the way of life. That confidence, in turn, arises first from the gospel of Christ's resurrection which we have heard and believed, secondly from the evident growth in goodness and holiness of Christ's followers whom we have known, and thirdly from our own experience: the evident "rightness" of such a pattern of life.

---

[6] Boros, Ladislaus, "Has Life a Meaning?", *Immortality and Resurrection*, Benoit, P. and Murphy, R. (ed.), p.16.
[7] Ibid., p.13.

16. I Peter 1:3-9 ♦ "A new birth into a living hope"

This passage centers around one powerful image: that of gold in the assayer's fire. The author compares the trials of our lives to the testing of gold and tells us that faith is tested in the same way but that faith which stands the test is more precious.

The implication of the author's argument is that "trials" come by God's plan in order to test and demonstrate our faith. Whether we are comfortable with such a picture of God or not, the fact is that, in this world, many valuable human qualities do develop as a result of hardship and are more valued by others when they see the suffering out of which they come.

Why should this be necessary? Why is there no easy road to virtue? We are no more able to understand this pattern than a child can understand why medicine always seems to taste bad. But we only need medicine if we are sick, and we only need to develop courage and patience and faith because the world is sick. The source of the problem is in the illness, not the medicine.

The danger, always, at the time of death is that we will focus our attention on the trials an individual has faced and the courage and faith and other qualities we have seen in their lives without recognizing that these are gifts given in answer to need. Because this passage is clear about our need and the source of the gifts, it begins with praise of God. That is the proper focus.

There seems to be no other way to heal this world's sickness than by acceptance of suffering. We may not understand this and might wish it were otherwise, but what we can see is that such acceptance enables God to work in us to purify and strengthen us. This is cause for thanksgiving.

17. I John 3:1-2 ♦ "When he is revealed, we will be like him"

Most people would put a dividing line between God on the one side and human beings on the other. St. John draws the line differently: between the world as a whole on the one side and God and God's people on the other. There is a fundamental inability of the world to understand us, and that should not surprise us. The world did not "see" or understand Jesus either. But we are called God's "children" and this fundamental relationship is leading us toward an adulthood in which our likeness to God will be fully realized. We can see tendencies in children without knowing what the full development of those tendencies will lead to. In the same way, we can see tendencies in ourselves that enable us to be called God's children without being able to see as yet what the full development will be. But we will be like God, as we were when the human race was first created. We will be restored to that first perfection. And meanwhile, we have seen in Christ something of what that perfection is.

18. I John 3:14-16 ♦ "We know that we have passed from death to life"

This passage makes three fundamental assertions which are essential truths to proclaim at the death of a Christian.

1) We have *already* passed from death to life. Death still hurts and separates, but we already met it, accepted it, and conquered it when we were baptized. Death is no longer final or hopeless (v.14).

2) Life depends on love. Death is triumphant only where there is no love. A Christian funeral, the gathering of Christians in sympathy, is evidence that love is real and life has conquered (v.14).

3) We know Jesus' love for us by his death. The cross or crucifix at the center of the church has been transformed from a symbol of death to one of love and life because Christ died for us. Those who have lived for others (and died for others) have shown us the power of love and that is neither forgotten nor overcome by the fact of death (v.16).

19. I John 4:7-18a ♦ "Everyone who loves is born of God and knows God"

The language of the Johannine writings is sometimes circular and repetitive, and it is not always clear whether the author is repeating himself or taking the argument to a further stage. Nonetheless, there seems to be a progression here from the love which is general among human beings to that which is specific to the revelation of Christ.

a. *"Beloved, let us love one another,..."* (v.7). We should not overlook the first word here. Common as it may be in church usage, the word is charged with significance. It is not the minister expressing his relationship with the congregation or St. John expressing his relationship with those to whom he writes. It is, rather, a recognition of our status in God's sight. "Beloved" is what we are because "God is love" (v.8) and we were made to belong to God. There may well be no more important statement that can be made at the time of death than this reminder that we are God's "beloved." Death would only be an ultimate tragedy if this were not true. In the light of this term, we can be exhorted to "love one another" because our love is then a reflection of God's love and renewed and strengthened by God's love. Loving one another is never more important than in bereavement. Death divides, but love unites. Hurt as we are by death's division, we need the life-giving unity which comes from God and which human love expresses and, by God's grace, creates.

b. *"...Everyone who loves is born of God and knows God...."* (v.7b). This could be a profoundly important statement to make at the funeral of one not noted for church-going behavior. Reluctant though some Christians may be to recognize it, there are indeed human beings who "know God" but do not find God in church. Love, fortunately, is not found only in Christians. Love pervades God's world and is sometimes more evident outside the church than in. And God is love. Where love is present, so is God. St. John's gospel makes the same point when it speaks of "the true light, which enlightens everyone" (John 1:7). Every human being has some knowledge of the light which comes from God. There is some room for love in the life of every human being. A funeral is often a time at which this can be acknowledged.

And this should not be done in a triumphalist sense ("Old Joe was really a Christian however much he denied it."), but in humility. We must recognize our failure as Christians to express God's love in such a way that old Joe could recognize it and be comfortable with our way of witnessing. Nevertheless, God was present and at work in this life and, perhaps, more powerfully than in the lives of many who do profess Christian faith and take part in the church's life.

c. *"...God's love was revealed among us in this way: God sent his only Son into the world..."* (v.9). This is, of course, the central claim of the Christian faith: that "the Word became flesh" (John 1:14), that the love of God was perfectly expressed in one human life. Our confidence in the face of death is grounded in this belief. Love is not a theory. The theory has been made flesh and blood and, in the life of Christ, we have seen love face death and overcome it. We can face death with confidence because we have seen God's love at work in one living and dying human being.

d. *"...In this is love, not that we loved God but that he loved us..."* (v.10). The temptation to "eulogize" at a funeral comes from a lack of confidence in God's love. We feel a need to prove to God that we are loveable, that the deceased merited God's love. But God's love for us came first and long before we had, in Christ, any claim on that love. This is our confidence and security in the face of death: that God's love does not depend on our love or our achievements. If it were otherwise, we would never be secure, never certain that our love was truly worthy. But God's love for us is all that matters.

e. *"...God abides in those who confess that Jesus is the Son of God, and they abide in God...."* (v.15). This verse (as suggested in the opening statement) seems to balance and move beyond what was said in verse 7. There we are told that "whoever loves, is born of God and knows God"; here we are told that "God abides in those who confess that Jesus is the Son of God, and they abide in God." It would seem that the one who loves has an implicit relationship with God, but the one who "confesses" has an explicit relationship. Such a person "abides in God" and that is an unchanging and unchangeable relationship. When we claim Jesus as our Lord, we allow him to bring us into a saving relationship with God which death cannot alter. Perhaps we can imagine a diagram in which there are three stages of the human relationship with God. First, all human beings belong to God by right of creation and have some knowledge of God's love though they may not be able to name that love or enter into a conscious relationship with God. Second, those who hear the gospel and respond, enter into a conscious relationship which is, nonetheless, limited by all the weaknesses of the human condition. Third, death opens to us a life of conscious and unlimited growth in God's presence. Those of us who have reached the second stage, can rejoice with those who have moved on to the third and final stage, the fullness of life for which God created us in the beginning.

20. Revelation 7:9-17 ♦ **"They will hunger no more, and thirst no more"**

a. *God keeps promises.* This reading might well be paired with the Beatitudes (Matthew 5:1-12a) since the picture presented here is, in many ways, a fulfillment of these words. In each passage a "multitude" is gathered, around Jesus in one case and the Lamb in the other. Among the promises made in Matthew and shown to be fulfilled in Revelation are:

"Blessed are those who are persecuted...for theirs is the kingdom of heaven" (Matthew 5:10).

These...have come out of the great ordeal;...for this reason they are before the throne of God" (Revelation 7:14,15).

"They will see God" (Matthew 5:8).

"The one who is seated on the throne will shelter them" (Revelation 7:15).

"Blessed are those who hunger and thirst for righteousness, for they will be filled" (Matthew 5:6).

"They will hunger no more, and thirst no more" (Revelation 7:16).

"Blessed are those who mourn, for they will be comforted" (Matthew 5:4).

"...God will wipe away every tear from their eyes" (Revelation 7:17).

Those who trust God will find that God is faithful and keeps promises.

b. *The vision of heaven.* Few portrayals of heaven can match the power and beauty of this, yet at the same time, this picture is the basis of the common caricature of heaven as a place where we will stand around in white robes playing on harps—like it or not. Since few people have much skill with a harp or much desire to stand around in white robes singing hymns, the picture, for all its power, may not be completely attractive.

Surely the key element here is praise. These are those who have praised God in their earthly life and now are privileged to do the same for eternity. But what was the substance of their earthly praise? Those in this picture are presumed to have been martyrs since their robes have been washed in blood. But martyrdom is only a moment at the end of life. While that may, in fact, be determinative, presumably they made a decision based on a life already given to God in many ways. And how do we praise God? By faithful service, by concern for the poor and outcast, by using the talents God gave us in business or labor or homemaking, by working for peace and justice, and so on. God is praised when we develop the gifts we are given as fully as possible. And those gifts are seldom musical. St. John's vision sums up God's praise in a portrayal of worship, the supreme offering of ourselves, but presumably this includes all other types of praise and self-offering. The vision is a summary and not meant to be all-inclusive. Nor can we imagine all the ways in which self-development and self-offering may continue hereafter.

Rudyard Kipling suggested that we might spend eternity, not singing, but painting:

> We shall rest, and faith we shall need it,
> Lie down for an aeon or two,
> Til the Master of all good workmen
> Shall set us to work anew...
> And each on his separate planet
> And each on his separate star
> Shall paint the thing as he sees it,
> For the Maker of things as they are.[8]

That is undoubtedly as valid an expectation as playing harps. The praise of God is never narrowing or limiting. Surely St. John would have us build on his vision to envision for ourselves the widest possible scope for the further development of our interests and abilities so that God may be praised in the infinite range of gifts that are given to God's people.

21. Revelation 14:13 ♦ "Blessed are the dead who...die in the Lord"

This passage speaks immediately to the circumstances of first century martyrs who can look forward to a heaven in which their earthly witness in time of persecution is honored in heaven and need not be continued. They rest from those labors because their deeds are known.

The idea of "rest from their labors" seems to have appealed to Christians much more in other centuries than it does today, though people of great age still often find it comforting. More often, it conjures up a vision of idleness which Americans, at least, (perhaps because of the so-called "Puritan work ethic") see as sinful or boring. Perhaps this passage should be paired with the second and third chapters of Genesis in which our ancestors were placed in the garden and told to "till it and keep it" but not told of sweat and wearying labor until after they had sinned (Genesis 2:15; 3:17-19). Work, it seems, need not be tiring. Indeed, those who are skilled at their work "make it look easy" and, in a sense, it is easy, because they enjoy doing it and do it well. Tiring work, drudgery, is work we are not fitted for or not able to do well. The "rest" of heaven ought to be understood as a place where whatever we do will never tire us because it will use all our talents in a way that recreates rather than exhausts us.

This passage might find appropriate use when the person who has died exemplifies this understanding in some way. It might even have an appropriate place in pondering the life of someone retired who had found joy in a "recreation" or hobby, a way of resting and being re-created after a lifetime of labor. Heaven should probably not be shown as a place where we can pursue our hobbies but as a place where we can finally develop our true skills and express ourselves perfectly through what we do. Worship, it might

---

[8] Kipling, Rudyard, *Collected Verse of Rudyard Kipling*, p. 131.

also be noted, is, at its best, refreshing, renewing, and restful. That is why the vision of heaven in Revelation centers on worship.

22. Revelation 21:1-7 "Death will be no more"

The proverb that says, "Two things are certain: death and taxes," is wrong. Death is a temporary phenomenon, and death has already lost its power. St. Paul points out that death no longer has dominion over Christ (Romans 6:9). Nor does death have dominion over those who are in Christ. "Death be not proud," says John Donne, "...For those whom thou think'st thou dost overthrow/ Die not, poor death, nor yet canst thou kill me..."[9] Death has its hold on human beings because of sin which separates us from God (cf. I Corinthians 15:56) and because, once separated from God, we are separated from the source of life. The forgiveness of sin which we are given through Christ is what destroys death's power and we accept that gift in baptism.

Revelation is filled with images of baptism and marriage. The white robes of the throngs around the throne must have reminded the first Christians of their baptismal garments. But here, where the new Jerusalem is "prepared as a bride adorned for her husband" (v.2), the marriage imagery predominates. Division is overcome, death and separation are defeated, and baptism and marriage, the symbols of unity, come into their own.

C. Gospel Texts and Commentary

1. Matthew 5:1-12a ♦ "Blessed are the poor in spirit"

It might seem to require a bit of nerve to choose this reading for a funeral, whether one's own or that of a friend or relative. Who would feel confident to be measured by this standard? But this is not a set of standards by which each of us is to be measured; it is instead another expression of Jesus' confidence that it is God's will to gather all human beings into his kingdom. The gospel accounts of Jesus show him setting his gospel in opposition to those who assume their behavior qualifies them for the kingdom. Seeing that ninety-nine think themselves to be in the fold, he will seek out the one remaining. Seeing that most people think themselves to be well, he will seek out the sick. The point of the Beatitudes is not to limit heaven to the poor, the mournful, and the persecuted, but to include even those the world would not expect to be included. Nor has 2000 years of the Beatitudes changed many attitudes. Respect and honor still go to the rich, the proud, and the

---

[9] Donne, John, *Poems of John Donne*, p. 297.

secure. Whether they will be included in the kingdom is not the issue. The point is that those who judge by another standard entirely, the standard of love and mercy and a concern for those in need, may be peripheral in the eyes of others, but they are central to Jesus' vision of the kingdom. Thus the important point is to be reminded at the time of death that our valuations and judgments are apt to be badly mistaken. We would do best to center our attention on God's promise rather than the apparent achievements of any human being. Our hope and confidence is in God's promise, not human achievements.

2. Matthew 9:18-19, 23-26 ♦ "The girl is not dead but sleeping"

Death is not God's will. Stories like this make that clear. God's will is life and Jesus brought life to countless people. But death is not abolished. Jesus still acts to heal and change human lives, and yet our lives remain set in the context of death. We have faith that death is defeated, but the reality of the moment is that death continues to cause separation and grief. How do we reconcile the reality of the moment with the sometimes less tangible reality of faith?

The value of a story like this is its concreteness. This is not "mere theology"; this is a real story about real people and may communicate better than any theological treatise the reality of God's purpose. God is the kind of God who acts in this way; therefore we can face the death of those we love with confidence. God's will is life and that will cannot be frustrated by our lack of faith or understanding.

3. Matthew 11:25-30 ♦ "Come to me, all you who are weary"

a. *"...You have hidden these things...and have revealed them..."* Death in all its forms raises questions we cannot answer. However we cannot excuse ourselves from making the effort. God gave us minds to use, and even in the face of the ultimate mystery, we should make every effort to understand. But the inevitable failure of that effort does not mean that we must resign ourselves to hopelessness. The mind can carry us just so far in any relationship and beyond that there must be love and trust. No relationship, of any sort, is complete without both elements. Oddly, we must look in opposite directions for help: to the wise for understanding, but to children for the simplicity of perfect trust.

Jesus pointed often to children to illustrate the sort of relationship God would have with us. This passage might well be appropriate not only for the funeral of a child, but for that of a teacher or anyone who showed a special care or sympathy for children.

b. *"...All things have been handed over to me by my Father;..."* (v.27). In various ways in his ministry, Jesus stressed the authority God has given him. Our lives are not in the hands of a seemingly distant creator, but in the hands of one who has shared our life and who knows us better than we know ourselves. At the time of death, especially, we should remember that it is Jesus, who was born for us and who died for us, who calls us and who has the power to give us life again.

c. *"...Come to me..."* (v.28). Death often comes at the end of a long siege of illness, much of it in the hospital. During this time, relationships are difficult. The patient is visited briefly and may not be able to respond. Doctors, nurses, and others may do their best, but they are professionals, not usually personal friends. This gospel reading reminds us that our faith is centered on a personal relationship with Jesus and that that relationship can be perfected at the time of death. Jesus calls us to himself and has time enough and love enough for each of us: more love than we have known in any human relationship.

4. Mark 10:13-16 ♦ "Let the little children come to me"

a. *Death and baptism.* This passage can be used at the burial of a child but its usefulness may depend to some extent on whether or not the child has been baptized. Since this passage is frequently read at baptisms, it makes an obvious and important connection. The child was given to God at baptism in order to share Christ's death and resurrection. Though it is usually not the aspect we emphasize when a child is baptized, still the reality of death is there and recognized and even accepted in advance. All human life must pass through death and the span between birth and death almost always seems too short, but if the child is baptized, we have, however unknowingly, prepared the child for death and accepted its final inevitability.

b. *Children and the kingdom.* Be careful! On the one hand, it is clear that a child has certain advantages at the time of death. Jesus points to the innocence and trustfulness and instinctive joy of a child as qualities needed for entrance into the kingdom. Jesus holds out his arms to welcome and embrace those who are childlike. On the other hand, there is nothing good about the death of a child. Even when a child is badly crippled or in pain and death is a merciful release, there is nothing good about the whole set of circumstances. More clearly, perhaps, at the death of a child than at any dying, there is a mystery in this evil that cannot be explained and should not be explained away. The gospel does not offer explanations; it tells us only that God shares our pain. That is good news, but it still requires of us a response of faith and trust. We respond to God's love, not God's logic. There is no reason to try to sidestep the evil. It can be faced. God has faced it for us and will give us all the strength we need to face it with him.

c. *Jesus and children.* The central message here is that Jesus will not let children be separated from him. His disciples roused his anger by even attempting such action. We cannot separate children from Jesus, nor can death itself. Jesus embraced no one but children anywhere in the gospel, but he drew them into his arms. He still does.

5. Mark 15:33-39; 16:1-8 ♦ "He has been raised; he is not here"

a. *Jesus' death.* The death of Jesus is central to the Christian faith. We are baptized into his death. Therefore, while the story of Jesus' death may seem an unusual choice for a funeral reading, it does, in fact, bring us face to face with the only story which gives our own death meaning and significance. Some may prefer to read only the second part of this passage, the sixteenth chapter, but where circumstances are such that a congregation seems likely to be able to absorb some real theology, a more important text to consider would be hard to imagine.

Oddly, though the significance of Christ's death is central to Christian belief, there has never been a single, universally accepted explanation of its meaning and value. One modern interpretation which may be helpful is that of Karl Rahner who points out, first of all, that human death "is never *merely* a natural process."[10] Death is a natural event, of course, but it also brings each human life to fulfillment and completion. Thus, death involves a "simultaneity of fulfillment and emptiness, of actively achieved and passively suffered, of full self-possession and of being completely dispossessed of self."[11] It is in Christ's death that we see this double character most completely. The words of Jesus at the moment of death in St. John's gospel, "It is finished," express it well (John 19:30). In St. Mark's gospel, we have the cry of abandonment and human emptiness balanced by the centurion's witness to a life filled with divinity. Our human deaths also have this double character, though imperfectly. It is the imperfection, the lack of completion and fulfillment, that darkens and saddens the event. It is the joining of our death with Jesus' death, that enables us to hope for fulfillment and completion for our humanity also.

A homily dealing with these themes might refer back to the moment of baptism in which our lives are first linked with Jesus' life, and our death with his death. "Baptism," says Rahner, "makes Christian death possible."[12] All life, after baptism, has the double character we have referred to: it finds fulfillment in self-emptying, in being directed toward others. The fulfillment of Christian life is discovered precisely in dying to self. Christ's death, then, is not only an example for us of obedience and trust, but the event in which our own death finds its completion. Our sadness at death is related primarily to death as a natural process, but Christians understand death as something more, and that knowledge provides hope and joy.

b. *Jesus' resurrection.* While St. Mark's account of the resurrection seems strangely incomplete because it includes no story of the appearance of the risen Lord, that very fact may make it the best resurrection narrative to read at a funeral. This is not an overpowering account of triumph, but a quiet, mysterious narrative which leaves many questions open and unanswered—as dying always does. (The use of verse 8, while not suggested by standard lec-

---

[10] Rahner, Karl, *On the Theology of Death*, p.38
[11] Ibid., p.40.
[12] Ibid., p.75.

tionaries, would seem useful to emphasize this note of mystery and unanswered questions.) Friends and family, at the time of death, are often in very much the position of the women at the tomb: confronted by events beyond understanding, afraid, and unable to tell others what they have seen and hope and feel.

This is an account of the resurrection which centers attention on the feelings of those who are left. How do they — how do we — go on from this point? It is helpful to understand that the resurrection is not presented as an instantly understood and transforming event. The framework within which life is to be lived has been radically transformed, but human lives are not changed overnight. It takes time to understand and assimilate traumatic events. This story "gives us permission" to be confused and fearful while reminding us that those who start at that point can go on to bear witness to the power of God, can experience the resurrection at work in their own lives, and can transform the world.

6. Luke 7:11-16 ♦ "The dead man sat up and began to speak"

There is a dramatic contrast between passages from the epistles suggested for funerals and those from the gospels. The epistles teach us about the meaning of death and the promise of life, but the gospels show God's will demonstrated in concrete situations. I Thessalonians 4:18 says "Comfort one another." This passage shows Jesus giving comfort. The epistles provide exhortation. The gospels provide example. This gospel passage demonstrates two things: 1) God's compassion, and 2) God's power.

a. *"...he had compassion for her..."* (v.13). Sometimes we think that the creator of the universe has everything planned to perform just as he wants it to; that death and evil are "God's will." But Jesus again and again responds to evil and death not by justifying God's ways but by tears (John 11:35), compassion, and even anger (Mark 3:5). God can indeed bring good out of evil, but God shares our pain at the evil.

b. *"...I say to you, rise"* (v.14). Jesus' own resurrection needs to be placed in context of stories like this and the raising of Lazarus. If Jesus had raised others and not been raised himself or if he had been raised but not others, these events would have little meaning for us. We should not dismiss Jesus' resurrection as insufficient on the grounds that "he was not like us," but there is a temptation to do it nonetheless. Jesus' resurrection combined with this story and others clearly demonstrates God's power over death and God's will that all people be set free from death's power and restored to life.

7. Luke 24:13-16, 28-35 (or 24:13-35) ♦ "Made known to them in the breaking of the bread"

a. How do we know the truth of the resurrection? The first disciples were only slowly convinced. We can see the process at work in this passage. First, there were reports from others who say they had seen an empty tomb, but that does nothing to break their sadness (vv.22-24). Second, Jesus walked with them, but they failed to recognize him (vv.15-16). Third, Jesus "was opening the scriptures" (vv.27, 32) with the result that they wanted to hear more (v.29). These disciples recognized after the fact that their hearts had burned within them as he spoke to them (v.32). Fourth, they invited him to stay with them and they knew him "in the breaking of the bread" (vv.29, 30, 35). Then, finally, "their eyes were opened," they knew him, and immediately set off to tell others (vv.31, 33).

Conviction of the resurrection comes slowly and against the deep resistance of human instinct. Reports from others, scripture, and sacraments have a cumulative impact. Jesus is at work in all of them, but we may recognize him as present only late in the process. Yet when we do recognize him, we have to share the news with others because that recognition carries with it the conviction that death has been conquered and life will never be the same again.

b. *"...Made known to them in the breaking of the bread"* (v.35). This verse may be worth discussing especially if a eucharist is a part of the funeral service. The "breaking of the bread" or "fraction" is a very brief moment in the eucharist, but so significant to the first Christians that they knew the whole service by that name (Acts 2:42). Once they had known Jesus' presence by his voice and appearance, but now a symbolic action communicated his presence. So, too, the bereaved must make a transition and change their relationship with the one who has died. What was once a matter of physical appearance, a kiss, a handshake, an embrace, must now be a matter of memories, photographs, and keepsakes. In the time of separation it seems to be all we have left. But it is not all. We still have in the eucharist a shared life conveyed by physical symbols. Jesus' followers had more than memories or they would have gone back to their fishing. They knew his presence in the breaking of the bread and shared his life still in the eucharistic bread and wine. The deceased once received that life in the eucharist but now shares it fully in the kingdom. And we, joining in the eucharist, are still joined with the departed in this common life which we share. The breaking of the bread reminds us of divisions overcome, life shared, and a reuniting promised.

8. John 5:19-25 ♦ "The Son gives life to whomever he wishes"

a. *"...Anyone who does not honor the Son does not honor the Father who sent him...."* (v.23). It is worth noting that in the verses just before this passage Jesus has called God his "Father" and so provoked the anger of his audience because to call God his Father was "making himself equal with God" (v.18). They understood that a son inherits his father's nature and that the actions of one are the actions of the other. Death illustrates this truth to us from the other side. Our human lives are bound up with each other by many ties, but most of all by family. "Every man's death diminishes me," wrote John Donne, but most particularly do we feel diminished by the death of a family member. In their death we feel our own since so many of our habits, so much of our nature, was shared with the one who has died. Death makes us aware of the way in which life is shared. That awareness, in turn, can help us see how God has acted in Christ to bring us life. It is the fact that Jesus shared God's nature that enables us also to share the divine nature. Baptism incorporates us into the body of Christ and, if Christ is the Son of God, then we share the divine nature through him. But the promise is more than that. One might think that the divine nature we have received will live and the human nature we inherited will die. On the contrary, since the human nature which Jesus took in his human birth was raised with him, our human nature also will be raised to new life. Thus, at a funeral, as we realize our human links with the departed, we can remember that those links are not broken. We are still bound to those who have died by our humanity as well as by Christ's divinity. The human bonding is now broken for a time by the barrier of death and that is the reason for grief. But we are still linked in the communion of saints and will be reunited with them at last. Our human unity helps us understand Jesus' unity with the Father through which our lives are given the deeper unity which transcends death and gives us the promise of life.

b. "...*Anyone who hears my word and believes him who sent me, has eternal life,...*" (v.24). There is a tension in the gospel between the "already" and the "not yet." Because the "not yet" is so evident, we do well to remember the "already." The signs of the kingdom are already present in the lives of Christians and in the church but the promise in itself transforms life already. Suppose you were in a lifeboat with other victims of an accident at sea and just before your only radio went dead you heard a message that said, "We have sighted your boat and help is on the way." Immediately life is transformed by that knowledge. There is no need to hoard and ration your limited supplies of food and water and no need to be fearful. You can relax and help others to relax because you know everything will be all right. In that important sense we "have" eternal life. Death must still be faced, but there is nothing to fear and, since there is nothing to fear, our lives are transformed now.

9. John 5:24-29 (or 5:24-27) ♦ "The dead will hear the voice of the Son of God"

The relationship between Father and Son is developed here in a way that makes clear their unity. When we come to Jesus and know him, we know God himself. This has a double significance: all the power of God is present in Jesus, and God is shown to be a personal God. In our need we find the strength we lack and we find the personal caring that makes that strength approachable. For most of us our experience of others seldom finds these two together. There are people with great power, but not accessible to us, and there are people of great sympathy who have little ability to help. In Jesus, the power of God has come near to us, and the God who first brought life into being promises new life to the dead.

10. John 6:35-40 (or 6:37-40) ♦ "And I will raise them up on the last day"

a. *"All that the Father gives,..."* It would be possible to spoil the impact of this passage by asking logical questions about it. Does the phrase "all that the Father gives me" imply that some are not given? Does "the last day" imply an interim period of waiting for those who die now? But the thrust of the language here is in a different direction. "Everything that the Father gives me will come to me" (v.37) stresses the inevitability of our coming to Christ. "I will raise him up at the last day" is a promise that runs through this passage like a refrain. It is repeated four times (vv.39, 40, 44, 54). The cumulative stress of this repetition is on the certainty that Jesus will accomplish what he has promised. At the time of death, the stress should be on the inclusiveness and certainty of the promise made, not on the secondary questions.

b. *"...I am the Bread of Life...."* (v.35). Many Christians will understand this phrase as a reference to the eucharist but others will see it simply as a vivid image like "the door" (John 10:7) and "the Good Shepherd" (John 10:11) meant to express the centrality of Jesus in the believer's life. Either way it is the kind of imagery we need most at the time of death. The physical reality of the deceased is gone but the reality of Jesus' presence is like bread and water to our need. If the funeral is a requiem eucharist, this reality will be central to the service and our need for tangible evidence of God's presence with us will be provided at the altar.

c. *"...Everything that the Father gives me..."* (v.37). Human beings, not unnaturally, tend to feel insecure about their relationship with God. What right have we to imagine that the creator of the universe would take an interest in us? Undoubtedly some of the grief we feel at the time of death is related to that insecurity. But Jesus tells us that we are God's gift to him—a gift, not a mere responsibility. Parents of small children normally consider them a gift, though they are also an enormous burden and responsibility. So God sees us as a joy and a gift in spite of all our failures. The gospel gives us every reason to be confident in offering back to God the lives of those we love. God loves them too.

d. *"This is indeed the will of my Father..."* In verses 39-40 the overwhelming stress is on God's will that we not be lost and on Jesus' promise to raise us to new life. In praying for those we love, we are asking God to do what God has always wanted to do, that is, bring us home for ever. God's will, accomplished in Christ, is to give us life. Our failures and blindness are to be placed in a balance with God's will. Our fears and doubts only have basis if they outweigh our faith in God's will. This passage breathes the confidence that God's purpose will be achieved—good news to proclaim when death seems to have won a victory.

11. John 10:11-16 ♦ "I lay down my life for the sheep"

One of the sources of grief at death is our lack of knowledge of each other. We wish we had known the one who died better, but somehow it seems as if we never gave it the time or attention it would have needed. We have the feeling that we haven't listened enough, haven't cared enough. The fact is that all human relationships are flawed and incomplete and no amount of time or caring is likely to produce complete satisfaction.

The image of the Good Shepherd, on the other hand, commends itself to us because it reflects the kind of knowing and caring we wish we could find and give. "I know my own," says Jesus, and we know that he does know each of us, that he is a personal Lord and Savior.

The image of Christ as the Good Shepherd inevitably reminds us also of Psalm 23 which refers to the "valley of the shadow of death"[13] and tells us that even there the Good Shepherd is with us and we need not fear. Not only so, but Jesus laid down his life for the sheep. He not only walks with us through the valley of death, he has gone through it before us and for our sake. He knows us, goes with us, and has faced our worst fears and conquered them.

12. John 11:17-27 (or 11:21-27) ♦ "I am the resurrection and the life"

No other story in the gospels shows us so fully how Jesus dealt with bereavement and grief; they provide a useful pattern both for ministry and for a homily. First, Jesus comes to be with the bereaved. Friends have already gathered to be with Mary and Martha, and Jesus adds his presence to theirs. Personal presence is a priority. Without it no ministry is possible. But presence opens us to pain. Jesus himself faces Martha's accusation that he might have come sooner and been more helpful. In our pain, we lash out even at those who want to be helpful. We cannot be helpful without understanding that this may be so and accepting it. Jesus accepts the accusation and moves the conversation forward with a dogmatic assertion of faith: "your brother will rise again." There are obvious, fundamental truths, which we know but need to hear repeated by others. They do not assuage our grief, they remind us of the faith without which our grief would be hopeless. Martha responds with an act of faith which, nonetheless, leaves her without immediate comfort: "I know my brother will rise...on the last day" (v.24). Faith, as intellectual affirmation, provides no comfort. Therefore Jesus draws Martha to himself saying, "I am the resurrection and the life" (v.25). Martha is directed to Jesus' presence rather than Lazarus' absence. Neither human presence and consolation nor the acceptance of creedal faith can fill the void in our lives. Jesus can. Perhaps this shows the difference between our consoling presence and his transforming presence. At last we need to be directed be-

---

[13] The NRSV says, "...the darkest valley..." The older translations may be less faithful to the Hebrew, but they are entirely faithful to Christian experience.

yond ourselves, beyond the one we have lost, to a power and presence always adequate to our need and from whom we cannot be separated.

13. John 12:24-26 ♦ "Those who love their life lose it"

a. *"...Unless a grain of wheat falls into the earth and dies, it remains just a single grain;..."* (v.24). A paraphrase of this verse might be, "A grain of wheat is simply a grain of wheat unless you plant it." It might equally well be said, "It is simply a grain of wheat until you grind it." A grain of wheat has no value unless it is used either for planting or for baking; to produce the next year's crop or to nourish life. Either way, buried or ground to powder, it loses its own identity and fulfills its purpose. Human life, Jesus suggests, is not very different from this. We can try to keep ourselves uninvolved but then how would we be alive? A life with meaning and purpose is one which becomes involved in the lives of others and is inevitably hurt and sometimes crushed, but those who give themselves most fully are those whose lives accomplish most. "I am involved in mankind," said John Donne, and that involvement means dying to self. "Those who love their life lose it," because the joy of life is in the giving and the losing.

This text can clearly be used to reflect on the meaning that can be found in the deaths of those who have truly given their life for others. It should be noticed that this giving process begins in baptism. There we are buried in water as a grain of wheat is buried in the soil and so made part of life's process. We are no longer alone; we are joined with others in the body of Christ; our life begins to interact with others and so, though we die in the process, we begin to grow and bear fruit.

b. Even more plainly, Jesus says, *"Those who serve me must follow me"* (v.26). These words appear in John's gospel as Jesus approaches his own death. To follow him is to go to Jerusalem with him and die with him. And yet to die with Christ is something completely different from merely dying since Christ's death leads to resurrection. The path we began to follow at baptism is one which leads not simply *to* death but *through* death to eternal life.

14. John 14:1-6 ♦ "Do not let your hearts be troubled"

a. Separation is the cause of "troubled hearts." How can we advise people at the time of death not to be troubled? Jesus himself was "troubled" as he looked forward to separation from his disciples. Being troubled in heart is evidence of love.

There is a technical point to be noted here about language. John speaks three times of Jesus being "troubled" (11:33, 12:27, 13:21). He says that Jesus was troubled in "soul" (*psyche*) and "spirit" (*pneuma*) while he quotes Jesus as saying "Let not your hearts (*kardia*) be troubled." Some translations do not observe these distinctions so that it appears that Jesus was "troubled in heart" not long before he advised his disciples not to be. On the other hand, John often varies his use of language for stylistic reasons and not to make a theological point. Not all scholars may agree, but it seems legitimate to speak of Jesus as sharing the turmoil of feelings which is the normal human response to approaching death and separation from those we love.

b. In life we move on and accept separation in order to respond to greater love. A child's love of parents doesn't end, but separation is accepted in order to respond to the love found in marriage. We accept (perhaps tearfully) separation from our children when they move out into marriage. So we can grieve at our separation while still understanding it as necessary if we are to know fully and personally the love of God in Christ. Jesus can tell the disciples not to be troubled because he can assure them of the greater love they will know in God's presence.

Those we love, from whom we are separated by death, enter into that place of deeper relationships and greater love. We are still united with them in Christ and at the altar. The question presented here is, "How do we deal with grief?" Christians don't avoid grief, but they do have resources to deal with it.

c. *"...Believe in God, believe also in me...."* (v.1). (The Greek word *pisteuo* is sometimes translated trust and should be understood to include a range of meaning including believing, trusting, and placing confidence in. The verb here could be either indicative or imperative and legitimately translated as a command or a statement of fact. Other standard translations say, "You believe in God, believe also in me.")

Many people build their lives around work and family. These are excellent reference points in purely human terms but not enduring. So it is not unusual to hear of people who retire one week and die the next, or of husbands and wives who die within days or months of each other. No one can live without a foundation or meaning for life: a job to do, a family to support, a love to rely on. What do we do when the love we relied on is gone? Christians believe in God as do most religious people, but Christians believe also in Jesus. Our faith is personal and based on direct relationship with the one we believe in. Jesus offers us a personal love and an undying life, a basis for continuing to live, here and hereafter.

d. *"...In my Father's house there are many dwelling places"* (v.2). The King James Version says "many mansions" (though "mansion" in those days might have been only a room in a cottage). This may convey the sense better to the modern ear than the RSV "rooms" or NRSV "dwelling places." The latter sounds small, but mansions sounds spacious. The sense is of spaciousness, room for all.

Some of our church buildings have many rooms and we can often draw people into those rooms whom we can never draw into the worship area. In that sense, at least, (though we try zealously to get people from the "outer courts" into the church itself) the church may be like heaven. Perhaps the question of what room we are in is less important to God than to us.

There's a message here for those who judge others on the basis of the room they are in; a message for those who fear that God's judgment may be too narrow. Our judgment may be narrow, but God's is not. Jesus promises to prepare a place for us, not set up standards to keep us out. This is a message of hope and love, not judgment and fear.

e. *"...If it were not so, would I have told you..."* (v.2). God is reliable. He wants us to know. He sends messengers of every kind to let us know his love and his care for us. We have the record in the gospel, we have the message in the church, we have Christ's continuing presence in the sacrament. Would God have sent us these messages, expressed the message in all these ways, if it were not so? God is trustworthy, reliable; we have no reason to doubt or fear.

f. *"...I go to prepare a place for you...."* (v.2). This seems to be spoken to each individual personally, "A place for *you*". The picture is not of an anonymous heaven with masses of people but a heaven in which each one of us is known and valued and where the door stands open and ready for each one.

g. *"...[I] will take you to myself..."* (v.3). The Christian faith is centered on a personal relationship with Jesus. It is not a doctrine or a system so much as a relationship into which we are drawn. This relationship reaches completion only hereafter. To come at last into Jesus' presence and know the fullness of his love: that is the purpose of this relationship and death opens the door to the completion.

h. *"...You know the way...I am the way,..."* (vv.4-6). In the early days the church was called "the Way" (Acts 9:2 et al) not only because it seemed to be a method, a way, of living, but because Christians alone seemed to know where they were going. Someone has said that "The best kept inns are on the through roads." It's the people who are going somewhere who make a difference along the way. Jesus is the Way not simply because he provides us a road to travel but because he gives us a goal toward which to move. So we move toward him with him. We never walk alone. Those who have died are not alone, nor are we. Indeed, our separation from those we love can draw us closer to Jesus' love, and through him to those who have died and are now nearer to him than they were before.

i. *"...No one comes to the Father except through me...."* (v.6). This saying sounds narrow, but it needs to be taken in context with verse 2—"In my Father's house are many rooms." Have you ever seen a picture of Jesus with his arms folded or hands closed? We see him most often with arms outstretched and reaching out to the whole human race. St. John calls Jesus "the light that enlightens everyone" (1:7). Whatever light we have comes from him and whoever responds to that light is responding to Christ by whatever name. St. John also says, "God did not send the Son into the world to condemn the world, but in order that the world might be saved through him" (3:17). When we come together at the time of death, we offer both our prayers and the one who has died to him who died for their salvation.

Death for some is a journey into the dark and the unknown. For Christians—all who have responded to the light—it is a response to a personal invitation to come home to the one we know. It is a response to Christ, who knows us already and calls us to himself.

15. John 20:1-9 ♦ "Mary Magdalene came to the tomb"

The story of Jesus' resurrection is, obviously, one of the most appropriate and powerful lessons that could be chosen for a funeral, especially in Easter season. It is only because of Jesus' resurrection that we can face death with confidence. One human life passed through death and, as a result, all life is changed. Perhaps the most telling sentence in this passage is the last verse, "as yet they did not understand the scripture,..." (v.9). This story tells of disciples who doubted because they had no expectation of resurrection. They had not read the Old Testament with that in mind. Therefore they came to the tomb with no expectation and were persuaded of the resurrection without the advantage of a reasoned framework of understanding. Reading the rest of the New Testament we become aware of the enormous change that has taken place since that original Easter morning. In the first years of the church's life, the disciples ransacked the Scripture to find all the clues they had missed. The result of that work is a New Testament studded with evidence of God's eternal purpose drawn from the Law, the Psalms, and the Prophets.

We lack the immediate experience of seeing the empty tomb and the risen Lord, but we do have the great advantage of the early church's exploration of scripture and the deepened understanding that has come through 2000 years of Christian living. Is it better to have the experience or the reasoned understanding? Our experience may be secondhand, but it is real and, now, of enormous diversity. Our faith is grounded on both experience and understanding and both begin here at the empty tomb.

III. Funeral Homilies

A. Death in the Midst of Life

Dorothy Lewis was director of the Altar Guild and a deeply devoted member of the church. In her early fifties she was stricken suddenly with cancer. Surgery was impossible and radiation treatment succeeded only in extending her life for about a year. She planned her own funeral except for the lessons and asked that the vestments be white and the mood one of joy.

"For everything there is a season, and a time for every matter under heaven" ♦ (Ecclesiastes 3:1)

There is, the Bible tells us, "a time for every matter under heaven; a time to be born, and a time to die;...a time to mourn, and a time to dance;...a time to embrace, and a time to refrain from embracing;..." What time is this? What time is it today? Is it, for example, a time for doubt or a time for faith? I could argue it both ways.

It is, inevitably, a time to question. What sort of world is it in which those we love are taken from us too soon; in which the good die young and those who have much still to give are allowed so little time in which to do it? The Bible itself is full of such questions. The psalmist asks, "How long, O Lord? Will you hide yourself forever? How long will your wrath burn like fire?" (89:46) Jesus himself asked "My God, my God, why have you forsaken me" (Matthew 27:46). Doubt and faith in the Bible are like two sides of the same coin. Because there is faith, there is doubt. Because God is known, God is questioned. A world without God would be a world without questions but, because the Bible tells us about a God of love, we ask, we doubt, we question. And so we should, because these doubts and questions draw us into a dialogue with the God who wants that dialogue and that relationship with us more than anything else.

We are here with our doubts because of our faith. This is a time to ask and therefore a time to believe.

Is it a time of separation or a time to gather? It is clearly a time of separation. The physical bonds that have held us have been dissolved. We cannot any longer touch and hold and embrace. There is an absolute form of separation. We are divided, alone, bereft. And yet look how that very division has brought us together.

Only under such stress do we really affirm our unity, tell each other how much we love them, say out loud what we seldom take time to say at all about how much their love means to us. This is, therefore, inevitably a time for gathering and, indeed, the separation that grieves us is itself a means of unity. Death is a separation from those who have died but, for the one who has died, death means a coming together with those who have already gone on, and that gathering is, of course, far greater than this separation. To be together today as a family, an Altar Guild, a parish, a community, is precisely to notice and remember those who are no longer here who were once so vital a part of our lives. And yes, they are divided from us, but not from each other, and certainly not divided from the Lord who loves them and has called them to come to him. And this is the place above all others where we are united with them now. In the words of the prayer we will say in a few minutes, we are here "with angels and archangels and with all the company of heaven." We are gathered here and united with them in love and fed at God's altar with the same food which is our common life.

Is it a time to mourn or a time to rejoice? Our instincts draw us both ways. How can we help being grieved? Quite apart from the sickness and death that have come to one we cared for and loved, we are sorry for ourselves because our own lives have been diminished, part of ourselves is gone. And yet Dorothy herself asked us to rejoice, to be glad; not so much, I think, because the sickness is ended and all pain put away but because life is always a gift and fifty years of living is a great gift and it would be a shame to spoil that gift by any failure to rejoice and give thanks to its creator for the gift God has given us all.

What time is it today? A time of mixed feelings and many emotions, a time to be separated and a time to gather, a time for doubt and a time for faith, a time to mourn and a time to rejoice, a time above all else to give God back the gift God gave to us with all our gratitude and all our love and all our praise.

B. Liturgy and Life

Gordon Newcombe had been a member of the parish since the age of seven and a lay reader for most of his adult life. He had been headmaster of a well-known private school and a gardener in his spare time. He loved to visit Wales, the land of his birth and photograph its castles and ancient churches. In his parish, he had served in every position of parish leadership, but he loved the liturgy above everything else. On his last Sunday in church, weakened by a three-year battle against cancer, he was able to come to the lectern and read from the fortieth chapter of Isaiah. His son read the same passage at his funeral a few weeks later.

"All flesh is grass...the grass withers, the flower fades, but the word of our God shall stand for ever" ♦ **(Isaiah 40:8)**

In the First English Prayer Book, the opening sentences of the burial service included a quotation from the book of Job: "We brought nothing into this world and it is certain we can carry nothing out." These words were always read until the 1979 **Book of Common Prayer** appeared without them. In my more cynical moments, I've pointed that out to people and asked whether it indicates that we have new information. And then a couple of days ago, I was thinking about it for some reason and suddenly realized that we do have new information. I realized that those words of Job are not the whole story. Yes, from a certain point of view, "we brought nothing into this world" and it is still very "certain we can carry nothing out." And that is something we all need to learn and remember. Material things have no lasting value. We need to learn again and again to let go, let go, let go of the material things that entrance us but that do not last.

Now that is a very familiar lesson for some of us. An English philosopher once said, "The purpose of a liberal arts education is to enable one to despise the wealth it prevents one from acquiring." So that part of it is made relatively easy for a schoolmaster for example. But still we do reach out for, admire, enjoy, contemplate, this world's beauty in whatever form it may be available to us: in music, in art, antiquities, books, an ancient cathedral or castle, our own garden. And we should. We were created for that purpose. These material things are God's creation, and all God made is very good.

Our calling is to be priests of this creation. All of us are called to reach out and take in, and then (and this is the part we resist) to appreciate thankfully, to share, to offer up, to give back to God the creator these good things which God made for our use. We are to take, to enjoy, and, most importantly, to offer. And as we do that something happens. The material world, as we do that, is transformed into what we refer to as spiritual.

It's hard to say exactly what that means but somehow the encounter with the good things of this world which leads us to offer them creates a change in them and in us. We are changed by offering. The child who comes squalling into the world concerned for nothing but food and sleep, who instinctively grabs away from others whatever attracts, who sets out to acquire property and possessions, almost inevitably somewhere along the way is drawn by love and begins to sense another perspective, and learns to care, to share, to give, to sacrifice, and so acquires—in or around or even in spite of material things—wisdom, compassion, judgment, integrity, honor, devotion. These are immaterial things, spiritual things, which we did not bring into this world but which we can and do carry out. These do not die. We do take them with us, and we also leave them behind. It's a kind of alchemy turning base metals into gold, the grass of the field into poetry and praise. And we are changed in the process, and the world is enriched in the process, and the kingdom of God is enriched by those who come into it bringing with them such gifts.

This process is also called "liturgy." We are sent into the world, as I said, to be priests of creation, to be liturgists, for what we do here in the liturgy is a paradigm of life, of life's meaning and purpose. We begin with wheat and grapes, basic foodstuff, and we process them into bread and wine, which are better food, more life-enhancing. But instead of sitting down to make a meal of them, we offer them, we give them away, and God takes them and makes of them something more, spiritual food, which then are given back to us as nourishment not simply for the body but also for the soul, nourishment not for this life but for eternal life.

Now, I could tell you today the story of a small boy who wandered into this church almost 60 years ago and discovered that pattern of life and in that pattern found something to give life a richer, fuller purpose and center, and whose life was transformed by that discovery, for whom life became liturgy and liturgy became life. But I think you know that story— or at least the outcome of it—and that's why you've come here today. And many of us have made that same discovery, and that story, therefore, is ours as well. So I don't need to tell you that story. We will tell it to each other. But what we do need to do today is to go on to complete that story because that story comes to fulfillment and completion here in the transition from death to life, in the giving up and putting away, the offering and transforming of this transient life into a new life of God's creation, a life which will endure.

Ladislaus Boros has said that "man is the being that can die into God."[14] We are that part of God's creation in whom that marvelous alchemy is at work so that in offering, in the giving of ourselves, we become something far

---

[14] Boros, Ladislaus, "Has Life a Meaning?", p.16.

more, far finer, something in whom God's own glory can begin to be seen. And at last that process is completed by dying into God, carrying back to God something more than the sum of all we have touched and held, and leaving behind us for others far more than we brought into this life at the beginning.

And that's why we are here today: to offer our thankfulness for the life God gave us in Gordon Newcombe, and for the life which Gordon offered back to God and shared with us. That's why this liturgy is a celebration in which our joy outweighs our pain.

C. Assassination

The assassination of John F. Kennedy was a traumatic event in the lives of all Americans. Many churches held special services and a requiem eucharist was celebrated in my parish as well. It was a time that required something to be said and, in the trauma of the moment, the words I found to say still seem to me as good a summing up of the Christian understanding of death as I have ever been able to articulate. I set it out in blank verse because it seems to fall into a pattern of speech-rhythms more marked than those in most sermons. (Because this was written when it was, and because the choice of pronouns was controlled by the fact that it was a man's death we were marking, the word "him" is used where today I would use inclusive language. To modify this now, however, would either destroy the original rhythms or require such extensive rewriting as make it almost a new homily.)

"Do you not know that all of us who have been baptized into Christ Jesus were baptized into his death" ♦ **(Romans 6:3)**

When a child is born,
his parents, desiring to do the best thing possible
take the child to the church
and place him in God's hands.

The child is seldom old enough to be aware of what happens.
What is done, is done for him by his family and friends
and by the whole family of God.
They say in effect:
>   We cannot give this child all he will need in life.
>   We cannot teach him, guide him, direct him,
>   defend him, strengthen him,
>   as we would like to do.
>   Our homes lack many of the things he will need.
>   So we bring him to a better home
>   and place him in better hands.
>   We bring him to the house of God
>   and place him in God's hands.

Throughout life, as we grow, each Christian person
will need to reaffirm that decision time and again.

Each of us must recommit himself to God,
> place himself in God's hands,
> ask God to hold him still.

So at the end of life
it is no new thing that we do.
We said at the moment of baptism
that there is no life worth living apart from God.
We gave up our natural life,
> we buried it,
> for the sake of the fuller life which God gives,
> into which we were born
> at the moment of baptism.
The natural life is buried,
> and we place ourselves in God's hands.

And if all this is true,
> then death cannot change it.
The natural life ends,
> but we gave it up long ago.
The natural body is buried,
> but we symbolized long ago
> our intention to bury it
> in the waters of baptism.
We can have no life apart from God,
> but we said long ago
> there was nothing else we wanted
> and we have said there is no life we care for
> now or hereafter
> apart from God.

This world is good.
God made it.
But this house, this earth, has been spoiled
> by human failures and weakness.
There is much that we need and desire
> that we will never find here.

So at the end as at the beginning
> our family, our friends,
> the church of Christ,
> will act for us
Seeing they cannot do anything more for us,
> they will bring us to the house of God
> and place us in God's hands.

And the life that we must have is here:
> the life we accepted in baptism,

the life we have received again and again at God's altar,
the life that sustains and strengthens us,
the life that unites us with God and each other,
the life we still receive and share.

Death has no power here;
this is the house of Life.
We are not divided here;
this is the house of Unity.

We come here to offer again to God
ourselves, our souls and bodies,
and to place ourselves and those we love
once again in God's hands.
And the same God who took us in his hands
at the first moment of life
will take us again in his hands and hold us
now, and at the end of our mortal life
and in the power of his eternal life
forever.

D. Free At Last

When Calvin Holland became the Sexton, his wife, Mary, was a vivacious and active woman who joined her husband as part of the parish. Over the next ten years she endured a series of crippling strokes that limited her more and more until finally she died of cancer. The funeral on Easter Even inevitably joined thoughts of death and burial with thoughts of resurrection and renewal of life.

"If there is a physical body, there is also a spiritual body." ♦ (I Corinthians 15:44)

God made us for freedom,
and all we ever have here and now
is a taste of freedom,
a promise of things to come.
God gave us bodies,
and these bodies can weigh us down.
They can't do all we want them to do.
They keep us from knowing real freedom.
None of us can run as fast
or work as hard
or dance as smoothly
as we'd like to do.
Our bodies tie us down,
all of us,
some more than others.
Some of us will never be athletes

and some of us can't sing very well
or dance at all
and some of us have bodies
            that just wear out too soon.
We get crippled
        and we have to count on others
        and we aren't free
            even to do the normal things;
        it gets hard even to walk.
But God made us for freedom
        and we will be free.

This Saturday before Easter
        Jesus was buried,
            his body sealed in the tomb.
But tomorrow is Easter
        and we know what happened then:
God raised him up and set him free.
God gave him a body
        that didn't hold him down,
        that could go where he wanted to go:
                push aside the rock,
                    go through closed doors,
        be with his friends
            wherever they were.
God gave him a new body,
        a resurrection body,
            a body to set him free.
And that's the evidence
        that God can also give us freedom,
        new bodies to set us free.
"There is a natural body
and there is a spiritual body..."
There is a mortal body
and there is a resurrection body.
God promises us a body
        that will truly set us free.

Now, that doesn't mean we can accept it
        when we see people who aren't free now.
We can't say,
        "God will set him free someday,
        so we needn't do anything now."
No, that's why we have the church.
        The church is the people that know
            what God intends us for.

The church is here to help us
find freedom now.
The church is here to reach out
and help anyone we see
who doesn't have freedom:
if they're sick, to visit them,
if they're crippled, to support them,
if they're poor to share with them.
And the church is here to tell us about freedom
so we'll never be satisfied with anything less.
The gospel tells us
that God sent Jesus to set us free,
as free as we can be in this world.
And when it seems as if there's no more we can do,
then we know that God can do the rest.
He will give their freedom
to all those who have suffered here
and all those who have had
only a taste of freedom.
Suppose you've been in a hospital room with someone
and the day comes when they can go home.
You may be sorry to see them leave,
but you can be glad they're finally free.
It's that way now when someone dies
after a long and painful illness.
We'll miss them.
We'll really miss them.
But we can be glad they're finally free.

If we know a prisoner who's been set free,
we can't grieve for them.
They can begin again to live.
But we can grieve for ourselves
who are still so limited,
still so far from free,
still so unwilling
to set people free when we can.

We need now to work together
and pray together
for all those who could have freedom here
if we would only help.
Now is the time for us
to care for the sick and the crippled
and troubled and bereaved
and the poor and the unemployed:

to lift them up
and share with them
all the freedom we can
so that here and now
we can begin to know the freedom
Jesus wants us to have
and taste the freedom he will give us all
when we also come to him.

We come here today
to thank God for the promise of freedom
and to thank God for the knowledge
that sets us free also
from the fear of death,
because when Jesus died on Good Friday,
God gave him life again
and set him free.
And those who believe in him,
who belong to him,
are promised that same life
and that same freedom.
We give thanks today
for the promise of Easter;
the promise of freedom and life.

E. A Member of the Family

Helen Ritt was a very private person. She lived with her daughter and son-in-law for almost ten years and never really revealed herself—her inner emotions, her cares, her love. When she became terminally ill, her daughter and son-in-law thought that at last there would be a time for sharing, for getting to know each other and expressing their deep feelings. But critical illness seldom changes personalities. It may reveal them more fully, but we tend to remain who we are. Helen Ritt remained a private person to the end and those who cared for her were frustrated of their hopes. This homily was intended to speak to that frustration and to set it in the light of the Christian hope.

"The sting of death is sin and the power of sin is the law. But thanks be to God, who gives us the victory through our Lord Jesus Christ" ♦ **(I Corinthians 15:56-57)**

Why do we hurt when someone dies? St. Paul tells us exactly why toward the end of that long and marvelous passage from First Corinthians. "The sting of death is sin..." It wouldn't hurt if there weren't something wrong. Christians aren't supposed to fool themselves into thinking death doesn't hurt. It does. It always will. And it's our fault, our sin, that makes it hurt. But for Christians, that isn't the whole story. What we've done or failed to do makes it hurt. What God has done in Jesus gives us victory nonetheless.

There's a dialogue toward the end of Ingmar Bergman's movie, *Scenes From a Marriage,* that expresses some of this hurt. The wife is saying, "The trouble is, I've never been able to love anyone and no one has ever been able to love me." And her husband says, "Well, I love you in my inept, selfish way. And you love me in your domineering, demanding way. We do love each other, not perfectly, but that's the way we are."

I think Ingmar Bergman and St. Paul both make the same diagnosis of our situation. We are made for love. We want to be loved. We want to be able to love. We want that more than anything in the world. But we never learn to love or be loved perfectly. That's the way we are.

Now, there's nothing more frustrating than working at something year after year and never completing it. There's nothing more frustrating than working at something for a long, long time and then having someone take it away from you saying, "Here, let me finish that for you." We may remember that happening to us as children and probably we've done it to our own children. And now, it seems, God does it to us. The difference is that this time we really have done all we can and if we really want it finished, if we really want those we love to be loved perfectly, only God can do it.

Our love for each other is inept and clumsy, demanding, selfish, domineering, inadequate. What we want, what we need, is a love that's better than that and wiser than that and stronger than that. And finally, it isn't in us to give or receive such love. Finally, we have to turn to God to find it and we have to trust him to complete what we've begun.

We talk about being separated by death. The truth is, we are separated by life—by life the way we live it, inept, clumsy, imperfect—because we don't understand each other well enough and we don't understand ourselves well enough. And we never really overcome those limits in this life.

The sting and grief of death is that we've lost our last chance to overcome these human failures. But we always knew we would. Try as we will, no other outcome is possible, because we are human. We can't do it all. And that's what hurts. But what Christians know is that death saves us from our failures. Christian death is an act of trust: trusting God to complete what we have begun, knowing God is able to give the love we have tried to give and not given.

I think it's a little like the process of letting go of our children as they grow up. We've given them the best love we could, but it's not enough. A certain age comes and they need another kind of love which only someone else can give. And we want them to find that love and we're happy when they do find it. But it hurts a little that we couldn't give it. We want to do it all ourselves.

So, too, at death, those we love need another kind of love, better than we can give. And we want them to have it, but it hurts that they have to go to God for that love we failed to give. That's the sting. But for Christians, what matters is not the sting but the victory.

We know, Jesus has shown us, the cross and resurrection have shown us, the love God wants us to have. And we know, Jesus has shown us, the cross and resurrection have shown us, that God's love does and will complete and perfect all our failures. We have tried to give love, and now perfect love will be given, not our inept imitations. We have come here today to remember what Jesus has told us and shown us, and to place our lives and the lives of those we love in his hands, and give thanks for the victory he has given us. We ask him to help us now to trust him to complete our love for each other and to help us to love each other through him: to love each other through him and through him alone.

F. Judgment

Paul Aurell had been a prominent figure in the foreign community in Tokyo, but his life had been troubled by business reverses and personal difficulties. When he killed himself, I had been in that community only a short time and not known him well, but I knew that he had been at one time a very active member of the church and instrumental in its building. Why should one rash act at the end of life over-shadow all the good that has gone before? God, we may firmly trust, sees our whole life in a truer perspective than we can ever attain.

At the time of this event, the Book of Common Prayer *provided only three choices of readings and we chose Romans 8:14ff.*[15] *The verse about judgment (8:34) might have provided a text, and was cited in the homily, but II Corinthians 5:10 seemed to provide a sharper and clearer statement of the essential theme and therefore was used as a text for the homily though it was not read in the service.*

"For all of us must appear before the judgment seat of Christ" ♦ (II Corinthians 5:10)

There is, in the psalms and lessons used at a Christian funeral, a theme of judgment. This theme is not central, not dominant, but it is present and unmistakable. We shall all be judged. And why not? It is, after all, a basic doctrine of the Christian faith. We state in the Apostles Creed itself our belief that Jesus Christ will finally come to "judge the living and the dead." St. Paul states it in the most uncompromising terms: "We must all appear before the judgment seat of Christ." But why should we want to think about judgment now? Why? Because we have no greater source of confidence. Nothing gives us more reason for hope.

What does judgment imply? First of all, it implies value. How many paintings are made and books written that are never judged by the experts, never reviewed or criticized? How many are worth judging? How much of the world's work or our work is thought by others, even our friends, to be worth any kind of comment? But "we must all appear before the judgment seat of Christ." In God's sight, each of us is worthy of judgment. Our lives have value. "Your labor is not in vain in the Lord" (I Corinthians 15:57).

---

[15] See commentary on Romans 8:14ff above.

Secondly, judgment implies knowledge. When St. Paul says we will all be judged, he is arguing that we have no right at all to judge each other. In praising or blaming, how much do we ever know? When it comes to another human being's motives and inner thoughts, abilities and disabilities, you and I are incompetent judges, no better able to judge another than I am to judge modern sculpture or painting. Leave such judgment to those who are qualified, who can measure the work on the basis of long experience and true understanding. Leave judgment to the creator.

And thirdly, judgment implies a judge. "Who," asks St. Paul in the lesson we just read, "is in a position to condemn? Only Christ; and Christ died for us, Christ rose for us...Christ prays for us" (Romans 8:34). He is our judge, the Lord Jesus, and he knows so well our weakness that he offered himself on our behalf. He is our judge, and he has judged us already, and paid the price himself.

This is the confidence we have. No human judgment matters. Whether good or bad, no one knows us so well or loves us as much as the only judge we must face. We can live in that confidence and die in it. We can trust those we love to that judgment and give thanks for that confidence and hope.

G. Murder

The circumstances of this homily are described in the introduction to the wedding homily "H. A Common Language" given at Margaret Everson's marriage to Lawrence Fossi. The shock of the tragedy described there throws a new light on the way in which baptism, marriage, and burial are all a kind of dying. All are acts of trust through which we place our lives in God's hands.

"Let the word of Christ dwell in you richly" ♦ (Colossians 3:16)

Less than two years ago I stood here and spoke about language. Larry and Meg were on their way to Italy to absorb language and culture, and I suggested that that was a lot like marriage. We acquire, with time and exposure, the ability to express ourselves in new ways, to live in new relationships. Now we are here again, needing a language to express ourselves. We've been searching for ways these last few days to say what we feel. The shock, the grief, the sympathy we want to express are not easily put into words.

It's natural, I think, to feel unable to say what needs to be said. No matter how long we've lived, no matter how familiar we are with this world of ours, we still stammer and grope for words like foreigners in a new country. It's as if we can't adapt ourselves to a world like this, can't learn the language we need in order to live with it. And, in a sense, we ought not to learn it or ever feel at home in such a place.

But there is a language I've been hearing from many of you, and I believe it's the language we come here today to use. It's the language God teaches us through our faith. And even though we haven't completely mastered it, it seems right. It feels like the language, the way of living, that we were really meant for. It's the language of thankfulness and trust and love which can look tragedy in the face and say, "Even so. This terrible event has happened, but even so there is much to be thankful for and that is what finally matters."

You see, we know something not everyone knows. And that is that life and love and talent and happiness are gifts, wonderful gifts. And the right response to gifts is a response of thankfulness always. In the words of the liturgy, "It is right, and a good and joyful thing, always and everywhere to give thanks..." Always, no matter what the circumstances, always to give thanks.

Not everyone is able to see it that way or respond that way. It's hard. It's a language we have to learn and it isn't easy. One way we learn it is by coming here and taking part in a liturgy that gives us words to say and hymns to sing. We learn to use words of thankfulness and to offer back to God everything God gives us. And gradually it becomes more and more natural to use this language. It becomes part of us. We talk differently because we are different. We speak of thankfulness because we are thankful.

And then when tragedy comes and words fail us, we begin to realize that we do have words to say after all. Not about this society of ours. Words to describe that are better left unsaid. Some things really are "unspeakable." No, the words we have to say are the words that express our underlying faith and our lasting thankfulness: the things that endure and uphold and sustain us.

This, too, is a world we are still learning about and with which none of us is as familiar and comfortable as we ought to be. But I think we do know that this is the language we most need and the world for which we were made. This is the language that enables us even now to thank God for all his gifts and, in particular, for the gift of life and love and happiness in Margaret Everson Fossi, and to offer that gift back, place it in God's keeping, knowing that God will keep and hold that gift for us now and forever.

H. Suicide

When the parish undertook sponsorship of a group home for the mentally retarded, John Paul Castagna was one of those who helped convince a reluctant community that this experiment would work. Cheerful and outgoing, he taught us that "retarded" is not a very useful label. Slow in some ways, he was quick in others and became involved in village life in several constructive roles. Perhaps, however, the cheerfulness concealed a deeper despair that he could function so well in some ways but not in others. And perhaps that helps explain why he woke up one day and killed himself by jumping from the balcony of the group apartment. John Paul's family took him home for burial but his adoptive community also requested a memorial service as an opportunity to give thanks to God for the life he had shared with them. Because this was a community event and included many non-church members, it seemed important to state a rationale for the lack of the eulogy which some would have expected.

"Beloved, we are God's children now; what we will be has not yet been revealed. What we do know is this: when he is revealed, we will be like him, for we will see him as he is" ♦ **(I John 3:1-2)**

There is a very strong tradition in the church against eulogies. Nothing should be done, the theory goes, to make a difference between people at the time of death. We are all equal in the sight of God and so there should be the same service, the same words, the same liturgy for everyone.

It's tempting to make an exception for John Paul, to say, "He was special." And he was special. But that would not only break a strong tradition, it would go against the whole purpose of our community residence. What we've been learning these last few years is that people are people. No one person is more special or less special, more precious than another or less precious than another.

We've been learning, I believe—and John Paul helped teach us—what God has been trying to teach humankind for a good long while: what matters is the love that all of us need and all of us are able to give. So let me do what I believe we should be doing now and that is to think about the love of God, about the way God loves us and the way God asks us to respond.

There are wonderful words in the passage just read from the First Epistle of John: "Beloved, we are God's children now; what we will be has not yet been revealed. What we do know is this: when he is revealed, we will be like him, for we will see him as he is."

That's a definition of who we are: God's children. And children are, by definition, an unfinished product. We ask children, "What are you going to be when you grow up?" They are in the process of becoming something new and neither they nor we can usually guess what that will be. But we know there is a potential to be many things, to grow in many different ways, to acquire many new abilities. And most of us along the way come to realize that however much we grow and learn, there will still always be more. We will probably never become as skilled as we would like to be as administrators, teachers, performers. There's much that will always lie beyond us.

There is a juggler in Ingmar Bergman's movie, *The Seventh Seal*, who says his son will learn "the one impossible trick."[16] None of us ever becomes all that he or she would like to become. The one impossible trick always lies just beyond our abilities.

One of the things that makes human beings different from other forms of life lies exactly here: that we have so much longer a period of childhood, of growth, of development. In a sense, perhaps, we never do fully grow up. We never do achieve completion.

St. Paul speaks of growing into a mature person: "into the measure of the stature of the fullness of Christ." That's the goal. But which of us could claim to be anywhere near it? Whether we die old or young, whether we

---

[16] Malmstrom and Kushner, *Four Screenplays of Ingmar Bergman,* p.106.

have acquired great skills or only a few, I think we are all still children, and
not that different from each other measured by that standard: the standard
of God's purpose revealed in Jesus Christ.

"Beloved, we are God's children now..." Yes, all of us are God's children.
"What we will be has not yet been revealed. What we do know is this:...we
will be like him." That's the promise, "we will be like him."

What is the gospel if it isn't a promise, a glorious promise of an opportunity to fulfill our potential, to become all that we could be not just out of
our own resources, but out of the limitless, infinite resources of God's own
nature? That's the promise, to all of us equally. And what can we become?
What kind of a musician could I be, if my fingers weren't quite so clumsy?
What kind of painter could you be, if only your eye for color were a little
clearer? What kind of scientist could you be, if you could only add and subtract and always get it right? What kind of basketball player could you be, if
you were only a few inches taller?

This world is a long and painful chronicle of what we accomplish in spite
of limitation: limitations of body and mind, limitations we never chose as
well as limitations we create for ourselves, limitations that prevent God's
good purpose from being made complete.

But it will be completed. It will be. God's purpose will be completed in
every one of us. God has promised. And we will be no longer children. We
will be like our Lord. This is the promise we come here to remember. And
it is food for this growth that we come here to receive.

The love we have seen in Jesus Christ, and glimpsed in John Paul and in
each other, in all God's children, will be fulfilled and perfected. We are here
to give God thanks for this promise and for showing us so much love.

I. Flight 007

*The Draughn family were members of my parish in Tokyo and later, again, in
Bronxville. They had moved again, to New Orleans, when their daughter Sarah, a
student at Tufts, went off to visit friends in Japan and was killed when Korean
Airlines Flight 007 was shot down. There was a service at Tufts and in New Orleans and friends in Bronxville arranged a memorial service for Sarah at Christ
Church. In order to make it possible for Sarah's family to attend the service, there
was a space of almost two weeks between the event and the service and, therefore,
somewhat more time than usual to reflect on the event and its meaning and the
needs of family and friends.*

**Then I saw a new heaven and a new earth;...Death will be no
more; mourning and crying and pain will be no more" ♦ (Revelation
21:1-7)**

I heard, as we all did, of the downing of Flight 007 almost two weeks
ago. It was a day or so later that I learned that Sarah Draughn was on
board. The next day, I left to take my son, almost Sarah's age, to his college
in the Finger Lakes region of New York. It's a long drive; six hours each
way. I drove up one day and back the next.

There are several ways you can go, but my favorite route is out across New Jersey, through the Delaware Water Gap, and then across the mountains to the Susquehanna Valley. The road winds along, high above the river, and the view, to borrow Alan Paton's words, is "beautiful beyond any singing of it."[17]

We headed north along the river and then up the whole length of Lake Geneva with its vineyards ripening in the early fall and the apples turning red in the orchards. And I thought about Sarah. I thought about the terrible contrast between her hopes and dreams, her family's hopes and dreams, and the sudden end those dreams have come to.

How is that right? How is it fair? What kind of justice is there in a world where such things can happen?

We have heard promises made in the Bible readings today. Isaiah, St. John, and Revelation speak of a new heaven and a new earth where there shall be no more tears, no more death, no more sorrow, "for the first things have passed away" (Revelation 21:4).

I found myself asking as I drove whether that helps at all. Does it help? Is there any way it can balance accounts, to lose all this and be promised a vision? And even if Sarah is well content with a larger and better life, if the books are balanced for her, what about her family and friends? Is it alright for them? Can anything make it right?

One of the problems is that the Bible has almost nothing to say about this promise. Including the passages we read today, you might find forty or fifty verses out of the whole Bible that mention this promise and even these are only suggestive, poetry not prose.

It's hard to see and understand when we're told so little. It's been said that the Bible is concerned with this world more than the next, and that's true, and so are we. But there are times all the same when we have to wonder, times when a little more information would help a lot.

As I drove back down Lake Geneva, heading home on a crystal clear September morning, I thought about a prayer which says, "O God, who has prepared for those who love you such good things as pass our understanding, pour into our hearts such love toward you, that we...may attain your promises, which exceed all that we can desire..."

As I looked across the lake with the sun glistening on the deep blue water, I thought to myself that the God who made that lake could indeed prepare for us "such good things as pass our understanding." The God who made Lake Geneva and the Susquehanna Valley could certainly do things I can't even begin to imagine.

But on this earth we have only a glimpse of that glory. Months and years can go by between the times we see for ourselves such evidence of God's creative power. And meanwhile we take the daily commuter trains down

[17] Paton, Alan, *Cry, the Beloved Country,* p. 3.

through the Bronx and ride the subways and walk the mid-town canyons, and no matter how long we live, there are only rare moments when God's glory breaks through.

Imagine, then, a world where God's glory is everywhere, always. That is God's promise. I'm not worried about Sarah. But I am worried about us because we have lost someone for awhile and it's hard for us, having only glimpses, only a little faith, to hold onto God's promise and say "Yes" to it, to accept the promise and to know that God can indeed make it right, can bring good even out of this evil.

And that's where we all have a part to play. Each of us may have only a little faith, but together we have a lot. And we can share that faith now and in sharing it, gain even more.

As we gather here in prayer, we are linked with many others at Tufts and in New Orleans and in Tokyo and London, and together we're an army, the Body of Christ, with power enough and love enough to hold each other up and even go on with new strength.

Our faith begins with the death, the defeat, of God's own Son. A hostile power, without regard for the value of human life, nailed him to a tree and he died. But God's power turned that day into a new beginning which speaks with more power today than ever.

In this same world, where fear is so strong and death so real, love is stronger still and is needed more than ever. God has promised. God can give life again. God can, indeed, send us out to begin again with all the strength we need.

J. Destination Unknown?

Lois Elliman was an active member of the parish well into her tenth decade. In her later years she was the central member of a small Bible study group that met weekly and she was especially interested in learning whatever she could of what the Bible said about heaven. She had strong views about heaven. She had been in her late eighties when a burglar broke into her apartment, threw her to the floor, threatened her with a gun, and demanded that she tell him where her valuables were. "Young man," she replied, "if you shoot me, I'll go to heaven, but you won't." He fled in confusion. Sometime after the age of 90 she finally stopped walking from her apartment to the church to join her Bible study group and the group began meeting in her apartment. When she died in Easter season at the age of 97 after some months of ebbing strength, she left behind a large circle of family and friends who were grateful that they had shared some part of her life.

"Behold, I make all things new" ♦ (Revelation 21:5)

Don't you think it's odd that Christians spend so little time thinking about life hereafter? Shouldn't we have an interest in where we're going? Would you buy a plane ticket marked "destination unknown?" Would you make plans to move to a new community without finding out first what it's like there? And yet we come to church and profess our faith and seldom ask what it's like where we're going. I think we ought to ask about it. I think we ought to learn what we can before the time comes for us to go.

The passage we read from Revelation gives us some important clues. It says, "Behold, I make all things new." What does this mean? Does it mean we will have new bodies, a whole new start? Would you want to begin again, be literally born again, and just start all over again in a new life in a new world? I know I wouldn't.

On the other hand, there was a time in the Middle Ages when theologians agreed that the resurrection body would be 35 years old forever. When I was younger, I thought that made good sense. Not any more. Suppose you lived to be 97, would you want to go back to being 35? Would you want to cash in two-thirds of your life, give it back, erase all the wisdom and experience and joy and pain of 62 years in order to be 35 forever? Or would you want to be 97 forever or live on for the mere sake of someday being 98 or 99?

I think the Bible shows us a God far wiser than any such theories or plans imagine. The Bible shows us a God who is never wasteful or cruel or inconsistent, who works in our lives steadily toward a purpose and who shows us what that purpose is and who invites us to share that purpose.

This vision of St. John, for example, shows us, first of all, the "new Jerusalem" coming down out of heaven. It's Jerusalem itself, not some place you've never heard of. It's Jerusalem, a real place, but made new, renewed, with all the evil purged out. There's no more death, no more mourning or crying or pain. All these are gone, but all the good remains and is given back. God accepts all the good, takes whatever is offered, cleanses it, and gives it back made new. That's the promise. That's the promise we came here today to hear again and remember.

Only once in the Bible, only in Genesis, do we ever hear of God starting out from nothing. Always after that God takes what we provide and renews it, makes it new.

When it came time to redeem the human race, God might have started all over, but that wasn't what happened. God called on a human being, the Virgin Mary, and of her flesh made a dwelling place among us. God took what was offered and made it new. When the time came for the resurrection, God might have taken a whole new body, some celestial body, but that wasn't what happened either. God took the dead body that was offered, with all its wounds and scars, and made it new.

Yesterday we heard in the gospel how Jesus appeared to the disciples after the resurrection and showed them the wounds in his hands and his side. It was the same body with the wounds still plain to see. But that body had been renewed and glorified and freed forever from suffering and pain and death.

I think that's one important thing to know about the life God promises, the life now opened to Lois, and the life that is promised to us. All that we give to God, all that we offer, God will take up and make new. I'm sure that doesn't mean that we'll be 35 forever. Nor does it mean we'll be 97 forever either. It means that all that is good will be renewed and given back, and we'll be who we are, but with all the sin purged out and all the pain. The scars, yes, the marks of the pain and all that we've learned and gained from what we've suffered: that will still be there. Everything of value will still be there. It will be our own life made new. And there will be opportunity, as one of the ancient prayers says, to "go from strength to strength in the life of perfect service."

That is God's promise to Lois and each of us. We come here to give God thanks for that promise of life made new.

K. Sowing Seed

Lawrence Rose grew up on a New England farm and went back to a New England farm in his retirement. Most of those who knew him, knew him as a teacher, as Dean of the General Theological Seminary. His grandchildren and neighbors knew him best as a farmer who took particular pride in his green peas and corn. But the two roles are not that different in some ways. The word "seminary" is derived from the Greek word for seed and a seminary is a "seed plot." The homily at his funeral almost inevitably centered on the biblical analogy of the seed and the resurrection body. Someone leaving church at the end of the service said, "You know, he never mentioned his name!" The reply was, "Well, he didn't need to, did he?" A homily should blend scripture and life together in such a way that names are not needed.

"...you do not sow the body that is to be, but a bare seed, perhaps of wheat or of some other grain. But God gives it a body as he has chosen, and to each kind of seed its own body." ♦ (I Corinthians 15:37-38)

"Very truly, I tell you, unless a grain of wheat falls into the earth and dies, it remains just a single grain; but if it dies, it bears much fruit" ♦ (John 12:24)

New England cemeteries are full of gravestones with slowly fading inscriptions carved a century ago whose theme is *memento mori,* remember death. For example:

"Remember stranger passing by
    That someday soon you too will die;
 As I am now, you soon will be;
    So now prepare to follow me."

Those old New Englanders were incurable teachers, and they had a point. Death also is a great teacher, and we have a lot to learn. But in recent years we've become inarticulate and we settle for a name and a date; no details, no message.

Occasionally the poems on those old gravestones might have included a few biographical details, but seldom were they eulogies. God, they well understood, does not read letters of recommendation. God has much more to tell us than we to tell God. God works constantly to gain our attention to instruct us. And death does instruct us.

God does not read letters of recommendation, but God does, perhaps, send them. The ways of God are recommended to us through a world of analogies, a world which reflects its creator every step of the way. Life reflects life. Creation reflects the creator. And one of the most powerful analogies God provides for our instruction is a seed.

The analogy of the seed occurs in two different ways in the epistle and gospel for this service and both are *memento mori*. Both have to do with the value of dying, the purpose of dying. Both tell us God has a purpose in us that is achieved by dying. God teaches us that in a variety of ways and, in particular, through a seed.

In the community where I live, people are often transferred to other cities and even other countries by their companies. They leave their homes to rental agents hoping someday to return, and the rental agent may lease the home to people from Japan or Hungary whose English is very limited. Suppose you moved into a borrowed house while the owner was away and it was filled with equipment you had never seen before and you had no idea how to use it. Pictures may communicate better than words. The owner, therefore, might leave little signs here and there with directions. Diagrams and pictures would help the tenants understand: a picture of food on the refrigerator, watery lines on the faucet. Sometimes, I think, we, too, are like strangers in a strange house.

How do we cope with a world full of events we don't really fully understand? We live in a world of separations. Someone we love is suddenly gone leaving only a lifeless body which we helplessly bury. It's frightening, isn't it? Suddenly we are cut apart; the ground cut from under us. What kind of a world is it where such things happen? What information has the owner left? Well, notice: over here is a farmer working his garden and he, too, is burying something. From this dead ear of corn he saved a few dried kernels. He digs a hole and buries them one by one. And then, behold, new life. A tasseled stalk of corn is growing up in the sunshine. Is God who created both the corn and us telling us something? Is there an analogy?

"Unless a grain of wheat falls into the earth and dies," Jesus said, "it remains just a single grain; but if it dies, it bears much fruit." Not only is there new life but more life, shared life, extended life. And it's true. Day by day, it's as we die to ourselves that we no longer remain alone, that life is enriched, fulfilled through giving to others: wife and children and grandchildren and colleagues and students and neighbors. Life is given, self is sacrificed, and we die. Each one of us dies daily in that giving we call love. And insofar as we have not held on to life but given it away in a lifelong process of dying to self, our dying bears much fruit. Life is enriched and fulfilled. God shows us that in a seed.

I used to think that the word seminary was derived from the Greek word for seed only because a seminary was a seed plot, a garden, a place for sowing and sprouting and nourishing. But now I've come to understand that a seed plot first of all is a place for dying. The common confusion between "seminary" and "cemetery" may be significant. A seminary is also a place to learn to die, to die to self so as not to remain alone but to bear much fruit.

A seed is a sign of God's purpose in sharing life through death. That's the gospel. It is also a sign of God's purpose for our future. The epistle develops that analogy. "Each kind of seed," St. Paul points out,"[has] its own body." When you sow, you plant "bare seed" and "God gives it a body as he has chosen."

Suppose you came from a world where there is no corn and no tomatoes or carrots or peas. Could you even begin to imagine the potential in one such seed? Could you imagine that that dried up kernel could become in a matter of weeks a tall stalk of corn to provide food for a whole family on a summer evening? Who could imagine that joy and the beauty and nourishment implicit in that seed? But bury it, let it die, and that's what happens. Who could imagine what God can do through death if we had no seeds? Who could imagine the potential hidden in this human body, if Christ had not been raised?

But God has given us these analogies, these letters of recommendation, this gospel, this ground of confidence to give us courage and hope and strength when we need it most. As we are asked to place ourselves and those we love in God's hands, so at this altar God's own life is placed in our hands. And if God's purpose in us is achieved by dying, we know that the Son of God already has died for us.

A seed is buried and dies to bear fruit and be clothed in its destined glory. Therefore today we give God thanks for showing us these things.

L. Many Rooms

Arthur lived just up the street from the church and came to church every week on Wednesday. He was an acknowledged alcoholic and the weekly meeting of Alcoholics Anonymous was the center on which he had rebuilt his life. Although he was a baptized and confirmed member of the church, Arthur had come to know God through A.A. He spoke often of his "Higher Power." But he never came to church on Sunday. We talked about that pattern several times but never got beyond discussion. We never managed to identify or resolve the problem that kept him as a church member from taking a full part in the life of the church. Every Wednesday found him downstairs in the church auditorium, but he only came upstairs to the church when he died.

"In my Father's house are many rooms" ♦ John 14:2[18]

It occurs to me that what Jesus said of his Father's house, might also be said of Christ Church. Here, too, there are many rooms, many rooms and many doors, and often the people in one room never meet those in another. We follow our separate routes, associate with our particular groups, and sel-

---

[18] The NRSV says "dwelling places," but this homily was written in the days of the RSV which says "rooms."

dom meet each other except, perhaps, in the hallways and stairways in between. The practical effect of that is that we seem divided although God's purpose and the church's purpose is unity, a manifestation of God's love.

Is heaven like that? Would heaven itself be composed of separate groups going their separate ways and seldom coming together? I doubt it. And I'm sure Jesus wasn't trying to tell us that we could go on like that forever. I think we know that instinctively. I think we hear this passage, as some modern translations put it, as speaking of spaciousness. I think the "many mansions" of the King James Version somehow conveyed that same sense of room for all.

The reason for all the rooms here is the diversity of human life and human experience, the impossibility of incorporating all that diversity in any single program or activity, or even one pattern of worship.

But God's is inclusive, not exclusive, love. No one is beyond the reach of God's love. Yet no human organization, not even the church itself, can reflect and act out that inclusiveness without many rooms, many programs, many means of reaching many people. Our love is limited and narrow. God's love is spacious and has room for all.

What else do we need to know? At the end of life, whoever we have been, whatever the way in which each of us has responded, if we have found any part of that spaciousness Jesus spoke of and tried to enter it, then death opens — what shall we say? — one more door or many doors into the spaciousness and all-embracingness of the love of God.

It is in that confidence that we come today to make our prayers and our offering, offering prayer for Arthur and for ourselves that no narrowness of our understanding, no limitation of our response, may separate us from each other either here or in the age to come.

Bibliography

Barrett, George W., and Casserley, J.V. Langmead. *Dialogue on Destiny.* Greenwich, Connecticut: Seabury Press, 1955.

Boros, Ladislaus. "Has Life a Meaning?" In *Immortality and Resurrection,* edited by P. Benoit and R. Murphy. New York: Herder and Herder, 1970.

Donne, John. *The Poems of John Donne.* Edited by Herbert Grierson. London: Oxford University Press, 1951.

Eliot, T.S. *The Complete Poems and Plays.* New York: Harcourt, Brace and Company, 1950.

The Interpreter's Bible. New York: Abingdon Press, 1956.

James, William. *The Varieties of Religious Experience.* New York: Macmillan, 1985.

Julian of Norwich. *Revelations of Divine Love by Julian of Norwich.* Edited by Roger Hudleston. London: Burns and Oates, 1952.

Kipling, Rudyard. *Collected Verse of Rudyard Kipling.* Garden City: Doubleday, Page, and Company, 1911.

The Lambeth Conference Report, 1958. London: SPCK, 1958.

Malmstrom, Lars, and Kushner, David. *Four Screenplays of Ingmar Bergman.* New York: Simon and Schuster, 1960.

Paton, Alan. *Cry, the Beloved Country.* New York: Charles Scribners Sons, 1948.

Phillips, J.B. *Letters to Young Churches.* New York: Macmillan, 1952.

Rahner, Karl. *On the Theology of Death.* New York: Herder and Herder, 1961.

Stegner, Wallace. *All the Little Live Things.* New York: New American Library, 1968.

Terrien, Samuel. *Till the Heart Sings: A Biblical Theology of Manhood and Womanhood.* Philadelphia: Fortress, 1985.

Thomas, Dylan. *Collected Poems, 1934-1952.* Dent, London and Melbourne: Everyman's Library, 1966.

Thoreau, Henry David. *Walden and Civil Disobedience.* Edited by Owen Thomas. New York: W.W. Norton, 1966.

80634